$27.50

Susan Colgate Cleveland
Library/Learning Center

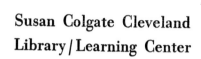

Presented By

Frances and William Rutter

Alphabet Books
As a Key
to Language Patterns

Alphabet Books
As a Key
to Language Patterns

An Annotated Action Bibliography

Patricia L. Roberts

Library Professional Publications
1987

© 1987 Patricia L. Roberts. All rights reserved
First published in 1987 as a
Library Professional Publication (LPP)
an imprint of The Shoe String Press, Inc.,
Hamden, Connecticut 06514

Printed in the United States of America

Library of Congress Cataloging in Publication Data

Roberts, Patricia, date.
  Alphabet books as a key to language patterns.

  Bibliography: p.
  Includes index.
  1. English language—Alphabet—Juvenile literature—
Bibliography.   2. English language—Alphabet—Juvenile
literature—Abstracts.   3. Children's literature,
English—Bibliography.   4. Children's literature,
English—Abstracts.   5. English language—Alphabet—
Study and teaching.   I. Title.
Z2015.A44R62   1987   [PE1155]   016.4281   87-3216
ISBN 0-208-02151-5

The paper used in this publication meets the minimum requirements of
American National Standard for Information Sciences—Permanence of
Paper for Printed Library Materials, ANSI Z39.48-1984.

To

James E. Roberts,
James Michael Roberts,
and
Jill Frances Roberts

Contents

Preface

Alphabet Books As a Key to Language Patterns is for parents, librarians, teachers, and teachers' aides—who meet and work with young children every day and who wish to get them off to a good start in the effective use of language. After the introduction outlining the role of patterns in supporting a young child's developing language, literacy, and learning skills, there is a bibliography of alphabet books arranged by features that may be presented as models of language patterns. Each entry in the bibliography is by author's last name, has an annotation, often including response activities, and notes the suggested age level. Most of the nearly 500 titles were chosen for analysis and inclusion as the result of a careful perusal of standard review media in the children's literature field, such as *The Horn Book*, the American Library Association's *Booklist* and *Notable Books* lists, *School Library Journal*, the journals of the International Reading Association, the *Recommended Readings in Literature: Kindergarten Through Grade Eight* of the California State Department of Education, and others. The author coupled the recommendations of specialists in the field with insights from her own experience as a teacher educator, staff development specialist, and classroom teacher in the elementary grades. Based on these considerations, some titles are designated "recommended".

Some of the ABC books annotated are appropriate for an older child or adult. Some titles offered by mass market retailers have been included, since it is possible that a relative has purchased one or more of these books for a young child and that they have been enjoyed in the home. It may well be that a young child will find some of the characters in these books interesting and attractive and adults who work with these children will want an opportunity to review available information about these books.

My sincere acknowledgments to the following people who helped make the research for this manuscript possible:

for her fine suggestions for the manuscript, Virginia Mathews, Vice President and Editor, The Shoe String Press;

for his contributions to the development of this material, Robert Whitehead, Professor of Education, California State University, Sacramento;

for her aid in bibliographic research, Roz Van Auker, Curriculum Librarian, California State University, Sacramento;

for her skills in the Inter-Library Loan Department, Kathryn King, California State University, Sacramento;

for their quiet interest during the typing of this material, my husband, James E. Roberts and my children, James Michael, and Jill Frances.

Introduction: The Role of Patterns in Supporting a Young Child's Developing Language, Literacy, and Learning Skills

What is the role of patterns in a young child's developing language, literacy, and learning skills? To respond to this question and to introduce the bibliography of alphabet books and their patterns of language that follow, it will be of value to list some of the generalizations about a young child's development in language, literacy, and learning skills and the role of patterns that have been published as a result of research and authoritative opinion. The interested parent, librarian, teacher, and teacher aide will want to know that

1. Pattern detecting is recognized as an essential function. A child recognizes letters as patterns, songs by the patterns of the tunes and the rhythms, and sees patterns in the actions of peers and adults (Hart, 1983). The child is a pattern-finder and a pattern-maker (Bronson, 1977). By reading and writing, a child intuitively may learn language patterns without verbalizing and without verbal formalizing of rules (Downing, 1969; Glass and Burton, 1973; Rosso and Emans, 1981; Tovey, 1980). Since a child is receptive to language from birth, an adult has an impact upon a child's language as talking, singing, and reading occurs (Carlson, 1985). Child-adult interaction is an instructional scaffolding that supports early language development (Lehr, 1985). Selective encoding (sifting out the important

from the unimportant), selective combining (assembling seem-ingly unrelated ideas together in a coherent manner), and selective comparision (relating the old to the new) are processes of insight that can be taught (Davidson and Stern-berg, 1986). An adult supports a child's language growth when an adult models mature word order in language (Cazden, 1972). A natural part of child rearing in our print-oriented society is to introduce a young child to books early (Lamme, 1980). Interacting with a book helps establish and maintain an adult's relationship with a child (Butler, 1980; Milner, 1951).

2. Patterns provide a foundation for oral responses and engage a child in oral language. Patterns build upon the speech of young children as they repeat pairs of rhyming words and as they play games with rhymes and repetition (Chukovsky, 1978). A child learns language by using it in meaningful experiences (Harms and Lettow, 1986) and has a natural interest in verses such as those from Mother Goose, where rich language is heard along with rhythm, alliteration, repeated refrains, and musical lilts. Rhymes may teach the alphabet, games, and a host of other subjects and lessons (Whitehead, 1984). The ability to hear beginnings and endings of like and different words is important and can be sharpened through the use of word lists, rhymes, jingles, tongue-twisters, poetry, or simple couplets (Chambers and Lowry, 1975).

3. Patterns provide relationships in language learning. It appears that there are relationships between riddling and language learning that capitalize on a young child's interest in riddle patterns (Geller, 1981). Riddles teach homonyms, double meanings, figurative and literal meanings, and intonation. Riddles provide high interest and a context for clues. The context clues in riddles introduce new vocabulary to a child (Cunningham, 1980; Gipe, 1980; White, 1980). Word play and logic are integral parts of language learning and cognitive development as a child categorizes speech sounds with the aid of rhythmic verse. By enjoying the nonsense of words, a child shows that he or she understands sense (Geller, 1985).

4. Patterns provide a foundation for reading. Environmental print (letter shapes seen in the surroundings) stimulates awareness of letters in preschoolers (Goodall, 1984; Wepner, 1985), and young boys or girls may grow into reading just as

naturally as they learn to talk (Downing, 1973–74; Holt, 1968; Huey, 1908; LeFevre, 1964; Smith, 1976). Sources indicate that a child needs to follow the patterns of words, to see the shapes of words, and to hear the words pronounced (Chomsky, 1976; Forester, 1977; Hollingsworth, 1970; Hoskisson and Krohm, 1974; Schonell, 1961; Tovey, 1976). A child develops concepts about print with patterned sentences (Combs, 1984). Hearing books read aloud increases a girl or boy's competence in many areas of language. Presenting language to a child appears to improve word knowledge, vocabulary, and reading comprehension (Cohen, 1968; Ruddell, 1965). Further, a child may learn complex sentence structure by playing with language (Blatt, 1978) and by recognizing a number of basic sentence patterns identified by linguists (May, 1986). These patterns are common ones and found in certain children's books (Pickert, 1978). Repeated reading seems to benefit preschool and elementary students (Wagner, 1986).

5. Patterns help begin the process of reading. An adult helps a child become a better reader not only by reading to the child but also by discussing stories, identifying letters and words, and talking about the meaning of words (U. S. Department of Education, 1986). A child's abilities to hear the difference between sounds, to see the difference between symbols, and to recognize letters have correlated significantly with early reading achievement (Barrett, 1965; Bond and Dykstra, 1967; deHirsch, Jansky, and Langford, 1966; Durrell and Murphy, 1962; Wingert, 1969). Encoding helps decoding, as well as oral language, listening, and questioning (Dinan and Dyson, 1980). High-frequency words may be taught from children's literature rather than from basals (Edds, 1985). Teaching sight vocabulary through patterns in language or structured language materials results in a young student's learning significantly more words than in a student's learning though pre-primers (Bridge, Winograd, and Haley,1983). The extent of the similarity of a child's oral language to the sentence patterns in the child's reading material affects the child's reading comprehension (Ruddell, 1965). Presenting words in semantic clusters may improve a child's knowledge about words and comprehension of them (Marzano, 1984). Wordless books establish a base for beginning reading (Ellis and Preston, 1984) and include pictures for a young child to read, provide an

avenue for a child to proceed toward an individualized oral or written text, introduce clues in illustrations, and allow the development of inference-making abilities (Whitehead, 1984).

6. Patterns provide a foundation for writing. Creative composition can begin in kindergarten (Mavrogenes, 1986). Frequent models of the functional use of reading and writing as well as opportunities to practice these skills may convince a child that reading and writing are important (Crowell, Kawakami, and Wong, 1986). One effective technique to encourage a young writer is to use the technique of patterning (Sharp, 1985). At an early age, children are able to detect phonetic characteristics of words that English spelling represents, use their best judgments about spelling, and invent their own spelling (Lutz, 1986). Some authorities state that sentence-modeling activities improve the quality of primary-grade children's written compositions (Odegaard and May, 1972), and others recommend that young children have oral and written practice in creating sentences that are similar to models in children's literature (Healey, 1978; May, 1980; Noyce and Christie, 1981).

Alphabet Books and Language Patterns

Language Patterns

In short, patterns from alphabet books, and other books, too, help a child make sense of what is heard, read, talked about, seen, and written. The patterns in alphabet books can be identified as models for certain uses and features of language. Among these models, patterns may be selected that present 1) creative uses of language, 2) words and meanings and actions of language, 3) ways of playing with language, 4) a foundation for oral responses, reading, and writing, and 5) a base for additional learning skills.

Patterns in Alphabet Books and Creative Uses of Language

Patterns of Language Sounds and Language Arrangements

Patterns in alphabet books may show a young child, or an older child, some of the creative ways in which our language is used. Our language contains not only sound-symbol patterns, word family patterns, and basic sentence patterns that can be transformed into other sentences but also created patterns of language sounds and language arrangements that can be identified for and by children. For example, language is presented creatively by an author when a pattern includes a repeated sound of consonants or vowels, words that indicate natural sounds, or words with similar ending sounds. In addition, an author creates patterns in language when the author's words accumulate, have rhythm, or are punctuated by a refrain. Patterns of language sounds in alphabet books are presented mainly with alliteration, onomotopoeia, and rhymes. Other patterns show different arrangements of language and include accumulation, repetition, refrains, and rhythm.

Alliteration

With alliteration, a child hears a repeating consonant sound at the beginning of words that are near one another or hears the assonance of repeated vowel sounds. Alliteration in alphabet books 1) presents vocabulary about a character's trip, or walk, or a family's activities; 2) shows a collection of objects or animals; 3) emphasizes sound-symbol relationships; 4) identifies and labels objects whose names begin with similar letters or sounds; and 5) introduces members within a group or category.

For instance, alliterative vocabulary about Alfred is heard in *Alfred's Alphabet Walk* by Victoria Chess as Alfred walks past alphabetical animals to learn his letters. Several curious cats call hello, while one dreadful dog does not call hello but growls instead. Continuing his walk, Alfred sees a quarrelsome queen bee, is frightened by a zebra, and is chased by a zoril. In another collection of objects and animals by Beau Gardner, a child hears a recurring initial letter sound in each phrase of *Have You Ever Seen... ? An ABC Book*. These phrases introduce an alligator with antlers, a banana with buttons, and a zebra with a zipper. Sound and symbol relationships, the idea that sounds are attached to letters, are emphasized in alliterative ways by different characters in *Dr. Seuss's ABC* by Theodor Geisel. In this one, Aunt Annie rides an alligator, a camel walks across a ceiling, and a Quack-a-roo is introduced. Monsters at a party are similar characters in Deborah Niland's *ABC of Monsters*. They portray actions for additional alliterative words. Each alliterative phrase for the members in this group begins with a word that ends in "ing." The monsters hum hymns, ink inkspots, and cuddle cats. Still more alliteration is found in Eric Carle's *All About Arthur (An Absolutely Absurd Ape)*. In each city visited by Arthur the ape, he meets other animals and objects whose names begin with a selected letter. Four friends are found in Fairbanks. There is Fred the frog, a fox named Fay, a falcon called Fletcher, and a fish known as Flora.

Onomotopoeia

With onomotopoeia a child finds words that imitate natural sounds. Some natural sounds are heard in a rhyming story about a day at the farm in *The Hullabaloo ABC* by Beverly Cleary. In Cleary's book, a boy and girl hear the cock-a-doodle-doo of a rooster's crow, the ding-dong of a ringing bell, and the drumming on a washtub. In another one, *Arf Boo Click: An Alphabet of Sounds* by Bijou Le Tord, a young child listens for other natural sounds. Unlike Cleary, Le Tord introduces such sounds as the eek of a mouse, the hee-haw of a donkey, and the oink-oink of pigs, without a story line.

Rhyme

Rhymes and verses in alphabet books center around the nonsense rhymes of Edward Lear, the traditional selections from Mother Goose, and around rhymes about animals, a popular topic of interest for young children. These rhymes may promote an opportunity for a child to use prediction skills, to solve simple problems, to gain vocabulary enrichment, to hear and see sound-symbol patterns and other patterns in words, and to begin a base for the invented or conventional spelling of needed words. Supporting prediction and problem-solving skills, the pattern of rhyming words in verses gives a child the clues to unfamiliar words at the ends of lines in verses and to the ways certain words sound. Sometimes, a boy or girl contributes a rhyming word for a key word within a line. In *I Used to Be an Artichoke* the verses written by Maureen McGinn and the illustrations by Anita Norman give clues which help a child complete the rhymes. In each rhyme the artichoke changes its shape. To finish a four-line verse about the artichoke who was unhappy about his change into a dandelion, what word will a child select? What word will be predicted by a child to indicate the artichoke's next unusual change? This predicting becomes a basis for observing other patterns the child will find in the yet-to-be-met forms of couplets, triplets, and quatrains.

With rhymes a child meets simple problem-solving situations. For example, a child sees and hears about problems in some of the Mother Goose rhymes. If the scholar used to arrive at ten o' clock and now arrives at noon, what should the scholar do? How may the black sheep deliver the wool to the master, the dame, and the little boy who lives down the lane? Why does Georgie Porgie run away when the boys come to play? What might help the king's men put Humpty together again? What causes Mary, Mary, to be always so contrary? What did the knave of hearts do with the tarts when he took them clean away? What will the butcher, the baker, and the candlestick maker do during their spree in a tub? If Little Bo Peep has not found her sheep, what does the child suggest to help the situation? If Little Miss Muffet is frightened by the spider, what could Miss Muffet do? A young boy or girl can plan resolutions for these rhyming problems through discussion or, if older, through writing.

Through rhymes a child also hears the emphasis on the similarity of ending sounds in words. There is rhyme in Fritz Eichenberg's *Ape in a Cape: An Alphabet of Odd Animals* and in Edward Lear's *Edward Lear's ABC: Alphabet Rhymes for Children* with its illustrations by Carol Pike. In Eichenburg's book a young boy or girl is introduced to internal rhyming words in all of the captions. The captions feature odd animals and include a unicorn who plays a French horn, a large whale caught in a gale, and a burdened yak carrying a large pack. In the second, Lear's nonsense rhyming, such as words "fishy" and "dishy" show that words can be created by adding an initial letter or by changing an initial letter. Rhymes such as these may begin a foundation for further recognition of word patterns (word families, phonograms), for future writing, and for spelling words in sentences by using initial consonant substitution or by identifying rhyming endings. For example: "This is a pig. This is a wig. This is a pig with a wig." A child begins to realize that if one can spell or write "pig" or "fishy," then by changing the initial letter, the word "wig" or "dishy" can be spelled or written. Additional vocabulary enrichment occurs as a child sees rhymes about favorite objects and hears the words with similar endings. For example, rhymes about one favorite subject, teddy bears, and their behaviors are found in *Alphabears: An ABC Book* written by Kathleen Hague and illustrated by Michael Hague. One teddy bear, Amanda, carries apples everywhere, young Bryon in bed receives a kiss on the head, and one old bear, Charles, carries his umbrella in the snow and protects a part in his hair.

Accumulation, Repetition, and Refrains

Gradually a young child begins to recognize the accumulation, repetition, and refrain patterns in the books that are read. As an accumulation pattern is recognized, a child usually enjoys these simple accumulating tellings. In these tellings, the idea, problem, or situation become interesting when details are added. In these tellings, a child sees an increase in the number of similar events or characters. To include these events or characters, the alphabetical story has accumulation as an important part of the story. The plot develops quickly, and the main character is introduced in the very first incident. As each subsequent character or event appears, all of the previous ones usually are repeated. The second incident builds upon the first one and adds more detail in an elaborative way. The accumulative telling quickly expands. Within some tellings there are refrains, those rhythmic words that cue a child into joining in to help tell the story. There is cadence. There is repetition. There is variation. Several of these variations can be found by careful readers.

● **Accumulation in the words with repetition in story or in refrain**

In this variation the incidents show the accumulation pattern by the sequential addition of repeated words in the story or in the refrain and by the incidents going forward to a point where the accumulation stops abruptly. One example is *C Is for Clown: A Circus of C Words* by Stanley and Janice Berenstain. Focusing on only one letter of the alphabet, the letter *C*, this book accumulates all of the previous words as the story moves forward until one final event abruptly stops the clown's circus act.

● **Increasing repetition of words and no refrain**

Here, without a refrain, each object is retained and added to an accumulating list. There is no refrain for the growing number of items. For instance, there is an increasing accumulation of items that is repeated as the objects are taken from Grandmother's trunk in Susan Ramsay Hoguet's *I Unpacked My Grandmother's Trunk: A Picture Book Game*. However, from acrobat to zebra, there is no refrain about any of the objects.

● Increasing repetition of words with retracing and no refrain

In this pattern the incidents, not just the objects, move ahead and accumulate from each preceding incident. In addition, the details are repeated from each previous incident to trace back all of the events to the original setting or back to the introduction of the first character. In one book, *The Berenstains' B Book* by Stanley and Janice Berenstain, the focus is on words that begin with the letter *B*. Events such as bumping into a banjo-bagpipe-bugle band, a baseball bus, and a bunny's breadbasket, are retraced within the story. The events are followed back to the first character, the big brown bear who is on a bicycle ride. Retracing usually is seen within a story but also can be found at the end of an alphabet presentation. For example, on the final pages of *This Is the Ambulance Leaving the Zoo* written by Norma Farber and illustrated by Tomie de Paola, the story about a yak's visit to a veterinarian is retraced and followed back to its beginning.

● Similarity of incidents with an accumulating
   or repetitive refrain

Here, without retracing, each incident is similar to a preceding one. It is the rhythmic refrain that is repetitive. The refrain in *All in the Woodland Early* by Jane Yolen is repetitive. To be read aloud or sung, the music and lyrics in this alphabet book are about one young fellow with a butterfly net who hunts and searches for something. Beginning with one ant to start the rhythmic search, the lyrics build and add the names of all of the alphabetical animals the little hunter meets in the woodland.

Repetition

Repeating words, phrases, or sentences on alphabetical pages, and other pages form dependable patterns for a young child, and reinforce familiarity with words. In repeating words, a boy or girl anticipates the familiar pattern, and the dependable words become known ones for a child. Dependability introduced with repeating words or phrases or sentences allows a child to read along with some confidence in alphabet books with repetitive patterns. These patterns may lead a child into creating other sentences from a basic sentence pattern. A basic sentence pattern allows a child to guess or predict, and then say, the words, phrases, or entire sentences. At times, with recognition of a pattern, a young reader can complete sentences or verses with or without print on paper. Other times an author will give predictable clues and will attract a young reader into the story as the reader becomes familiar with the words. For instance, one author, Vee Guthrie, gives predictable clues in her book *Animals from A to Z*. Here a young reader sees repetitive lines and easily remembers the names of animals and what objects the animals like. Sometimes a child may hear an unfamiliar sentence pattern, too, one that becomes recognizable after it is found in the story several times. For example, there is a patterned sentence with a subordinate clause in *As I Was Crossing Boston Common*, one ABC written by Norma Farber and illustrated by Arnold Lobel. This pattern is heard each time the slow-moving turtle meets an unusual alphabetical animal while crossing the Common.

Rhythm

A young girl or boy responds to the rhythmic pattern of the alphabet song about the startled bunny in *The ABC Bunny* by Wanda Gág. Additional rhythm is enjoyed in the familiar ABC song in *The True to Life Alphabet Book Including Numbers* by Johan Polak or in Demi's version of a music box book, *The ABC Song*, illustrated by Leonard Shortall. To the tune of this popular ABC song, an older child may sing the different animal names from *A Peaceable Kingdom: The Shaker Abecedarius* and see the accompanying illustrations of animals by Alice and Martin Provensen. By the time a singer recites all of the animal names in this alphabetical and rhythmic listing, he or she may be ready to go to other ABC books and hunt for more names that match the rhythmic pattern, perhaps even to prepare another musical rendition.

In contrast to the rhythm in the previous book is the soothing rhythm in a short excerpt from the John Keats sonnet "Oh! How I Love!" The words are from *If There Were Dreams to Sell*, compiled by Barbara Lalicki and illustrated by Margot Tomes. To some children, Keats's words about the balmy breeze and the resting clouds will have their own attraction because the words reflect the visual calmness of a cottonlike cloud. The gentleness of the words are in contrast to the rhythmic quickness one uses to say the words in *A Peaceable Kingdom*. Listening to this excerpt from

Keats's sonnet may establish a reflective thoughtfulness for a girl or boy when the words are read aloud. Then, in Tomes's accompanying illustration a young viewer finds another contrast. There is more than one way to look at this situation. There is another happening, one that is different from the experience the words convey. A boy or girl sees clouds in the shapes of sheep that float across a gray-blue sky. The child looks again and observes that some of the clouds are in the shapes of other animals, too—an elephant, a lion, and a whale. After a first listening experience with this excerpt, a child may then create an original picture to go with the author's words. When the words are read again, a child can look to see if a second story can be created, one based on the animal-shaped clouds in Tomes' s illustration. For a related activity, is a child interested in lying on the grass and watching clouds to find shapes in the sky?

Patterns in Alphabet Books and Words, Meanings, and Actions of Language

Presenting Words

Patterns in alphabet books also provide new words and meanings and actions for a young child's vocabulary enrichment. Terms such as the *Mediterranean Chameleon*, the *Nine-banded Armadillo*, and the *Rockhopper Penguin* may be new ones to some children as they hear these and other names of animals in *Animal Alphabet* by Bert Kitchens. More nouns are found facing Leonard Baskin's illustrations in *Hosie's Alphabet.* Accompanying the nouns of *eel, fly,* and *octopus* are alliterative adjectives for a child to hear and say that are as colorful and precise as the ones an adult might choose to describe the selected animals, e.g., *electrical, furious,* and *omnivorous.* In another title, *ABC Book* by C. B. Falls, there are still more nouns that introduce the illustrations of familiar and unfamiliar animals. A child meets an *antelope, bear,* and *cat,* as well as an *ibis, yak,* and *xiphius* (fish). Other ABCs may introduce other parts of speech. For instance, a child finds verbs in *A to Z* and still more adjectives in *A Is for Angry: An Animal and Adjective Alphabet,* both by Sandra Boynton.

Presenting Meanings

Patterns of writings in alphabet books can present not only words but certain meanings to a young child in the context of an ABC rhyme or story. With a story, a word association pattern, or a rhyme, an adult focuses attention on a selected key word in the alphabetical sequence. The adult can decide where the key word occurs and can judge the extent of the material needed for clarification. The adult also judges the extent to which the key word needs elucidating beyond the book, that is, a need for the adult's further explanation of the meaning. The informational material on the page often begins with an illustration, a sentence in a paragraph, or a line in the verse. At times the necessary words range through the paragraph or the verse. At other times the desired information requires the total poem or story. For instance, in Donald Crews's *We Read A to Z*, only one illustration for each word choice is needed as a clarifier to illustrate the meaning for "almost," "corner," "horizontal," and other concept words. In Alan Sloan's *The Sea World Alphabet Book*, only one rhyming sentence is needed to provide the meaning of the key word for *D*, "dolphins," when it is defined as "very small whales." However, in Thomas Mattiesen's *ABC: An Alphabet Book*, two sentences are needed for a discussion of "clocks," the key word for *C*. The term is followed with words about how clocks help us and how we learn to tell time. In another book for an older child, *The United Nations from A to Z* by Nancy Winslow Parker, several paragraphs are needed for clarification of the term "security council." The subject for *S*, "security council," is described as a group whose members are responsible for keeping international security and peace. Seven paragraphs are needed to present useful information. In this account both "security" and "council" are explained in the text that follows the first appearance of the term. After reading all of the paragraphs, the older child or adult may point out the beginning paragraph where the illustration of the permanent members of the council is displayed. The first paragraph may be repeated aloud, and then a listening older child may be asked to tell in his or her own words the meaning of the term.

Presenting Actions

Alphabet patterns also can serve as vehicles for actions. Some invite a child's participation. With these patterns a child may develop fluency by meeting a single situation with multiple responses. A child may develop flexibilty by changing, adapting, and responding in a variety of settings. A boy or girl moves to the music in a favorite ABC song or pantomimes certain words or actions from George Mendoza's *The Marcel Marceau Alphabet Book* or from *The Mime Alphabet Book* by Nina and Cathy Gasiorwicz. Behaviors—getting dirty, feeling itchy, and being sleepy—from Kate Duke's *The Guinea Pig ABC* can be talked about or mimed. Portraying more actions, words that end in "ing" are found in Janet Beller's *A-B-C-ing: An Action Alphabet*. In this one, boys and girls, smiling, giggle together, hang from a playground exercise bar, and whisper to one another. Other actions occur in *Join In with Us! Letters: An Action Alphabet* by Karen O'Callaghan. The letters appear in pictures with motions that a young child can demonstrate. Children move with their shadows, make themselves flat to go under chairs, and follow a zigzag path. In Charlene Schade's *Move with Me from A to Z*, there are alphabetical animals that initiate different types of movements. Instructions are given to help a child imitate movements such as walking on all fours like an anteater, swaying one's arms to portray an elephant's trunk, and waddling like a mallard duck.

Presenting Interactions

ABC books that encourage a child's participation or response to the pages can serve as initiators for a child's interaction with the print and pictures on paper. In one interaction a child pulls a tab in Robert Crowther's *The Most Amazing Hide-and-Seek Alphabet Book* to find the animals hidden behind the letters. For another interaction a playground game can be recreated from chanting the repeating alliterative patterns recorded by Jane Bayer and illustrated by Steven Kellogg in *A My Name Is Alice*. In still another interaction distortions of animals and objects by Mitsumasa and

Masaichiro Anno come into their proper porportions when seen with a viewing tube. The tube is formed from a silver mylar sheet included in *Anno's Magical ABC: An Anamorphic Alphabet.*

Patterns in Alphabet Books and Ways of Playing with Language

Figurative Language, Idioms, Puns, Riddles, and Visual Games

Patterns in alphabet books also provide several ways of playing with language. In certain books a child sees the figurative language of similes and metaphors—idioms where the playfulness of language is based on the meanings of words—and puns, where the play is on words that have the same sounds but carry different meanings. A child also responds to riddles, a popular source of language play, and finds visual games in which words and objects are changed, transformed, or manipulated in some way.

Figurative Language

An author can use figurative language, particularly the word pictures of similes and metaphors, in language play in a way that blends into the telling of an alphabetical story or into a descriptive ABC verse. As one example, a young boy, Adam, and his father in Dale Fife's *Adam's ABC* take an evening walk along the river that flows through the city. Adam paints a word picture when he says that the river at night looks like a thin dark ribbon. Hearing Adam's words about the river, a child finds an example of the playfulness of our language. In Djuna Barnes's *Creatures of the Alphabet,* an older child may find other examples of figurative language. There are metaphors: an elephant is similar to four unplanted trees, a hippo suggests a type of traveling trunk, and a walrus is defined as a cow who sits on ice alone. More metaphors are found in *All Around the Town* written by Phyllis McGinley and illustrated by Helen Stone. A subway is seen as a dragon who snorts, a jaywalker as a human jeep, and umbrellas as mushrooms of many colors.

Idioms and puns

Another area of language play in alphabet books is based on the meaning of words—the use of idioms and puns. Some of the books take a look at the literal meanings or the interpretation of words used as idioms. Others include puns. With puns a young boy or girl hears a play on words that have the same sounds but that carry different meanings. When puns are considered, a child sees that a pun will use different applications of a word for a witty or clever effect. For instance, in *A Phenomenal Alphabet* Cooper Edens and Joyce Eide show some puns in a visual way. Edens's words, "lying in the sun," are found in the caption beneath Eide's illustration of a golden lion in the sun. With examples of idioms a child finds that the total meaning of an idiom cannot be determined just from the separate meanings of each word contained in an idiomatic expression. McNaughton shows this in his *Colin McNaughton's ABC and 123*. McNaughton illustrates words literally. The words "elbow room" are illustrated with a large elbow intruding into one room of a house. "Flying off the handle" labels a modern Icarus leaping from the handle of a water pitcher, and the words, "lets off steam," are illustrated with a teakettle steaming with boiling water.

Riddles

Most boys and girls, particularly those four years old and up, like riddles. Riddles are found in several alphabet books and give short word mysteries, ones solved by guessing. Selecting the title by Mary Elting and Michael Folsom, *Q Is for Duck: An Alphabet Guessing Game*, a child predicts the answers to the riddles about why a selected letter stands for the name of a certain animal, and finds the missing information on a following page. After reviewing the riddles, a child may create a riddle or may want to write one remembered from the book. Writing the selected riddle on a slip of paper, the child inserts the paper into a small brown bag and leaves it on a shelf in the classroom book corner for others to read and answer. After reading Jan Garten's *The Alphabet Tale*, the child may select a riddle tale, one accompanied with an illustration of the tail of one of Batherman's unknown animals. The child selects a riddle, one he or she appreciates, tells it to others, and shows the illustration. When listening to a child tell, write, or answer several riddles from a source such as Ann Bishop's *Riddle-iculous Rid-alphabet Book*, an adult receives firsthand information about the level of simplicity or complexity of the material the child selects, asks, understands, and enjoys. With this self-selection of riddles and his or her responses, a child demonstrates language interests, oral language skills, and comprehension abilities.

Visual Games

Some authors and artists play visual games in certain ABC books and invite a child to participate in some way with the alphabet, the text, or the illustrations. In *Demi's Find the Animal ABC: An Alphabet Game Book*, an animal for each letter of the alphabet waits to be found in an identical drawing in the accompanying illustration. Each pair of upper- and lowercase letters introduces an animal. Answers are included at the back of the book along with one more visual challenge—a child is asked to find one outlined cat somewhere in the pages of the book. Another visual game, one of secrets, begins with Satoshi Katamura's *What's Inside? The Alphabet Book*. First a child sees two boxes near a brick wall and asks the question, what's inside? The child predicts a response and turns the page to see the answer. One four-year-old laughed the loudest over the prediction for *C* and *D*—two objects hidden in a large trash can. In a street scene on the next page, the objects are discovered. A black-and-white dog barks at a comical, wide-eyed cat perched on top of a corner lamppost.

Patterns in Alphabet Books Provide Ways of Seeing the Symbols of Language

Code, Rebus, Environmental Print, Finger Spelling and Body Sign Language, Word and Letter Changes

Patterns provide ways of seeing the symbols of our language with or without a printed page. For instance, symbols of our language are seen in a child's daily surroundings and in print in the environment. There are finger spellings and body signs used in sign language. A code or rebus can be deciphered. Word and letter changes, or transformations, can be reviewed and observed. With all of these patterns available in alphabet books, and in others, a child may explore several ways of seeing different symbols for our language.

Code and Rebus

Authors may use a rebus or code pattern to show certain symbols of language. One author, Lorna Balian, uses a cipher, or code, to show the ABCs. In *Humbug Potion: An ABC Cipher*, a homely witch is delighted to find a secret recipe for beauty in a number code. The recipe is written entirely in code. A young viewer helps the witch change the numerals into words. A child recognizes the letters of the alphabet and substitutes the letters in every numeric sequence.

Like this code approach, a rebus approach also offers a visual game with language for the child to see. One rebus pattern is found in *From A to Z: The Collected Letters of Irene and Hallie Colletta* by Irene and Hallie Colletta. This one combines words and pictures in the syntax of a verse. To comprehend fully all of the Collettas' sentences, a reader names the illustrated objects in the sequence in which the objects appear in the lines and then reads all of the words that come before or after each rebus picture. In some cases the child reads parts of words that appear before or after the rebus picture, because the rebus picture is necessary to complete the entire word. An adult may invite an older child to look at the rebus rhymes in the book and then select one to decipher. The older child may want to work with a friend as a team of two to break a code or to synthesize the combinations of pictures and the syllables in words to get meaning from the rebus clues. Using the books by Balian and the Collettas as models, a boy or girl may want to create original rebus rhymes or codes and challenge a friend or another team to decipher them. What other rebus rhymes or codes may be developed? These language approaches are most appropriate for the reader with a knowledge of sound-symbol relationships, which is required for completing all of the rhymes and for reading a deciphered code.

Environmental Print

In certain ABC books a child notices the language symbols in man-made shapes, in environmental print, and in certain objects in nature. In her book *Arlene Alda's ABC: A New Way of Seeing*, Alda provides examples of letters found in a child's environment. In colorful photographs a turning dirt road forms an *L*, a garden hose twists into an *R*, and the wooden bracing on a garden gate forms a *Z*. Unlike Alda's full-color illustrations, black-and-white photographs are used by Bruce McMillan to show parts of musical instruments in his book *The Alphabet Symphony: An ABC Book*. The parts of the instruments form the shapes of letters for a child to see. Other man-made objects, such as a street barricade, a traffic signal, and the handle of a cup, replicate still more shapes of letters in Barry Miller's *Alphabet World.*

Finger Spelling and Body Sign Language

In other ABC books some authors show the symbols of language through finger spelling and hand signs. In *Handtalk: An ABC of Finger Spelling and Sign Language* by Remy Charlip and Mary Beth Miller, a member of the Theater of the Deaf, there are full-color photographs. These photographs show signs for selected words such as *angel, bug, crazy,* and for the arrangements of the finger positions that are needed to communicate each letter of the alphabet. More finger signs are in the sketches of *Handmade ABC: A Manual Alphabet* by Linda Burke and in the photographs of *Sesame Street Sign Language ABC.* In the latter, Linda Bove, an actress who is deaf, signs words for each letter, beginning with *alligator, bird, cat,* and *duck.*

Word and Letter Changes

Another visual game, or visual play with language, shows word and letter changes to a child. These changes occur when authors and artists illustrate words in ways that signify the meanings of the words. With these books a young girl or boy sees changes that create meanings, not only for words but also for sound and symbol relationships. One type of change, or transformation, that a child sees is introduced in *Talking Words: A Unique Alphabet Book.* To demonstrate this graphic change, Ashok Davar selects a noun for each letter of the alphabet and lets the noun itself tell a child what it means by the way it looks on the page. For instance, to let the word, "cat," tell a child what the word means, Davar adds whiskers to the word. Looking at other nouns, a child sees the way they look when they are changed. There are spots on the letters in "leopard" and crowns of royalty rest on top of each letter in "king." In *Owl and Other Scrambles* Lisl Weil uses all of the capital letters that make a particular noun and draws a cartoonlike character from the stylized shapes of the capitals. The letters for "LION" turn into a cartoon figure of a lion, the letters for "WITCH" form a witch who rides a broom through the sky, and the letters for "HORSE" carry a child as they gallop across the page. Like Weil, Sybil Rebman also changes the look of words with her stylized capitals in *Animal Alphabet.* For every letter in the alphabet there is a key animal whose shape is created from all of the letters in the animal's name.

Not only words but single letters are changed, too. This second type of change is seen in *Action Alphabet*. In this one, Marty Neumeier and Byron Glaser select a letter and then let the letter itself show a child the selected key word or action for the letter. The letter *J* jumps across the page, a *C* has a crack is its shape, and a butterfly net is made of *N*s.

For a third type of change, other authors take the shapes of letters and turn them into objects or animals whose names begin with the original letter. For example, in *A Is for Anything: An ABC Book of Pictures and Rhymes*, Katherina Barry takes a *C* and creates a canoe, while Crockett Johnson's *C* becomes a cake in *Harold's ABC*. In *Alphabatics* Suse MacDonald includes the shape of a letter in every illustration. *A* is found in the illustration of the ark. *C* is somewhere in the shape of a clown and *J* is the body of a jack-in-the-box. In every picture each letter becomes an integral part of the final object. Sometimes the letters turn into animals only. Don Freeman adds lines to a *C* to make a curled cat in *Add-a-Line Alphabet*, while in *The Alphabeast Book: An Abecedarium*, Dorothy Schmiderer changes all of the letters into alphabet beasts. Schmiderer's letter *B* becomes a butterfly, and she turns an *E* into an elephant.

Other letters are the recipients of unusual turns and are formed with the help of the animals in the illustrations, the accompanying objects, or the animals' actions on objects. In *Ed Emberley's ABC* and in Monica Beisner's *A Folding Alphabet Book*, it is the animals and the accompanying objects that together make the shapes of the letters. In Emberley's book the actions of the alphabetical animals create the letters: a parrot paints a pink letter *P*, a quail arranges quilt blocks into the shape of a *Q*, and a turtle helps a tiger form the letter *T* from small wooden sticks and perforated wheels. In Beisner's folding book the actions of the animals or the placement of objects shape the letters. Two weasels stand on their hind feet back-to-back and tail-to-tail to form the letter *W*. The strikers for a xylophone are crossed into the shape of an *X*, and the upheld arms of a yeti form the branched letter *Y*. In another one, *Q Is for Crazy* by Ed Leander, a child sees that it is the shape of the object, and not always the name of the object itself, that guides the alphabetic sequence. Here *X* is for examining and not for the turtle waiting to be examined. The legs of the turtle are posed and form the shape of the letter. One bite from the center of a chocolate popsicle shapes the Y, and a policeman holds his wooden baton over his head to help form the shape of Z. There are more unusual turns with letters when the size of the letters change. For instance, in *Alphadabbles: A Playful Alphabet* Marjorie Price shows a child how to use a crayon, pen, or pencil, and expand a letter into a design by magnifying, minifying, or stretching the letter. These dabbles show a child still another way to see symbols of language.

Patterns in Alphabet Books and a Foundation for Oral Responses and Informal Drama

Telling a Story

Patterns in alphabet books elicit oral responses. Sometimes a child will return to a favorite ABC book again and again. As an adult reads aloud from these favorites, the young listener hears colorful descriptions, listens to the flow of language, and finds that there is clarity in words. When favorites are reread, the words and illustrations are discussed. Comments are made. A young listener may contribute additional language by adding words, giving proper names to unnamed characters and otherwise expanding on the author's sentences. Basic sentence patterns are read and reread. Some favorite adjectives may be added orally before certain nouns. Adverbs may be suggested to support selected verbs in the story patterns.

Additional oral responses to these books for a boy or girl consist of telling stories or repeating part of a story, participating in choral reading or story theater, improvising and interpreting in informal drama, making masks and puppets, and engaging in role play. For example, an ABC book can lead to oral responses as a young child talks about the book with a friend. Questions about the book can be selected, asked, written, and answered. Does the child have something special to say about what was seen or heard? If so, an opinion of the character, the actions, or the illustrations can be dictated. Does the material lend itself to a presentation for story theater? Is there a special part of the story that is suitable for a short choral reading? Is an audiotape recorder available to capture the words? When the recorder is placed nearby in a classroom book corner, the tape may be played again and again by the child and classroom friends.

Improvising and Interpreting Characters

Patterns in alphabet books can stimulate the use of oral responses in informal drama. There are several books that offer opportunities for interpreting and improvising in this way. For instance, certain story patterns lead to improvisation. With a selected story a child improvises as he or she changes the story or creates an original episode. A child uses a familiar character, a problem, or an idea from an alphabet story and with these elements, builds a different short story. From Tasha Tudor's book *A Is for Annabelle*, the idea of using a doll like Annabelle as a selected play object begins an improvisation. A child will imagine leaving the inside play corner for the outside playground. Returning to play with the doll, Annabelle, the child finds the doll is broken. The improvisation starts when the child returns for Annabelle, discovers that the doll is damaged, and acts out what to do. After the short action there can be discussion of feelings about the broken doll and the action that was taken. If desired, a girl or boy repeats the situation and shows another way to resolve the situation created by the broken doll.

Slightly different from improvisation with an ABC story is interpretation in an informal drama situation. A young child interprets a story by helping to dramatize the story in a different way. One story that has been a favorite of some boys and girls is *The King's Cat Is Coming!* by Stan Mack. The townspeople wonder what the king's cat will be like, and they name possible traits for the cat in alphabetical order. This story can become a story theater presentation and be the focus of a child's interpretation. For instance, an adult may tell or read the story and let a young child mimic the cat's traits. The child shows the actions of one of the townspeople, demonstrates the actions of the cat as each trait is announced, or interprets the actions of the young king waiting for the delivery of his newly acquired cat.

Acting with Puppets and Masks of Characters

Patterns of language in alphabet books also support a child's interaction with puppets and masks of characters. Sometimes a young child who is reluctant to speak as a character in front of others is much more comfortable with a puppet or a mask to help interpret an ABC story. With a puppet or a mask the emphasis is on the prop and the character who is speaking through it and not on the girl or boy holding the puppet or mask. If needed, a puppet or a mask can be made by a young speaker to represent the character or certain objects in the story. Puppet actions can be introduced with a story or with the verses found in certain ABC books. As an adult reads some of the verses from *Mother Goose ABC* by Kinuko Craft, the puppet can show the action. What movements with the puppet will a child make to show Georgie Porgie who runs away? Humpty Dumpty as he falls? And Wee Willie Winkie as he raps at windows and cries through the locks? A puppet can be made easily from various items, such as a large wooden doorknob covered with plastic modeling clay, a sock, a shoebox, a sack to place over one's hand, a paper character to hold, or a styrofoam cup to slip over a finger. Another puppet is made from an oven mitt with Velcro attachments. One small piece of Velcro on the mitt adheres to a second piece of Velcro on the back of art-paper cutouts of characters or objects. Other puppets are made from a small paper bags, round plastic lids, or magazine illustrations to attach to cardboard tubes saved from depleted rolls of paper towels, wax paper, or plastic wrap.

A child may concentrate on the talking in a story with the aid of masks. A mask can be made of large pieces of colorful nylon net that are seen through easily and large enough to cover a child's head and drape down to the shoulders. Other masks are large pieces of cardboard that cover the front of the child's body. The adult may outline the body shape of the wearer on a large sheet of white paper to make one of these cover-the-body masks. This large body-mask has an opening cut out for the speaker's eyes, nose, and mouth. Still other masks made from paper plates or paper bags or art paper cover the face; have the required openings for seeing, breathing, and talking; and are tied at the back. If needed, inexpensive plastic headbands form a base for the ears of animal masks.

At times, making these puppets and masks can be an independent activity for an older child. To organize a puppet-preparation activity, there is *A Resource Guide for Elementary School Teaching: Planning for Competence* by Richard D. Kellough and Patricia L. Roberts, which outlines step-by-step procedures to help the teacher prepare a student's self-instructional packet for making a puppet as an independent learning activity. A similar sequence of steps may be prepared to lead a child through the steps in preparing a desired mask.

Playing the Role of a Character

Certain story patterns in alphabet books present a base for the use of role play, a situation where the child plays a character and interacts with others. For example, some ABC books provide a beginning for role play that does not follow the plot line of a particular story. The role play activity may be organized around an alphabetical character or an idea from an ABC story. A child is given the part of one character but plays this character in a situation that is different from the one in the alphabet story. The child plays the situation as if he or she were the character. If *Curious George Learns the Alphabet* by H. A. Rey is the selected story and the child plays the part of the man in the yellow hat, the child might be told that it is now one year later and the day of George's birthday party. The man will teach the curious little monkey, George, something new and different at the party. Discussion follows. What will the man in the yellow hat teach George? A birthday party game? What might he need to teach? Of course the child who plays George must decide what to do, too. What does George want to learn? Not want to learn? Will George learn easily? Be a cooperative learner? Continue to be curious?

Role playing in this manner helps reading become visual and real to a young child. Playing a role of a character asks a child to understand how someone else might see things and is most appropriate for an older boy or girl, age 7 and above. Sometimes during these role play situations, an adult notices that a child, though wearing a character's name tag, responds with his or her own reactions and not "in character." When this happens, a child should be encouraged to participate in more role play experiences, and the pictured reactions seen in *Feelings Alphabet: An Album of*

Emotions from A to Z by Judy Lalli might be useful preparation for them. A child selects a guiding letter, shown with a photograph and a caption, that illustrates a feeling—afraid, brave, proud—and portrays a reaction for the feeling. However well a player's reactions convey or do not convey those of a certain feeling or character during role play, a child should be given the opportunity to engage in future role play situations because they provide opportunities for the boy and girl to listen, talk, respond to others, show feelings, and to state thoughts and reactions aloud in front of classroom or neighborhood friends.

Patterns in Alphabet Books and a Foundation for Reading

Process, Sound-Symbol Relationships, and Comprehension Activities

In addition to presenting samples of language from alphabet books to a child, an adult can support a child's developing skills by providing many opportunities to *use* language. Along with participating in informal drama, a child should speak and listen during conversations with others about alphabet books, discuss topics found on the pages, and engage in reading and writing. These opportunities support a child's understanding of the reading process, as well as the building of sound and symbol relationships and related comprehension activities.

Process

Reading alphabet books aloud can be organized by the adult with modeling that helps a young child understand the process of reading. During the times when a boy or girl watches an adult look at pages, turn pages, talk about illustrations, and read stories or verses from the pages, the child begins to understand that there is meaning on a printed page. When a child hears favorite verses over and over again from *In a Pumpkin Shell: A Mother Goose ABC* by Joan Walsh Anglund, or from Walter Crane's *An Alphabet of Old Friends* and *The Absurd ABC*, the child begins to realize that the meaning from the verses stays on the pages of the ABC book. Understanding about certain terms related to reading begins to develop. The terms of *letter, word, page, picture, sentence,* or *line* all begin to take on meanings. Directional concepts may be introduced as a child hears words such as *beginning, ending, first, last,* or *middle.* Watching the type as an adult reads, the child begins to associate the symbols with the words. When an adult reads the words that are touched, the child associates what is heard with what is seen on the line.

At times the child sees the adult model the ways in which prediction is used in reading. The adult points out that a word is going to be guessed before a page is turned or before the end of a rhyming line is read. Perhaps the adult models the use of an initial consonant and a picture clue to predict the name of an object. The adult might cover a word or a part of a word and predict the word for the child. Post-it tape may be used to cover a particular word in a story and is easily placed, replaced, and removed without damage to the book. At other times the adult asks a child to read a word or a phrase with the adult. For example, a boy or girl becomes an echo and repeats the word or words right after the adult reads them aloud. The adult and the child take turns in a you-read-to-me and I'll-read-to-you arrangement. There may be a reading duet where both the adult and the child chant or read familiar material together. For a sibling duo, an older child may read along with a younger one. The older one will read and point to the words. Listening to an audiotape of favorite verses or stories while looking at the illustrations or reading along with the tape also supports a child's interest. With these repetitions, and others, a child recognizes repeated words and develops an awareness of language. This awareness includes the words and patterns on the pages of selected alphabet books. As part of this awareness, a child begins to recognize the many words and patterns that are common to speakers and writers.

Sound and Symbol Relationships

Patterns in alphabet books provide the sound and symbol relationships in our alphabetic system. With repeated looks at alphabet books, a young child begins to read our symbol system. The pages that a child selects will be ones that hold the child's interest. This interest motivates response to the meanings of symbols that are the letters of our alphabet. Interestingly, the symbols are seen in different ways in these books, since in each book different techniques and materials are used for the illustrations. Various type fonts are seen, occasionally found on different pages of the same book, notably *An Edward Lear Alphabet* by Carol Newsom. Sizes of type are noted. With these differences, a child sees what someone else thinks or says or imagines and how variously it is expressed. These ideas may be internalized or interpreted by a child, who may want to draw what he or she sees, or perhaps wants to talk about some of the objects. After discussing certain pages, such as those created by Lear and presented by Livingston and Low in *A Learical Lexicon: A Magnificent Feest of Boshlobberbosh and Phun from the Vorx of Edward Lear*, an older child may explore his or her own inventional spelling. The boy or girl meets regular and irregular sound-symbol relationships while looking at the words and listening to the reading of the pages. During reading, some skills in word recognition may begin to be used. Words are pronounced and may be written according to a child's inventional spelling for a language experience, or later, written according to the words' conventional spellings. On some pages there will be word and sentence patterns that are familiar ones for the child, while on other pages, new ones will be discovered. These may be words or sentences found by the child that do not follow the patterns he or she recognizes, and they can provide a discussion beginning.

Comprehension Activities

Word association patterns in alphabet books support comprehension activities. A boy or girl listening to or reading an ABC book may see in the clusters of words or chunks of concept materials the associations that make up most of the phrases commonly used in English. With these word association patterns, a child takes in and integrates ideas. After one of the attractive word association books catches a young reader's interest, a child may want to extend any personal meaning gained from the book by expressing the meaning in a unique and personal way. Does a young viewer want to talk about things that he or she knows and can discuss about the topic? Discuss other things to be known about the topic? Discuss things that are alike and things that are different? About what happens in the illustrations and in the print? About organizing ideas and information from the alphabet book? About using an alphabet book as a reference book? Does a child want to talk about the book as an example of entertaining reading? Or for planning a personal story? For one example, an adult may record the child's stated thoughts as the child watches the writing. A child might decide to dictate a short ABC episode to entertain a friend or relative. In organizing an episode or story, a young reader sequences ideas, develops characters, selects settings, and passes along knowledge gained. All of these activities, and the many others that go into the preparation of a story, demonstrate a child's comprehension and help the young reader to accept information from others into his or her thoughts.

Patterns in Alphabet Books Provide a Base for Writing

Writing

What can the patterns in alphabet books do for a child's writing? Gradually writing development moves from simple scribbles and dictating material done for others to writing materials independently. With this development a pattern in an alphabet book may generate an idea for a child's writing, provide a model for writing, or initiate a way of responding. For instance:

- In selected alphabet books, patterns are available to elicit a child's response with a language arrangement of accumulation, alliteration, and repetition. Accumulation patterns can emphasize the power of repetition and often introduce a child to refrains. Pages on which alliteration occurs are models, too, of strong ways to sequence words together in phrases and sentences.

- In alphabet books with letter-object-word patterns, the patterns can serve as identification sources, resources for written labels, and as references for sound and symbol relationships.

- In alphabet books with rhyming patterns, there are similar word endings for a child to hear and say, which provide an introduction to word families and rhythmic rereadings. Books with rhymes and songs emphasize the rhythm found in the placement of words.

- In alphabet books with progressive stories, a child sees the model of narrative writing with its forward movement of the story line as well as the forward pattern and movement of the alphabetic sequence. Common sentence patterns are seen.

- In alphabet books with word associations, the sequence supports semantic clusters and becomes a base of information from which a child can write. This base of information includes a variety of topics, from being entertained, observing the city and the ways we travel, to considering views held by others. This base supports writing styles: descriptive, expository, narrative, and persuasive.

- In wordless alphabet books the work of the artists presents the material upon which a child can rely when creating individual patterns of language. The illustrations introduce information and clues on the pages and provide opportunities for a child to observe, ask questions, respond, and develop abilities for making inferences.

- Turning to an alphabet participation book, a child can be encouraged to respond to an author's or an illustrator's pattern through writing and other actions. The child's favorite books show different ways to see ordinary things, and one title may provide a stimulus for choosing, planning, and implementing a unique response.

Ideas

Alphabet books that encourage a child's participation can provide guidance into a writing response. One title, *Easy As Pie: A Guessing Game of Sayings* by Marcia Folsom and Michael Folsom with illustrations by Jack Kent, encourages a response to each saying in writing. How does the young writer want to finish the phrase, straight as an ——? Or snug as a ——? Or cool as a ——? A young writer gives an ending to one of the phrases, selects other choices for endings, or discusses why the ending selected seems to be the best from all of the other alternatives considered. Often the young writer dictates the responses, and an adult records them in writing. An older child records his or her own written responses to the saying or serves as a scribe for a younger sibling or friend.

Models

The variety of alphabet books supports different curriculum areas and topics of interest. With the word associations in these ABC books, a child acquires language by discovering that every object has a name. These word associations help a boy or girl see the world in a different way or see what is in the world for a different reason. In these books may be found word associations about 1) being entertained, 2) the city and ways we travel, 3) conservation and ecology, 4) country and farm, 5) incredible animals, and 6) names and occupations. Within these associations a child realizes that certain words are used to describe an object's color, shape, and size. Other words will tell about the object's texture, or if applicable, its sound and scent. At times several meanings can be associated with a single word, e.g., "train." A conductor on a fast-moving train applies the brakes in *Alphabet Cat* by Floyd Black. A toy train is found in *ABC and Counting* along with the verses by Harriet Lane. Officers and police dogs train together in *Police Officers A to Z* by Jean Johnson. The long train of a queen's robe and gown are seen in *Picture Book ABC* written by Helen Jill Fletcher and illustrated by Jennie Williams. Other variations of the word "train," are found, too. A child sees the engineers guide their trains under electrical lines and through crossings in *Ride with Me Through ABC* by Susan Bond. Katie, the kennelmaid, walks a well-trained dog in *Adam the Astronaut: A Name and Occupation Book* by Donald Smith, and Mr. Lion holds a ringmaster's whip for trained circus animals in Pam Adams's *Mr. Lion's I Spy ABC*.

Patterns in the alphabet books not only provide word associations for a child's interests but also serve as writing models and as beginnings for good writing. For instance, when a child is interested in a certain topic in a word association book, the related words form a framework from which to write. For a child's descriptive writing purposes, there are several models available in alphabet books. If needed, these ABC models can be a useful source for a young author wishing to record the details of a particular character, situation, or object and write in a descriptive manner. Relying on James Tasker's *African Treehouse* or on *Incredible Animals A to Z*, the latter edited by Howard Robinson, a child describes, orally or in writing, a selected animal and how some of the world's most unusual animals look and act. An interested viewer can tell about a favorite character in a descriptive manner. Favorite objects selected from *Brian Wildsmith's ABC* or *Bruno Munari's ABC* may be described. Perhaps one child will be interested in recounting a scene from *Helen Oxenbury's ABC of Things* or in telling what one Zoophabet is like from Robert Tallon's *Zoophabets*. After reading these models of descriptive writing and developing an interest in it through these activities, the child finds there are other ways of writing that might be of interest—expository, narrative, and persuasive writing.

Sometimes a child may be interested in explaining the way something is done and will begin expository writing. For instance, an interested listener hears about the effects of pollution from Harry Milgrom's *ABC of Ecology* and begins expository writing about some of the effects of pollution in the environment the child has seen. In another situation a child reads some of the recipes arranged alphabetically in *Mary Poppins in the Kitchen: A Cookery Book with a Story* by P. L. Travers or in *The A to Z No-Cook Cookbook* by Felipe Rojas-Lombardi, and explains, for others to read, the steps in preparing one of the foods.

In addition to modeling descriptive and expository writing, a word association book, such as one of the previous cookbook titles, may serve as a first reference book on a particular subject. For a reference when the subject is dinosaurs, a child may select Jill Kingdon's *The ABC Dinosaur Book* or Pat Whitehead's *Dinosaur Alphabet Book*. However, when the alphabet book has a progressive story as does Whitehead's, it introduces a child to simple narrative writing. The story also can be a model for common sentence patterns or for recording another story or a part of a story. To experience narrative writing with an alphabet book, a young author might listen to the first part of *Albert the Alphabetical Elephant* by Roger Hargreaves and then dictate or write an original ending for it. After hearing Leo Lionni's *The Alphabet Tree*, a child listens again carefully to Lionni's ending and then considers a different conclusion. Just as in the book's ending, the child's writing could include thoughts about what to include in a sentence that would mean something important. Perhaps a boy or girl will select the character of Clifford, the big red dog, from Norman Bridwell's *Clifford's ABC* or the character of Babar, the big gray elephant, from *Babar's ABC* by Laurent De Brunhoff and write another short episode for the character. A child's interest in an alphabet story such as Margaret Friskey's *Indian Two Feet and the ABC Moose Hunt* may lead to a new written adventure about the little Indian boy and thus another experience with narrative writing. Expanding on an interest in narrative writing, a young author might enjoy a picture variation of a folktale. There are several tales illustrated by John O'Brien in *Macmillan Fairy Tale Alphabet Book* by Nancy Christensen Hall, ones to launch a child into narrating an original folktale or into labeling objects for the narration.

At other times, an older child might like to write persuasive material to convince a friend of something or to persuade a peer to consider the value of a certain topic or a certain point of view. For instance, after reading *A Is for Aloha* by Stephanie Feeney or *ABC of Australian Animals* by Robert E. Smith, a boy or girl might write several sentences in the style of a travel brochure. A reader might prepare illustrations to make a visit to Hawaii or to Australia appear attractive to others.

Wordless ABCs

If wordless ABC books are available, they can serve as visual images and stimulus for the telling of a story in a new way or for creating a plot that is different from the one seen in the illustrations. These wordless stories may develop a young writer's interest in more writing, for each wordless book holds an unwritten story or a future rhyme to be recorded from a child's point of view. With a wordless story such as Rockwell's *Albert B. Cub and Zebra: An Alphabet Storybook*, a child has a beginning for writing stories or verse at home or at school. With the pictures and patterns of plots they hold, wordless books can expand language for a child. A child observes the illustrations to gain information. Words are added to the young viewer's vocabulary as the child describes the illustrations and talks about what his or her imagination produces after seeing the pictures. A girl or boy uses words to tell about the shape, size, color, and texture of things that are seen; names objects and characters; makes the objects and characters move with words; and gives characteristics to the items. Sounds, scents, and tastes are added. With these books, a child continues to develop fluency and may meet the given situations in the illustrations with a variety of responses. A child continues to develop flexibility, adapting and responding to the variety of settings in the pictures. With these books a child labels pictures independently and tells a story orally. If needed, a girl or boy reviews a wordless ABC book, or another alphabet book, to find models of letters and experiments with words and ideas while writing prose and poetry.

Jim Arnosky's *Mouse Writing* is a wordless presentation that may inspire a girl or boy to build upon the illustrations as a base for an episode or a short story. The observer of Arnosky's illustrations may contribute the narration with the dialogue of the characters and some description for a story line or for verses. Will the young author select a favorite feature of language to include in the story? What feature seems to be an appropriate one? Accumulation, alliteration, or a refrain? A progressive pattern or a participation pattern? Rhymes? What features could be combined? To organize a verse or a story based on a wordless book, a child gets an idea, examines it, and organizes it in some way. Before beginning a short written story or a verse, a child looks through books that are remembered because they hold a favorite pattern, looks at the books friends have produced, browses through other books with a similar format, or through books on the same topic. Perhaps the child dictates a story and sequences events, or chooses to prepare a written draft. Sentences about the events may be written on paper strips. The child moves the strips around in different arrangements for different sequences. A different color strip may be used for the dialogue of each character in the story. Later the child edits the writing to refine the story or polish the verse. In preparing the written draft, a child learns to paginate and to read or display a final story or poem for others to enjoy.

If interested, a child may create illustrations for the story, too. Looking at other illustrations, a child may find similarities in alphabet illustrations and compare the effects of different media and techniques of artists. Differences are found when the pictures are contrasted. After seeing what other artists have done, original illustrations may be made to accompany the child's words. After the book is completed, it may become a valued contribution to the home or classroom reading corner.

Additional alphabet books with letter-object-word arrangements are word charts between covers. They contain labeled objects that become spelling aids, visual aids, and word lists to support the child's writing. Other ABC books of the child's choice provide the phrase or sentence patterns to be enjoyed. These have great value when they are seen as one-of-a-kind patterns by a child for reading, for review purposes at home, or as a resource in a classroom writing center.

Varied Responses

Patterns in alphabet books can be categorized by features of accumulation, alliteration, refrains, repetition, rhymes, progressive stories, letter-object-word arrangements, or word associations. All of these categories can be found in certain ABC books, which may initiate different ways of responding for a child. At times a special talent or special interest leads the child to respond to an individual topic. After seeing the fine art collection in *ABC, Museum of Fine Arts, Boston* by Florence Cassen Mayers, a child writes or dictates a column of words on a tall, narrow card or chart to describe a favorite selected work of decorative art: It may be Steinlen's *Cats*, Renoir's *Dance at Bougival*, or Gauntt's *Two Children*. From another book, *On Market Street*, with pictures by Anita Lobel and words by Arnold Lobel, a child identifies all of the items in a selected picture that are repesented by the key word. One key word, "toys," becomes the heading for a list of items as a child categorizes miniature toy trains, soldiers, sailboats, and other toys. In *Celestino Piatti's Animal ABC* the animal illustrations by Celestino Piatti and the English rhyming text by Jon Reid may interest a young writer in recording several lines from the rhyming patterns. Another reader may enjoy Karen Ackerman's *Flannery Row* and elect to record some of its verses about Commander Ahab, his wife, and the alphabetic names of their twenty-six heirs. After reading the rhythmic names for the children in *One Very Very Quiet Afternoon* by Patricia Lillie, more rhythmic names of children, real and imaginary, may be created.

Instead of always responding to one of these alphabet books through a writing activity, a boy or girl may select other ways to repond. There are several ways of putting one's own ideas about a book into an overall presentation. For example, the child's presentation may be the painting of one picture or several pictures to show modern artistic shapes similar to the shapes in the bright paintings in *Sonia Delaunay Alphabet*. Other artistic shapes may be created after seeing the museum art in another one of Florence

Cassen Mayers's ABC books. In *ABC, Museum of Modern Art, New York*, Mayers selects Pinin Farina's bright red automobile for *A*, Jim Dine's bathrobe for *B*, Claes Oldenburg's two cheeseburgers for *C*, and other works of modern art for other letters. A favorite from this collection may generate another child's paper sculpture or drawings. Perhaps a boy or girl will organize a collage after seeing the ones arranged by Elizabeth Cleaver in *ABC* or will develop a section of an alphabet frieze modeled after *The ABC Frieze* by Dick Bruna. Different ABC pictures or words are developed after seeing the unfolding pages of bouncy children around the apple pie that makes its way down an extended table in Tracey Campbell Pearson's book, *A Apple Pie*. Still another boy or girl will choose to paint with watercolor on wet paper or will model a kitten from clay. The kitten may resemble one from Clare Turlay Newberry's *The Kittens' ABC*. The watercolor and wet-paper technique is the technique Newberry uses to create her attractive illustrations of kittens. These activities, and others, encourage each child to organize ideas into a special way of responding to the work of a favorite author or artist.

Patterns in Alphabet Books
Provide a Base for Additional Learning

Additional Learning

With alphabet books a young child, and an older child, too, may learn language patterns by accepting the language heard from a book. An ABC book may serve as an available language model. An ABC book can be a colorful file of letter, word, or sentence patterns. This file is personal, portable, filled with pictures and examples of language, and protected by hard covers. While interacting with such books, a child asks and answers questions, recalls information, and listens to the words of another reader. Directions may be followed. A boy or girl may discuss a mental picture, the image found in one's head, in what Shakespeare called "the mind's eye." These learning experiences contribute to the child's developing syntax, semantics, and a phoneme-grapheme base.

To continue to develop a syntax (the way words are sequenced along together in a sentence to make sense), a semantics base (the development of the meanings that words have), and a phoneme-grapheme base (the relationships of symbols to sounds), a young boy or girl should see examples of language, should hear examples of language, and should have many opportunities to use language. Alphabet books can make a contribution by providing these examples and by being the visual focus of these opportunities. With alphabet books and their patterns of language, an adult can generate some of these language opportunities for a child. After selecting and interacting with favorite alphabet books, a child finds that:

- language patterns created with sounds of language (alliteration, onomotopoeia, rhymes) and with arrangements of language (accumulation, repetition, refrains) are presented in alphabet books. Common letter, word, and sentence patterns are found.

- language patterns—which include figurative language, idioms, puns, riddles, and visual games—show ways of playing with words in alphabet books.

- language patterns—such as those found in codes, in rebus arrangements, environmental print, sign language, finger spelling, and word and letter changes—may use alphabet symbols in different arrangements or may use symbols that are different from the child's familiar alphabet. These patterns in alphabet books create additional ways to see language.

- language patterns—such as those found in ABC word association books, participation presentations, progressive stories, or those created from the illustrations in wordless alphabet books—build a base for additional learning.

Since the skills in language arts are symbiotic, i.e., mutually beneficial, the child's experiences in speaking and listening support a positive relationship with experiences in two other areas— reading and writing. With these parallel activities the child speaks, listens, and increases developmental skills in reading and in writing the words heard and said. With these opportunities, a child is involved in developing literacy, language, and learning skills through all of the areas of the language arts. With the variety of alphabet books available and with the extended range of language patterns seen in these books, a young girl or boy should be encouraged to interact often with various types of alphabet books. Opening the covers of alphabet books begins to unlock words and to release the patterns of language that the pages hold for a child. Indeed, for a receptive girl or boy, alphabet books may be a key to an early acceptance and a confident use of language.

Alphabet Books
As a Key
to Language Patterns:
A Bibliography

Accumulation

Berenstain, Stanley, and Janice Berenstain. *The Berenstains' B Book*. Illustrated by the authors. New York: Random House, 1971.

In this beginning section of the bibliography, alphabet books with accumulation patterns are found. In the Berenstains' ABC book, a big brown bear goes bicycling. As the bear rides, the book centers on one letter of the alphabet, *B*. The repetition of words that begin with *B* encourages a child to see the alliterative pattern as it builds on each page: *B* words tell about a big, brown bear, a blue bull, and a beautiful baboon and are repeated as the words accumulate. The names of the objects they bump into are repeated. Finding this pattern easy to read, a boy or girl may be encouraged to look for other books with alliteration and repetition. The accumulation may entice an older child to dictate an original accumulating story about these characters or other invented ones. In addition, lists of created names of imaginary characters whose names begin with *B* can be written. This writing suggestion may be typed on an index card and inserted into a paper pocket that is pasted inside the book's back cover. Kept in the pocket, the suggestion always is available when it is needed. If this is a favorite story, an adult may read it with a child over and over. A child joins in with recognized words. An adult or child points to a word. They talk about the word. The child frames it with fingers and if writing skills are developed, writes the word on paper. As this favorite story is read again and again, language is expressed over and over in an accumulative pattern. The boy or girl may join in and point to known words. Ages 5–6.

Pattern: Language can be expressed and arranged in accumulative ways. The alliterative and repetitive *B* words accumulate with each page. Basic sentence pattern: noun, verb, noun.

Berenstain, Stanley, and Janice Berenstain. *C Is for Clown: A Circus of C Words*. Illustrated by the authors. New York: Random House, 1972.

In answer to a question about how much Clarence the clown can catch and carry, the Berenstains offer an alliterative and accumulating answer. Words that begin with *C* predominate as Clarence catches and carries such things as cats, canes, and collies. Within this repetition a child recognizes the objects and the word pattern that is built in a way similar to the well-known and often-chanted "This Is the House That Jack Built." Using words such as "These are the things that Clarence caught, " a boy or girl adds phrases during a chanting or a retelling. For example, one child begins with "These are the collies above the cats that were some of the things that Clarence caught." With this story and its pyramid of animals, an adult may want to discuss certain terms that relate to the story and to the task of reading, such as *first, middle, last, before-after,* and *above-below.* Ages 5–6.

Pattern: Language can be expressed in rhythmic ways. First, there is the accumulation of animals and their possessions, the objects, that are caught by the clown. Second, there is the repetitive and the accumulating question that forms the refrain. Last, there is the alliteration in *C* words. Basic sentence pattern: noun, verb, noun.

Farber, Norma. *As I Was Crossing Boston Common*. Illustrated by Arnold Lobel. New York: E. P. Dutton and Company, Inc., 1973.

Recommended. Farber's rhymed account of a turtle crossing Boston Common is an ABC book, an unusual animal book, an accumulative story, and a circular story. This is a book with many patterns, one that invites a child's participation by making agreed-upon sounds of animals as the animals accumulate. One man leads a small West African lemur, called an angwantibo, who in turn leads a boobook, a small Australian owl. The owl tows a coypu, a

South American rodent with webbed hind feet. The coypu pulls a desman, a molelike animal. More unusual animals follow. The animals all wear their names on their collars and hold on to a long guide rope to form a parade in single file. After a second reading, some children will begin to be authorities at identifying the patterns. There is a pattern in the accumulation of animals, a pattern in the circular effect of the story, a pattern in the italicized names of alphabetical animals, a pattern of rhymes in the story, and a pattern in the playful polarized use of words with opposite meanings, common and uncommon. These boys and girls will know that the turtle is always going to be crossing so slow, so slow, and that the turtle will always see another animal in alphabetical order. They realize that the alphabetical sequence is an accumulating one and that the uncommon animals consistently will be real animals. The animals' names will be identified by the italicized type style.

Finally, some children will be aware that the story wraps itself back around to the beginning character by circling again to the man in the vest who was the leader of this parade. The last animal in the parade is a civet cat from India, the zibet. The zibet leads the same man who first passed with the angwantibo. The polarization pattern of language with word opposités, or word contrasts, is found, too. There is back-and-forth play between the words, common and uncommon. For instance, it is an uncommon sight for the first man, the leader of this parade across the Common, also to be the last one in the parade. What is uncommon for a child to see? It is uncommon for these unusual animals to be in Boston and on the Common. Towing one another with a long, long rope is uncommon. Wearing collars is uncommon for these unusual animals. In contrast to these uncommon animals, some common animals—pigeons, squirrels, and sparrows—line up in a common row to see the uncommon animals and comment with "How uncommon."

The circular quality of the story is emphasized in additional ways. The animals form a circle for a final activity, a last turn of uncommon events. The animals walk in a circular pattern for their final parade around and around the Common, leading one another. The circle and the concept of roundness is emphasized by the round moon, the round glow of the lamps placed around the edge of the Common, and by the circular towing that Lobel shows in a final illustration.

For a guided activity, perhaps a child will identify a sound to make for each animal as it is introduced in the story. Another child may want to discuss or dictate or write about the unbelievable animals he or she imagines while passing a town square, local park, or green belt area. Still another might be interested in matching the definitions to the animal names. Who can find the small reddish deer with the simple spikelike antlers? (Pudu or POO doo.) Or the ostrich with three toes on each foot? (Rhea or REE A.) Or a large antelope with curved horns from South Africa? (Sassaby or SASS a bi.)

Rhymes are heard. The word pattern for the family of words ending in "ow" is featured with *snow, bow, know, grow, crow, row, overflow, slow, tow,* and others. Each animal is illustrated in a large drawing as it appears. On two final pages of the book, a child sees all of the animals in smaller pictures and reads the animals' names again as their names introduce brief definitions. A clear pronunciation guide is included for every one of the unusual animals. What sound patterns can be discovered? The guide concludes with xenopus (XEN o pus), a tongueless african toad, a yaguarundi (yag war UN di), a grayish unspotted wildcat, and a zibet (ZI bet), an East Indian civet cat. Names of unusual animals in italics guide the sequence in the rhyming text. Ages 5-up.

Pattern: With subordinate clauses, accumulation of uncommon animals supports a circular story with repetition and rhyming.

Farber, Norma. *This Is the Ambulance Leaving the Zoo.* Illustrated by Tomie de Paola. New York: E. P. Dutton and Company, Inc., 1975.

Recommended. Farber's alphabet is an accumulative story that introduces city scenes in an ABC order, beginning with an ambulance leaving the zoo. Why is the ambulance leaving? Where is it going? A bus stops to let the ambulance go by. There are cars, drivers, and emergency signals. The ambulance rushes through the city. A child sees ABC sights and may predict answers to certain questions. What or who is in the ambulance? What has happened? Word choices such as funeral procession, green lights, highways, and intersection are repeated and always seen a second time in following sentences. In capitals and bold type, each word choice leads to the introduction of the next key word in the sequence. The sentence pattern includes "This is a ———" or "These are the ———" on every page. The two final pages hold a review of all of the words in a retracing of the sequence of the story from Z to A, in alphabetical order and in rhythmic phrases. There are no single letters to guide the sequence. Ages 5-up.

Pattern: With narrative writing and retracing, accumulation is guided by word choices. Basic sentence: pronoun, linking verb, noun, verb.

Hefter, Richard. *Everything: An Alphabet, Number, Reading, Counting and Color Identification Book.* Illustrated by the author. New York: Parents Magazine Press, 1971.

Hefter shows a different accumulation pattern with a physical addition of words. At the letter A a child reads one word and sees one apple. At B a child reads two words and sees two objects, and so on. On the Z page Hefter writes twenty-six words about zebras who run a race at full gallop. Since the words are written in a column arrangement, an adult demonstrates where to begin reading the book, where to begin reading a page, and where to turn to continue reading when the page is completed. With this arrangement terms may be discussed: *letter, sound, word.* Later, with other readings, more terms may be added to the discussion: *sentence, line, page, picture,* and *illustration.* Is an older child interested in rewriting Hefter's words and changing them from a column format to a horizontal one? If so, what is the punctuation pattern needed? Ages 6–8.

Pattern: Words accumulate with successive letters.

Hoguet, Susan Ramsay. *I Unpacked My Grandmother's Trunk: A Picture Book Game.* Illustrated by the author. New York: E. P. Dutton and Company, Inc., 1983.

Recommended. A young acrobat unpacks Grandmother's trunk in this notable Children's Trade Book for the Language Arts (National Council of Teachers of English) and finds a bear, clown, and other alphabetical objects in an accumulating pattern within the ABC sequence. Five other patterns may be seen, too. First, there is the pattern of unifying features. For instance, the blue trousers and sweater of the acrobat are decorated with stars and crescents and turn into the acrobat's blue leotards that are decorated again with stars and crescents. In addition, the handprints of the acrobat turn into the pawprints of the brown bear. Second, there is a replication pattern—e.g., the design of the three-quarter page replicates the opening of the lid of an old trunk. As more and more objects appear, the trunk opens wider and wider. Third, there is the use of white space, which intensifies the appearances of the ABC objects. Next, there is the pattern of parallel postures between the young acrobat and some of the animals. The brown bear mimics the sitting posture and the handstand of the acrobat. A kangaroo tries similar handstands. The ostrich copies the acrobat's tumble in the air. Last, there is the pattern of visual humor in some short subplots. As each animal or object appears, humorous events take place. For example, a child notices the actions of the mouse who appears for *M* and the subsequent actions about the nest, the fainting queen, and a curious, helpful tiger. What rhythm for these accumulating words can be introduced to form a chant, e.g., "Acrobat, bear,———? Players may turn this title into a game by adding new objects for the sequential letters after reciting all named objects. Ages 5-7.

Pattern: Accumulation of nouns, unifying features, replication, parallel postures, and some visual humor. Basic sentence: Pronoun, verb, noun.

Morse, Samuel French. *All in a Suitcase*. Illustrated by Barbara Cooney. Boston: Little, Brown, 1966.

Full-page illustrations in full-color offer a young viewer a guided fantasy trip through Boston by seeing animals in alphabetical order. Morse encourages a child to review the accumulating sequence of the letters as various animals are introduced. At Boston Harbor a child meets a starfish. At the ocean there is a vole, and on Boston Street there is a xenopus to meet. Ages 1-3.

Pattern: With alphabetical animals the letters are seen and reviewed in accumulating sections of verses.

Waller, Barbara K. *I Packed My Trunk*. Illustrated by Carl Koch. New York: Follett, 1965.

In this accumulation a trunk is packed for Squintums with objects in alphabetical order. *A* for a hanging red apple and *B* for a book wearing glasses open this ABC series of objects. After seeing the zoo that concludes this alphabet, a teacher asks what variations might be written or said about *I Packed My Trunk*. The teacher suggests a recall activity with this accumulative pattern to second-grade students. A student thinks of a title and suggests, "I Took My Tote Bag could be the name of this game." The teacher records these words on the chalkboard: I took my tote bag and I tucked in an———. The title motivates other students to dicate their title choices for their individual patterns of writing. Some of the students' titles were these: I Vamoosed with My Valise; I Flew with My Flight Bag; I Blew into Town with My Backpack; I Borrowed a Beachbag; and I Brought a Basket. Ages 7–8.

Pattern: With compound sentences, accumulating objects appear in alphabetical order with no key letters to guide the sequence. Basic sentence: Pronoun, verb, noun.

Yolen, Jane. *All in the Woodland Early: An ABC Book*. Illustrations by Jane Breskin Zalben. New York: Philomel/Putnam Publishing Group, 1975.

Recommended. Yolen writes an alphabetical story in verse that can be sung to the included music. From ant to zemmi, Breskin positions the animals around the shapes of the letters in the illustrations. Yolen and Zalben show four patterns: a) the alphabetical sequence in which the animals appear; b) the spoken, rhythmic refrain in a question-and-answer format that is repeated several times; c) repetition of additional phrases; and d) rhyme. The rhyming words point out some of the characteristics of the animals. For example, the phrase about a quail's wings rhymes with the phrase about a raccoon's rings. Words about a king snake that is fast rhymes with words about a mink who hurries past, and the ending word in the line about an oppossum that plays dead rhymes with the final word in the line about a partridge flying over one's head. After a few readings some children will become expert at identifying the patterns. For instance, a child realizes that the little boy is going hunting and that he would always say the same words about going hunting. A child knows that the animals accumulate and that the animals consistently respond with the same words about where they are going. The end of the spoken, rhythmic refrain always signals the next sequence of alphabetical animals. A child is aware that the story ends with an invitation to play. An adult may record the refrain on paper to be read again. Most children sing or say each refrain briskly each time. Ages 5–8.

Pattern: With variety in sentence patterns, animal names in alphabetical sequence, question-and-answer refrain, repetition of words and phrases, and rhyme are seen. Basic sentence: Pronoun, verb, adjective, noun.

Alliteration

Amery, Heather. *The Alphabet Book.* Illustrated by Colin King. London: Usborne Publishing, Ltd., 1979.

Nonsense pictures illustrate alliterative sentences. Angry alligators chop apples, baby bears peel bananas, and a cowboy cat rides a camel. Uppercase letters are in red and lowercase letters are in blue, making the symbols easy to distinguish in the corners of pages. A child looks for letters in words, finds letters in the scenes, and traces letters on a final page. Several high-frequency nouns by Allen and Allen in *Teacher's Resource Book: Language Experiences in Early Childhood* are found in plural patterns:

apples	bears	beds
cats	dogs	elephants
houses	jellies	kites
queens	televisions	umbrellas

Short phrases may be created orally or in writing from the longer alliterative sentences in the book. Nonsense alliteration in a sentence may be extended with a pattern of adding words that begin with *a*, one by one, to a first sentence, then adding *b* words in a second sentence, and so on: This is an alligator. This is an———— alligator. This is an————alligator————. (This is an angry alligator acting.) In the short phrase, *Aa,*————alligators, which word will a child choose to describe the alligators? Alliteration may be promoted through nonsense writing similar to this. Does a child want to introduce a title for some additional nonsense sentences? Does an adult want to introduce another title and an introductory sentence as a model? Ages 7–8.

Pattern: Alliterative sentences accompany upper- and lower-case models for manuscript letters differentiated by color. Basic sentence: noun, transitive verb, noun.

Boynton, Sandra. *A to Z*. Illustrated by the author. New York: Simon and Schuster, Inc., 1984.

Near the animals in these scenes are outlined block-capital letters. For instance, for *A*, one aardvark admires himself in a mirror, a beaver sails with balloons for *B*, and with a broom, pail, and cloth, cats tidy around the letter *C*. With the exception of the word choice for *U*, words that end in "ing" are the key selections, e.g., "admiring," "ballooning," and "cleaning" (present participle verb form). This form of a verb describes the action going on in the illustration, but can also describe action in the past or action that will be going on in the future. Does an older child want to search for a word that begins with *U* and ends in "ing" to complete this pattern? Can the searcher find such examples as "unpacking" and "uncovering"? Ages 5-up.

Pattern: Each outlined block capital is followed by a key word that ends in "ing."

Brown, Mik. *Little Simon ABC*. Illustrated by the author. New York: Simon and Schuster, Inc., 1982.

Framed in lavender, turquoise, and yellow, the illustrations depict various small scenes where animals introduce the letters. For some unusual uses of words with *D*, a child reads about a dizzy dormouse, a detective who disguises himself as a deer, and a dog who does not hear the doctor. Capitals and lowercase letters are centered on each page with phrases placed by each scene. Alliterative words are illustrated with Brown's humorous pictures and tell of animals and their behaviors. A frog falls flat on his face, a jellyfish jumps to jazz, and a porcupine policeman pours porridge into pajamas. Some prepositional phrases such as "at an ant," "in an airplane," and "for the baby badger's birthday," are seen. The phrases may form short sentence strips for a reading display. Accompanying word cards can be matched to similar words on the sentence strips and to the labeled objects on the pages in the book. There is an animal quiz. A child is asked to look at a second sequence of ABC pictures and find objects that begin with a selected letter. A culminating end page shows upper- and lower-case letters sequenced in blue. Can a child identify the conventional pattern of needed capital letters at the beginning of sentences and needed punctuation at the ending? Does any student want to respond to the effect of some favorite alliterative words as the words are read outloud? After the words are read, the child indicates the effect the words have. Is the sound pattern a silly one? A soft one? A happy one? A musical one? A slow one? Ages 6–8.

Pattern: With prepositional phrases, sentences with alliterative words begin without capitals and end without punctuation marks. Basic sentence: noun, verb, noun.

Carle, Eric. *All About Arthur (An Absolutely Absurd Ape)*. Illustrated by the author. New York: Franklin Watts, 1974.

Recommended. As Arthur travels, he is seen in a bright collection of illustrations. In accompanying sentences about Arthur, a pattern of information can be heard and discussed. A child finds environmental print in photographs of buildings, clothing, and street signs. The young child reads and hears the names of animals Arthur meets, the names of cities to which he travels, and the actions of the animals in alliterative words. To begin Arthur's travels, *A* is found in a neon building sign and again in the words "autumn," "Atlanta," and "accordion-playing ape." There are other words that begin with *A* for a child to find on the page. In Cincinnati, Arthur sees a calico cat named Cindy. In Denver he meets a dalmation named Danny, and in Evansville Arthur finds an enormous elephant named Eddie. A child's patterned response may be repeated as each acquaintence is met: In the city of———, Arthur met a———named ———. Ages 6–7.

Pattern: With shapes of letters in photographs of environmental print, alliterative words identify cities, behaviors of animals, and objects. Some parallel sentence construction with basic sentence: prepositional phrase, noun or pronoun, verb, noun.

Chess, Victoria. *Alfred's Alphabet Walk*. Illustrated by the author. New York: Greenwillow, 1979.

Recommended. When Alfred's mother tells him to learn all of his alphabet letters, Alfred hides his book and leaves the yard. On his walk Alfred learns the alphabet. As Alfred plays ring-around-the-rosy with rabbits, sees a sloth snoozing, and watches a tortoise and a toad toss tiddledywinks, he reviews the guiding letters. In this review a child sees capital letters in color and some alliteration within the sentences. For example, capital *T*s are found in the sentence for *T* with the words, *Tiddledywinks*, *Tortoise*, and *To*. Alfred walks past such animals as an iguana, a juggling jaguar, and a kangaroo who flies a kite. Each sentence contains certain words that begin with the same letter highlighted in the same color. This pattern of finding similar letters may be emphasized by presenting to a child a sentence containing blanks for each alliterative letter: One _azy _ion _aps water by a _ily pond.

During a short walk with an adult, a child may collect his or her own alliterative words about items found near home, the school, or the neighborhood. In addition, an adult may invite the child to dictate what was seen and organize the child's responses in an *A* to *Z* manner. Ages 5–8.

Pattern: With capitalization, punctuation, and variety in sentence patterns, alliterative words show capitals in color.

Children's Television Workshop. *The Sesame Street Book of Letters.* Illustrated. Boston: Little, Brown, 1969.

This book offers letters with similar shapes in groups. The letters are shown in a nonalphabetical sequence. *O, C, Q,* and *G,* for example, are all variations on a circle and are shown in a group because they share the same basic shape. *D, B, P,* and *R* are members of the straight line and half-circle group. Humorous jingles with alliterative words accompany the letters. A child reads about giving a cat a candy-coated codfish, grumpy goats galloping toward green grass, and oily old balloons. Letters in black are found again at the foot of each page. A letter identification review and matching letter game are included. Ages 5–7.

Pattern: With alliterative jingles, letters are grouped by shapes and presented out of sequence.

Coudrille, Jonathon. *A Beastly Collection.* Illustrated by the author. London: Warne, 1974.

There is alliteration in the text and appealing beasts in the author's black line drawings. In this collection the animals and objects are arranged around a topic or theme for each letter of the alphabet. For example, a rabbit is surrounded with *R* words: "rapid," "race," and others. For an older child this book includes such words as "piquant," "exactitude," and "vanity." Ages 8-up.

Pattern: Alliterative words about animals in verses and accompanying objects in illustrations contribute to central scene or episode.

Coudron, Jill M. *Alphabet Stories*. Illustrated by the author. Belmont, Calif.: Pitman Learning Inc.,/Fearon Teacher Aids, 1983.

Coudron writes stories to read or to tell for each letter of the alphabet. During a story the child identifies the sound-symbol pattern and makes the sound of a selected letter at specific times. A child identifies the pattern of the letter and its appropriate sound by adding items to the story that begin with the selected letter. Each story is divided into eight short parts. With these story parts, a child may assemble the sequential pattern of each story into a small book or paste the parts in order on a narrow paper strip or frieze. For variety the story parts may be placed on a poster in a left-to-right pattern or assembled into an accordion format for a child's individual book. Ages 4–6.

Pattern: Short stories incorporate ABC characters, the letters, their shapes, and sounds.

Cox, Palmer. *The Brownies' ABC*. Illustrations by Palmer Cox. Text by Robert and Pam Kraus. New York: Windmill Books, 1980.

Introducing a child to brownies and other beings, Cox's small book includes drawings created over a century ago. Alliterative sentences describe the behavior of the brownies. For *B*, they balance badly; at *C*, one cooks chili; and *G* is for gliding gracefully. Other small imaginative creatures are mentioned in the text: dwarves dance, leprechauns leap, gnomes glide, and pixies pull peppermint candy. Beneath each small illustration is the serif capital in blue to lead to each alliterative sentence. These alliterative sentences are short ones and are composed of three, four, and five words each. Ages 7-up.

Pattern: Illustrations described by alliterative sentences are guided by serif capitals in color.

Craig, Bobbie. *A Comic and Curious Collection of Animals, Birds and Other Creatures*. Illustrated by the author. New York: Modern Promotions, 1981.

Craig's collection of comic animals are shown in ABC order on double-page spreads and are discussed in alliterative sentences. For each upper- and lowercase letter, there is a list of animals and a curious alliterative situation. For example, an ox, otter, and octopus play in an orchestra; a turkey, toucan, and toad toboggan in twos; and a walrus, woodpecker, and wolf wash clothes on a windy day. Nonsense alliterative sentences such as these can be restated aloud or rewritten as questions: Is that an ox, an otter, and an octopus playing in an orchestra? Do you see a walrus, a woodpecker, and a wolf washing clothes on a windy day? Is it true that a turkey, a toucan, and a toad can toboggan in twos? With these arrangements, a child begins to see that language can be expressed in declarative sentences and in interrogative ones. Ages 6–7.

Pattern: After each capital and lowercase letter, there are traditional sentence beginnings such as "*A* is for————" and "*B* is for ————" that lead to alliterative sentences about animals in curious situations. Basic sentence: letter name, linking verb, prepositional phrase.

De Brunhoff, Laurent. *Babar's ABC*. Illustrated by the author. New York: Random House, 1983.

Here is De Brunhoff's alphabet book for a child's Babar collection. Babar and others in Celesteville introduce the ABCs. From Arthur's accordion to Zephir, the little monkey who zips the zipper on a sleeping bag, each object represents a key word that is displayed in an alliterative sentence. For *A*, Alexander plays with a bow and arrow and aims at an apple on a tree. There is no connected story line to accompany the large illustrations or the unrelated small inserts at the foot of each page. However, in the sentences, a child sees the key words in boldface. In turn, these words name the key objects and introduce the letters. Unrelated smaller illustrations show sentences to give a context for the words that begin with a selected letter. Some prepositional phrases with *in*, *on*, *to*, *of*, and *among*. Ages 4–6.

Pattern: Uppercase and lowercase letters lead to key nouns in large illustrations. Basic sentence: noun, verb, noun.

Eastman, Philip D. *The Alphabet Book*. Illustrated by the author. New York: Random House, 1974.

Large serif capitals in black introduce the alliterative words found in these short nonsense phrases, where animal characters demonstrate unusual behaviors and incongruous situations are seen. Some animals show the behavior of humans: a bird rides a bicycle, a cow drives a car, and an octopus rows a boat with all eight of its arms. An alphabet frieze along the right and left margins of the pages identifies the selected letter for the page with colorful highlighting. Using word cards to match to the words in the phrases, a child points to individual words as they are found and read. Ages 4–6.

Pattern: Capitals are repeated in alliterative words in nonsense phrases and in the ABC frieze in the margins.

Gardner, Beau. *Have You Ever Seen...? An ABC Book*. Illustrated by the author. New York: Dodd, Mead, and Company, 1986.

Full-color illustrations show Gardner's images in bright graphics. There is a ladybug who rides a lightning bolt, an inchworm on ice skates, and an octopus who eats oatmeal with spoons held by all eight arms. Both upper- and lowercase serif letters guide the sequence and are found in the corners of colorful pages. These letters are matched to initial capital letters in alliterative words about the humorous situations. Ending with a question mark, each phrase completes the question in the title and emphasizes the words that begin with the page's selected letter. Ages 2–6.

Pattern: Alliterative phrases complete title question. Basic phrase: noun, preposition, noun.

Gretz, Susanna. *Teddy Bears ABC*. Illustrated by the author. New York: Follett, 1974.

Gretz's key words end in "ing" and emphasize the activities of six teddy bears. The teddy bears and their dalmatian, Fred, see a red airplane with animal passengers, who are traveling to the zoo. The bears invite the giraffe, two kangaroos, a yak, and one very cross owl home with them for some fun. With these invited guests, *G* is for gargling when the giraffe gets a sore throat, *W* is for washing the yak in the shower, and *P* is for painting a mural with the help of a kangaroo. On the *E* page the bears *enjoy* a picnic. The bears are surrounded with the foods from a large basket: mustard, hotdogs, fruit, and bottles of soft drinks. Phrases such as "arriving in an airplane," "yelling at a yak," and "zipping off to the zoo" present additional words that begin with the same letter and sound. Does a child notice the similar "ing" endings in the words? Ages 4-6.

Pattern: Guided by single lowercase letters, alphabetical activities and verbs with "ing" endings for actions.

Heide, Florence Parry. *Alphabet Zoop*. Illustrated by Sally Mathews. New York: McCall Publishing Company, 1970.

Alexander the alligator adores asparagus. Bertha the bear believes in brussel sprouts. Cauliflower is craved by Clarissa. A pattern of alliterative animals and foods is seen in each of Mathews's illustrations. In each pattern is a child able to name some of the animals and the objects that have the repeated consonant sound in their names? Any activity seen in one of the drawings may be selected as the middle of a pattern for a short story for an older child's oral dictation or writing. As the child dictates information about the activity, the information is recorded on a 5 X 7 card. From this a child creates a short story aloud or in writing from either a) a beginning direction or pattern or b) an ending direction or pattern. The card information is the center of the story. For example, on the page for J Jeremy jumps for joy over jelly rolls. Two jaguars sit at a dinner table in the middle of a jungle. A jujube-eating jackal and a jug are nearby. Would any of these activities form the center of a story? If so, from which direction does a child want to create a story? From a beginning direction? An ending direction? What help does a child need to start dictating or to begin writing? Ages 7-8.

Pattern: For each capital, alliteration in print and in names of objects in illustrations. Basic sentence: noun, verb, noun.

Ipcar, Dahlov. *I Love My Anteater with an A*. Illustrated by the author. New York: Alfred A. Knopf, 1964.

For every letter (e.g., A) Ipcar writes alliterative sentences about an animal (Aristotle the anteater), tells why he likes it (affectionate) and dislikes it (argumentative), names its country of origin (Afghanistan), and identifies the occupation this anthropomorphic animal has (abstract artist). Ages 8-up.

Pattern: Within parallel writing, alliterative sentences found about anamophoric animals.

Knight, Hilary. *Hilary Knight's ABC*. Illustrated by the author. New York: Golden Press, 1961.

Language is expressed with more sounds of alliteration in this one, and there is a visual pattern in the pictures as well. Alliteration is heard in the names of the objects in Knight's humorous double-page spreads. For example, at *A* there are acrobatic alligators in airplanes and questions that suggest looking for objects beginning with the letter. On a concluding page is a list of objects to be found for each letter. To discover any similarities in the patterns of the artwork of two artists, show an older child the illustrations in Knight's book and in *All Butterflies: An ABC* by Marcia Brown. Does a child see any similarities in the color patterns in the two sets of illustrations? Is there a similar use of line or a line pattern in the artistic work of both Knight and Brown? Ages 6-9.

Pattern: Manuscript and cursive models of letters and objects to identify.

Kraus, Robert. *Goodnight Little ABC*. Illustrated by Neils Mogens Bodecker. New York: Windmill Books, 1972.

Saying the word signal that is a farewell acknowledgment is fun with these animals whose names are alliterative. A young listener says good night to Xenophon Xerxes Xiphosura (a horseshoe crab), Yelva Yacobowsky Yak, and Zorba Zachary Zebra. After reading these sentences, a child may choose a substitute word for the evening farewell, good night. This farewell pattern may be replaced with another signal and the patterned sentences read or chanted again. Some word signals to consider for the substitution are good morning or hello for welcoming greetings and please and thank you for courtesy signals. Ages 4-6.

Pattern: Large uppercase and lowercase serif letters in white are introduced with repetitive sentences and alliterative animal names.

Law, Felicia, series advisor. *Animal ABC*. Illustrated by Peter Woodcock. London: Octopus Books, 1980.

Written with alphabetical phrases about such animals as acting armadillos, bathing bears, and yelling yaks, this book shows the large animals on double-page spreads. The spreads provide ample space for the oversize guiding letters in black and make it easy for a child to locate the words that end in "ing": "driving," "eating," and "flying." These phrase stems give a child the opportunity to expand a basic phrase pattern and to insert a verb auxiliary such as "are" (yaks are yelling) and "were" (bears were bathing) into the phrases to see other patterns. Does a child see one exception (excited) in the "ing" pattern? Can a child restate a word that fits into the "ing" pattern? Ages 7–8.

Pattern: Alliterative phrases introduce words that end in "ing."

Mills, Carol. *A-Z and Back Again: An ABC Book*. Illustrated by Susanne Ferrier. London: Tiger Books International, 1986.

Originally published as *The A-Z of Absolute Zaniness* (Australia: RPLA Publishers, 1984), this alphabet introduces each pair of letters with an unusual personality, from Auntie Ada and Barney Bear to Yolanda Yallop and Zebedee Zebra. For each personality there is an alliterative and rhythmic text with capitalization and punctuation inserted in the full-page illustration. Large sans serif capitals and lowercase letters introduce the names of the personalities. In Africa on an adventure, Auntie Ada meets Albert the alligator, who gives Auntie an apple. (Later Auntie ate the apple and Albert ate Auntie.) Barney the bear buys a bee in a bottle and a beetle in a box. Cousin Clara's chubby cat is Charlie, who catches a cold and eats some creamy custard. Other personalities to meet are Goobly Goblin, who grows grapes, gladioli, and gooseberries; Mungo Monster, who lives in a muddy marsh and hums to the moon; and Weirdy Old Witch, who wiggles a wobbly wand. Ages 6-up.

Pattern: Alliterative rhymes introduce zany personalities.

Nedobeck, Don. *Nedobeck's Alphabet Book*. Illustrated by the author. Milwaukee: Ideals, 1981.

Does a child want to see Merrill the monkey nibble nutritious nuts? Or Pudgy Paul, a pig, who plows through a pail of pears? Or the quail quintet that belongs to Queen Quintessa? Large full-colored illustrations show these characters with alliterative names. In a column arrangement the capitalized words in black emphasize the pattern of alliteration in each sentence about the animal. On each page their initial letters may be matched with the large red serif letter that guides the sequence. Does a child understand that the pattern of the color of the letter does not affect the matching process on these pages? Ages 5-up.

Pattern: Capitalized alliterative words in column format describe actions of characters. Initial letters in words in column match single guiding serif capital in red.

Niland, Deborah. *ABC of Monsters*. Illustrated by the author. New York: McGraw-Hill, 1978.

Recommended. Monsters at a party do some unusual things. One monster ogles an ogre, two quake, and all zigzag all the way back home. Can a child identify the pattern of the phrases and see that each phrase begins with a word that ends in "ing?" The phrases represent chunked material, words that can be read as a meaningful unit of language. After reading the chunks, can a child create a second pattern for the phrases by using the model of changing "annoying" into "annoy"? By eliminating each "ing" suffix whenever it is seen in a word? With these changes, the monsters and their activities lend themselves to another extension of language. Ages 4-6.

Pattern: "Ing" verbs in phrases presented as units of language.

Obligado, Lilian. *Faint Frogs Feeling Feverish and Other Terrifically Tantalizing Tongue Twisters*. Illustrated by the author. New York: Viking Press, 1983.

In alliterative phrases the names of animals, along with their actions and selected words that tell how the actions are happening, are seen and read. A child sees words that end in "ing" and "ly."

There is an admiring anteater, a bear who acts badly, and some chattering chipmunks. These phrases, like the ones in the previous book, organize words into meaningful language groups, or chunks, for a child. Each language group is separated by spaces and is easy to identify. Forming a pattern of words that end in "ing" and "ly," these language chunks are ready for a child to see, to hear, to repeat, or to read. Ages 7–8.

Pattern: Alliterative words name animals and describe actions with words that end in "ing" and "ly."

Patience, John. *An Amazing Alphabet.* Illustrations by the author. New York: Derrydale Books, 1984.

With alliterative phrases both upper- and lowercase letters are introduced. Anxious animals wait in an anchored ark, a baker with bread walks toward an unseen banana skin, and a crazy cat drives a car. Beginning with similar letters the words are in bold type and are easy to identify. For each key character the scene changes on the endpapers. Several guiding letters are found again in different alphabetical scenes or poses on the endpapers—e.g., the letter *A* labels a large red apple, the letter *B* takes the shape of a baker carrying a lowercase *B* on a tray. What questions can a child generate after looking at each picture and caption? Ages 4–6.

Pattern: Oversize capitals and lowercase letters are introduced by phrases with alliterative words.

Peter Piper's Practical Principles of Plain and Perfect Pronunciation with Manifold Manifestations. Illustrations created by Marcia Brown. New York: Scribner's, 1959.

Each alphabetical question is an alliterative one and is asked for each letter in the alphabetical sequence. Each question tests a student's ability to repeat a series of alliterative words without tangling his or her tongue over the pronunciations. The questions may be rewritten into alliterative declarative sentences and used as headlines. The headlines become ideas for a child's illustrations, story, or poem. Ages 9-up.

Pattern: Short alliterative phrases are followed by alliterative questions.

Portugal, Jan. *ABC Sillies.* Illustrated by the author. Palo Alto, Calif.: Wild Horse Publishing Company, 1983.

Portugal's small book introduces the Wuppies of Zoobi, who are small hobbitlike people with dark eyes. The Wuppies do all the things that non-Wuppies do. Jeremiah and Josephine journey in their jalopy, Rudolph and his relatives go to a reunion, and Willie accompanies Wilma for a walk in the woods. Capital and lowercase serif letters in red precede alliterative phrases in a text of purple. At the foot of each page is a frieze of the alphabet, in both upper- and lowercase letters. In the frieze the selected letter is shown in boldface type. For *A*, alligators do not admire Alonzo's artwork. At *B*, Buddy buys a breakfast of bread and butter, and with *C*, Custer catches a catfish and a cold. Additional story sentences about alliterative characters may be dictated or written: Cousin Custer———. Ages 7–8.

Pattern: Alliterative sentences show capitals at beginnings and punctuation at ends.

Sendak, Maurice. *Alligators All Around: An Alphabet.* Illustrated by the author. New York: Harper and Row, 1962.

Alliterative two-word phrases describe the alphabetical activities of the members of an alligator family who are quite busy. In the sequence a key word with an "ing" ending introduces each phrase. The alligator family is bursting balloons, doing dishes, and quarreling. To create a second pattern, an older child might be encouraged to delete the "ing" ending from each one of the introductory words to create a second list of verbs. The word "keeping" becomes "keep," "looking" becomes "look," and "ordering" becomes "order." Here is additional material chunked into phrases representing proper language units for a child's listening or reading. Ages 7–8.

Pattern: Alliterative phrases about an active and humorous alligator family contain words ending in "ing."

Seuss, Dr. *Dr. Seuss's ABC.* New York: Random House, 1963.

Recommended. In this one a child sees that language may be used for fun and nonsense. Dr. Seuss (pseud. for Theodor Seuss Geisel) asks the question, "What begins with———?" and the answers are alliterative ones. A lazy lion licks a green lollipop. There are bubbles near a bumblebee. A camel walks a ceiling. The author's words could be the beginning of tall-tale talk for a child. In addition, a child hears the nonsense words created by the author— another exciting aspect of playing with language—in Fiffer-feffer-feff, tuttle-tuttle, and Ubb. Nonsense words and illustrations lead to discussions of questions from another point of view, one similar to this: "If this illustration about the camel shows nonsense, what do you think an illustration about a camel would look like if it showed something sensible?" Ages 5–6.

Pattern: Uppercase and lowercase letters are followed by key nouns, nonsense, tall-tale talk, and rhythmic alliterative sentences.

Tallon, Robert. *Zoophabets*. Illustrated by the author. New York: Bobbs-Merrill, 1971.

Recommended. Humorous drawings show alliterative creatures who in turn introduce the letters of the alphabet. Beginning with *A* a child recognizes that language includes original words. The first zoophabet is an alpok. Living in an attic, an alpok eats objects that begin with *A*. Each subsequent zoophabet introduces another letter in a similar way. Alliterative sentences such as these serve as short stories. Within each story-sentence a noun can be deleted so a listener can contribute an original one to complete the thought. Ages 7-up.

Pattern: Twenty-six creatures, the zoophabets, introduce letters in alliterative sentences.

Tempest, Margaret. *An ABC for You and Me*. Illustrated by the author. London: The Medici Society, Ltd., 1948.

Clothed in trousers, shirts or dresses, each animal in these alliterative sentences has a proper name that begins with the same letter as the object word. What does David have? A duck. Edward? An elephant. And Freddy? A flag. Is the capitalization of the proper names noticed? During a second reading, an interested child may respond to such questions as What is this animal's name? What does this animal have? Does a child want to create an illustrated page to show his or her knowledge of words that begin with the same letter or sound? Ages 5–6.

Pattern: Each sentence shows:—— (proper name) has a ——
(name of object). The proper name of the animal and the name
of the object begin with similar letters and sounds.

Letter-Object-Word Arrangements

Letter-Object

Bruna, Dick. *The ABC Frieze*. Illustrated by the author. London:
Methuen Children's Books Ltd, 1971.

Single objects such as duck, fish, and grapes are outlined in
black and introduce each lowercase serif letter. These are the same
objects the child sees in *B Is for Bear: An ABC* (also by Bruna).
Some unusual noun choices for children to recognize in this letter-
object arrangement are "jigsaw," "eskimo," and "yawn." Ages 4–5.

Pattern: Lowercase letters, objects, and names of objects.

Happy Helper ABC. Illustrated by June Goldsborough. Racine,
Wisc.: Western Publishing Company, Inc., 1971.

For *A*, one green alligator juggles apples, a bear shows the
letter *B* to a bird, and a cow joins a cat as passengers in a car with
the letter *C* on one door. All of the nouns that identify the objects
are listed in alphabetical order on the last page. Ages 4–5.

Pattern: Objects and nouns introduce stylized capital letters.

Hoban, Tana. *26 Letters and 99 Cents*. Illustrated by the author.
New York: Greenwillow, 1987.

Full-color photographs are seen on recto pages and large
uppercase and lowercase letters on verso pages. For example, *Uu*
is for a photograph of an umbrella. Hoban's book is one a child
may read to say the letters of the alphabet, and then turn it over to
find more photographs of coins that represent counting from 1 to
99. For instance, one dime and two quarters are pictured by the
value for sixty. Ages 4–8.

Pattern: For each pair of uppercase and lowercase letters
there is a full-color photograph of an object.

Hyman, Trina Schart. *A Little Alphabet*. Illustrated by the author. Boston: Little, Brown and Company, 1980.

Hyman's little alphabet features one large beige serif capital as the center of each small page. Each letter is surrounded by a black line drawing that shows a boy or girl using objects that begin with the letter. For the letter *R* a child roller-skates through the rain with a rabbit and a rosebush nearby. The names of the objects are listed on the endpapers and provide a self-checking list. Is a boy or girl ready to look at any object and name it? Or look at the written noun and then pronounce it? Is any boy or girl interested in hearing the word, seeing it, saying it, and then writing it? Ages 5-7.

Pattern: Capital letter emphasized by objects whose names begin with the letter's sound.

Kitchens, Bert. *Animal Alphabet*. Illustrated by the author. New York: Dial, 1984.

Recommended. A young viewer guesses the identity of each animal. The large capital gives a clue to the initial sound of the animal's name. On plain white backgrounds the carefully detailed animals give visual insights to a young viewer. X-ray fish swim in blue water held by the intersecting sides of the *X*, a snail climbs up the curved shape of the *S*, and the rhinoceros attacks an *R* with his horn. For a self-check the last page lists the animals, from armadillo and bat to yak and zebra. Since Kitchens's ABC is an alphabet book that links an animal with the capital letter beginning the animal's name, a comprehensive, concluding list gives a child the opportunity to verify the names of the animals. Does a young child identify each letter aloud as well as locate each letter by pointing? Ages 5-up.

Pattern: Initial letter in name is matched with large serif capital in black.

Lionni, Leo. *Letters to Talk About*. Illustrated by the author. New York: Pantheon, 1985.

Lionni presents several active mice to help a child learn the letters of the alphabet. There are no objects or key words for the letters. A child sees only colorful manuscript capitals. One mouse poses near each letter. The letters are carried by mice, stood upon, and ridden like a unicycle. Are any actions of the mice in ABC order? Ages 3–4.

Pattern: Colorful capital block letters in sequence.

My First ABC's. Illustrated by Linda Bound. New York: Starlog Press, Inc., n.d.

In a flip-flop format this book shows the objects from one apple through several nails. On the back side are additional objects such as an ostrich, sun, and vegetables to see. On the pages that fold up in an accordion arrangement are children's blocks with capitals in colors. Each key object poses near one block. Each capitalized key word shows at the foot of the page. Ages 2-up.

Pattern: Full-color objects introduce key nouns and serif capitals in colors.

Pienkowski, Jan. *ABC.* Illustrated by the author. New York: Harvey House, 1981.

Pienkowski's small volume contains bright backgrounds of fuschia, blue, green, and orange. One object per page reflects the initial sound needed to match the capitals and lowercase manuscript letters. The letters are found in the lefthand corner of each page. Two unusual noun choices are "die" (singular of dice) and "number" (on a telephone dial). The beginning sound of each noun is related to the accompanying symbol. On a final page are boys and girls from various ethnic groups. Each one wears a shirt that shows one letter of the alphabet. Is a child ready to hear the sounds in a name of a selected object and then, with an adult's help, blend them to pronounce the name? As auditory discrimination skills develop, is a boy or girl ready to hear the name of an object and then say the phonemes (sounds) for the word in order? Ages 4–6.

Pattern: Objects introduce pairs of uppercase and lowercase letters. Beginning sound of each noun may be matched to accompanying symbol.

Rojankovsky, Feodor. *Feodor Rojankovsky's ABC: An Alphabet of Many Things*. Racine, Wisc.: Western Publishing Company, 1971.

Rojankovsky's ABC letters are shown on separate pages. The letters face illustrations of such familiar objects as an airplane, a button, and a clown. An adult may label several of the pictures for a child. In some cases the adult covers a beginning letter of the object's name and asks the child to fill in the letter. Ages 3-up.

Pattern: Letter-object arrangement.

Teddy Bear's ABC. Photographs by Michael Plomer. London: Deans International Publishing, 1985.

Teddy bears pose with cutout letters of the alphabet on every page. To emphasize which lowercase letters in white the bears hold, the same letters are shown again a second time in blue in the alphabet frieze at the foot of the page. Ages 3-4.

Pattern: Lowercase letters are repeated in ABC frieze.

Wynne, Patricia. *The Animal ABC*. Illustrated by the author. New York: Random House, 1977.

On the thick durable pages of this ABC, a wooden alphabet block with a capital *A* is the first in the sequence to introduce an accompanying animal. Frogs leap on and around the block for the letter *F* and two African frogs (xenopus) pose near the block for *X*. Ages 3-5.

Pattern: Capitals on alphabet blocks are related to initial sounds of animal names.

Object-Word

Beller, Janet. *A-B-C-ing: An Action Alphabet*. Illustrated by the author. New York: Crown Publishers, Inc., 1984.

Using children in pictures, Beller illustrates actions. Beller shows twenty-six ing words for the actions. Each word is at the foot of the page and is accompanied by a black-and-white photograph that freezes the action. There is climbing, reading, and zipping. Each word is in lowercase serif letters in black. Since there are no single letters to guide the sequence of the alphabet, a child should know the letters of the alphabet or should recognize the first letter in each action word as a guide to the sequence. Ages 4–7.

Pattern: "Ing" words for actions form sequence without single guiding letters.

Cartwright, Mary. *Mary Cartwright's ABC*. Illustrated by the author. New York: Rand McNally and Company, 1981.

Bright blue letters trimmed in gold braid introduce this alphabet with the key words *admiral* and *anchor*. Dressed in his admiral blue uniform and hat, one teddy bear admiral sits with the anchor of his ship. Does a child notice that this illustration is framed with the shape of *A*s? At *H* the letters take the shape of a green hedge and show a red helicopter delivering a sculptured hedge to someone's garden. Does a child notice the apparent texture of the capitals and lowercase letters? Closing key words are *xylophone*, *yak*, *yucca*, *zebra* and *zoo*, and are found beneath the accompanying large full-color illustrations. Ages 4–6.

Pattern: Upper- and lowercase letters are introduced by illustrations with single-word choices.

Gundersheiner, Karen. *ABC Say with Me*. Illustrated by the author. New York: Harper and Row, 1984.

One tiny girl illustrates "ing" words to introduce this imaginative alphabet. Gundersheiner's presentation uses word choices such as "asking," "balancing," and "cleaning" to support the illustrations. For the unseen letter *E* the key words are "eating" and "egg." On top of a red-rimmed drum, the small girl holds a white daisy and dances. In other illustrations the girl is floating with a feather, giggling in a grape cluster, and hiding under a hat. A young viewer seees the little girl and the objects in an action described by the verb. The illustrations supply the context for the verb used on each page. Printed in capitals, the verbs are emphasized visually. The combined illustrations provide a small language file of "ing" words as the little girl moves through the ABCs. Like Beller's book, there are no single letters from the alphabet as a sequence to guide a viewer. The alphabetical order is led by the initial letter in each word choice. Ages 3–4.

Pattern: Key "ing" words label actions.

Lalli, Judy. *Feelings Alphabet: An Album of Emotions from A to Z.* Illustrated by Douglas L. Mason-Fry. Graphics by Nancy Snyder. Rolling Hills Estates, Calif.: B. L. Winch and Associates, 1984.

In language, feelings can be named and described, and Lalli names feelings in this alphabet. A one-word caption and a black-and-white photograph emphasize one feeling or emotion experienced by a young child. Stylized words from *afraid* (of a snake) and *brave* (climbing high) to *excited* (receiving gifts) and *zonked* (sound asleep) are seen. Some of the letters that spell the words help tell a child what the word means with creative use of print. For instance, shaky letters spell the word *afraid*, a question mark dots the letter *I* in *curious*, and the letters in the word *unhappy*, are accompanied by a teardrop. Ages 5–6.

Pattern: Photographs show children's feelings and emotions and lead to key words, initial letters, and sounds.

Letter-Object-Word

A Is for Apple. Illustrated by Lynn N. Grundy. Loughborough, Eng.: Ladybird Books, Ltd., 1980.

Some of the colorful objects (apple, ball, cat) outlined in black that are seen in *The Big ABC and Counting Book* can be found again in this smaller ABC. The objects introduce their names and the lowercase letters in colors. There is one object per page. A favorite word may be discussed as a child listens for the beginning sound of the word. With discussion a child accepts that every letter in a word has a name. The name of the letter that is the symbol for the beginning sound of each noun is identified. When ready for more advanced listening activities, a child listens for a medial or a final sound in the word. Ages 4-up.

Pattern: One object per page presents key noun and single lowercase letter.

A. B. C. Illustrated. Los Angeles: Price/Stern/Sloan Publishers, Inc., 1981.

On each page of this colorful, sturdy book are frames that embrace three letters, words, and objects. Lowercase letters (similar to manuscript) are seen again in the labels of objects, e.g., "ant," "balloon," and "clown." After the labels are introduced, the separate objects are regrouped in an illustration. For example, the clown is seen again holding one yellow balloon while the ant crawls along the string. Stick drawings on a classroom chalkboard may be labeled as a child dictates the names of the objects. There are several high-frequency nouns from the Allens' List of 100 Nouns: *balloon, elephant, ice cream, clown, girl, queen, duck, horse.* Ages 4–5.

Pattern: Lowercase letters in black are introduced by objects found a second time in additional scenes.

ABC. Janine Amos, ed. Illustrated by Anni Axworthy. Paulton, Briston, Great Brit.: Purnell and Sons, Limited, 1982.

Large objects—e.g., one green apple, one yellow balloon, and one red cat—are centered on white backgrounds. Does a child notice any size discrepancy? The apple is as large as a boy, the fox is as large as an elephant, and the dustbin is as large as a car. Block upper- and lowercase letters in black are related to initial letters in the one-syllable and two-syllable key words. A child in the United States hears the language of Great Britain when the word "dustbin" identifies a large trash can. Some high-frequency nouns are shown: *apple, balloon, boy, car, cat, dog, elephant, horse, kite, oranges, queen.*

The endpapers and the back cover show a review of objects—such as a jigsaw puzzle, the unicorn, and a zebra—in a left-to-right sequence. During a rereading, an adult might show that the letters in words are written in this left-to-right sequence, too. Does a child notice that a blank space separates one word from another? Ages 3–5.

Pattern: Black block capitals and lowercase letters are models for letter identification, matching, and manuscript writing.

ABC. Illustrated by Patti Boyd. New York: Simon and Schuster, Inc., 1985.

This small apple-shaped book opens to one object per page beginning with a shiny red apple, a blue and yellow tugboat, and a blue-eyed cat with yellow fur, in full-color on white backgrounds. Upper- and lowercase san serif letters and capitalized key nouns are introduced by such objects as one Easter egg, one jack-o'-lantern, and one purple yo-yo. Ages 3-up.

Pattern: Colorful objects introduce capitalized key words and pairs of letters.

ABC. Illustrated by Joseph Cellini. New York: Grosset and Dunlap, 1980.

Cellini's board pages hold clear objects and letters. Large capitals, decorated with colorful spatters, can be matched with the first letters in the words for such drawings as a red cadillac, Santa Claus with his pack of toys on his back, and a child's backyard, complete with a red ball, sand pail, and swing set. Words that label objects may be dictated by a child and written by the adult. The adult calls the child's attention to the left-to-right sequence in which the letters are written. Before an additional word is written, all of the words previously recorded may be read aloud in a repetitive pattern. Ages 1-5.

Pattern: Initial letters and sounds in names seen in lowercase letters may be matched with objects and large block capitals in colors.

ABC. Illustrated by Cornelius DeWitt. Racine, Wisc.: Western Publishing Company, Inc., 1951.

A colorful collection of objects on each page introduces the names of the objects and the first letter that is similar in all of the names. Each selected letter is shown in three ways—once as an oversize block capital in color, then as a lowercase block letter, and again as a lowercase letter in italics. A child will be able to turn to these letters for models for writing. All of the objects selected for a particular letter are integrated into one illustration. For *E*, an

Eskimo carries a large decorated egg while riding on the back of an elephant. Ages 4-up.

Pattern: Objects introduce names with guiding letter as a block capital, as a block lowercase letter, and as a lowercase letter in italics.

ABC. Illustrated. London: Ramboro Books, n.d.

Two full-colored objects per page help point out the sequence. Serif capitals are in three colors. Nearby objects are labeled with names in black capitals. Some unusual choices of objects to see: one white swan, a country village, and the signature of Elizabeth Regina, Queen of England. To review, a child selects names of objects, and the adult records the names. With each name, the first and the last letter may be located. As more names are dictated, an adult assists the child so all of the words that are found that begin or end with the same letter or sound are discussed. Ages 3-up.

Pattern: Sounds or shapes of colorful capitals related to sounds or shapes of initial letters in capitalized words in black.

ABC. Illustrated by Gerald Witcomb. Loughborough, Eng.: Ladybird Books, Ltd., 1978.

For a younger child, key words are given for vowels. The key words for *A* and *I* are "bag" and "ink." Each verso page holds one lowercase manuscript letter and the name of an object. Each facing page holds one clearly illustrated object, but the relative size of an object when compared to other nearby objects is not shown. For instance, the elephant is as large as the black cat, and the jeweled ring is as large as the wristwatch. After a child dictates names of selected objects and the adult records the names, a specific word is located. A young child is invited to place his or her hands around the word and to look at the shape of the word. Since a standard school pronunciation guide for the alphabet begins this book, an older child is encouraged to tell how an unfamiliar word may be pronounced as it is shown in the guide. Ages 4–5.

Pattern: Key objects and initial letters in names introduce lowercase letters.

ABC and Counting Rhymes. Illustrated by Mary Horton. New York: Wonder Books/Grosset and Dunlap, Inc., 1980.

A is for airplane, *B* is for boat, and *C* is for a mother cat carrying her kitten. More than one object is seen on a page. There are block capitals in black. Key words are capitalized. Following this alphabet are several counting rhymes, including "One, Two, Buckle My Shoe, " and " Ten Little Blackbirds." Ages 4–5.

Pattern: Single capital letters relate to capitalized initial letters in one-syllable and two-syllable names of objects.

Anderson, Walter. *An Alphabet.* Illustrated by the author. Jackson: University of Mississippi Press, 1984.

For this alphabet Anderson carved the illustrations from linoleum blocks. Each letter and object had to be drawn and cut backwards so the positioning would be correct when the illustrations were printed. Does a child notice the reverse position of the capital *Z* for "Zebra"? Ask an older child to help find Anderson's word choices of "Oppossum" or "Persimon" in the dictionary. The correct spellings are "opossum" and "persimmon." What animals and other objects can be found in the swirls of designs that surround each letter? Is that a snail hidden in the waves of the sea on the *S* page? Ages 5-up.

Pattern: Colorful capital letter, key noun, and key object arrangement.

Animal ABC. Illustrated. Tokyo: Froebel-Kan Co., Ltd./Heian International, Inc., n.d.

On the pages of this sturdy board book, a young boy or girl sees uppercase and lowercase block letters in bright colors. The letters stand beside the animal that introduces it. Key nouns are shown consistently in block capitals in black: "ALLIGATOR" for *A*, "BEAR" for *B*, and "CAT" for *C*. One word choice to discuss is *X* for "Xmas turkey." Ages 4–5.

Pattern: Animal name in capitals introduces pairs of upper- and lower-case letters.

Baby's First ABC. Illustrated. New York: Platt and Munk, 1960.

With a letter-object-word arrangement, a child begins to realize that in language the words he or she says are written with letters of the alphabet. Familiar full-color illustrations of objects and their labels introduce the capital block letters to a young child. In this one with its yellow backgrounds, *A* is for "APPLE," *B* is for "BIRD," and *C* for "CAT." The child sees words such as" egg," "fish," and "goat" written with capital letters. Ages 2-up.

Pattern: Objects and their names in capitals introduce single block capitals.

Baskin, Leonard. *Hosie's Alphabet*. Illustrated by the author. Words by Hosea, Tobias, and Lisa Baskin. New York: The Viking Press, 1972.

Recommended. A child begins to look at these pages and sees the guiding letters and descriptive phrases that face the illustrations of the animals. Here is a belted and Amazonian armadillo, a bumptious baboon, and a carrion crow. There are other rich words—"incredibly scaly," "quasi," and "omnivorous"—to describe such animals as the iguana, kiwi, and locust. What meaning will a child give to these words? Can the words be explained and defined, perhaps with the help of a dictionary? The creative use of print is seen as different fonts, and different-size styles are found for each letter and phrase. In a consistent pattern capitals are used to introduce the first word in each phrase. A child may want to finish some of the phrases and make complete sentences. Ages 5-up.

Pattern: With different fonts and sizes, single guiding letters are introduced by animals and descriptive phrases.

Bradbury, Lynne J., compiler. *The Big ABC and Counting Book*. Illustrated by Lynn N. Grundy. New York: Modern Promotions/Unisystems, Inc., 1981.

In pairs, capitals and lowercase letters in colors are found in the lower right-hand corners of the page. When an object's name begins with a vowel in this book, that name begins with the short sound of the letter (*A* as in "apple," *E* as in "egg," *I* as in "ink") and not the name of the letter (*A* as in "Amy"). Consonants are introduced with colorful objects outlined in black. Key words are in lowercase boldface near the objects, and their initial letters are easy to match with the selected lowercase letter. The selected lowercase letter is consistently located in the upper left-hand corner of the page. After seeing the final zebra and zipper, a child is invited to name selected objects (sun, fish, key) and to identify the sound with which each one starts. There are letters in a similar color pattern to match. Does any child notice a size discrepancy among or between the objects that are shown? Is a house key as large as a kangaroo? Is a cat often the same size as a car? Ages 3-up.

Pattern: Guided by upper- and lowercase pairs, objects introduce key names and initial lowercase letters.

Brett, Molly. *An Alphabet.* Illustrated by the author. London: The Medici Society, Ltd., 1980.

Oversize serif capitals are the centers of pages encircled with full-color illustrations of plants and animals. Beneath the illustrations are the word choices to introduce the letters. For *A*, a child sees" acorn," "adder," "ant" and other selections. After *L* there is a double-page spread that reviews all of the letters within the illustrations near the objects. Ages 4–6.

Pattern: Capital-object-word arrangement.

Broomfield, Robert. *The Baby Animal ABC.* Illustrated by the author. New York: Puffin Books, 1964.

Baby animals introduce the letters of the alphabet. An anteater cub introduces lowercase serif *A*, a bison calf is for *B*, and a donkey foal is for *D*. Some young animals are called cubs, e.g., the lion, tiger, wolf. Other young are called calves—the young of the yak and the rhinoceros. Still others are foals—zebra and ponies. Which animal young have names that are applied only to them? On each page the name of the mature animal is in capitals, and introduces the capital letter that begins the animal's name. The name of the baby animal is in lowercase letters and introduces the lowercase letter on each page. A noun that is used frequently, such as an animal's name, may be extended with other related nouns for additional language experience. Under two headings, a) Adult Animal Names and b) Baby Animal Names, the child's dictated nouns may be listed. To pronounce the words in an oral pattern, a child may want to say the name, in capitals, of the adult animal in a "capital" voice (high, loud) and say the name of a baby animal, in lowercase letters, in a low, soft voice. Ages 3-up.

Pattern: Animals in full-color and their names introduce large upper-and lowercase serif letters in color.

Burningham, John. *John Burningham's ABC*. Illustrated by the author. Chicago: Bobbs-Merrill, Inc., and Jonathan Cape Ltd., 1964.

Burningham's collection is guided by capitals and lowercase sans serif letters. There are illustrative words on the verso pages. Bright pictures with boldly composed figures are on the recto pages. For *T*, the word "tractor" is seen in lowercase letters, which face a colorful picture. A tractor is driven by a seated workman. Ages 4-up.

Pattern: Letter pairs and names of objects face illustrations.

Burningham, John. *John Burningham's ABC*. Illustrated by the author. New York: Bobbs-Merrill, 1967.

In this attractive book, capitals and lowercase letters on verso pages face Burningham's illustrations. One green apple introduces *A*, one golden orange introduces *O*, and animals at the zoo introduce *Z*. Ages 4-up.

Pattern: Objects in color introduce both uppercase and lowercase letters.

Burningham, John. *John Burningham's ABC*. Illustrated by the author. New York: Crown Publishers, Inc., 1985.

Here is another Burningham ABC book. One small child joins animals, objects, and people on the full-color pages. The alphabetical nouns that accompany these objects introduce the upper-and lowercase serif letters in black found in the corners of the pages. The child pushes an elephant, is bumped by a goat, and rides the back of a hippopotamus. The endpapers hold a review of all of the lowercase letters in purple. Burningham's topic of animals lends itself to a discussion: Would you rather meet a ——— or a ———?

It also lends itself to stick drawings on a chalk board or paper to represent words that a child dicates about animals. Ages 4–5.

Pattern: Capitals and lowercase serif letters relate to initial letters in key words.

Charles, Donald. *Letters from Calico Cat*. Illustrated by the author. Chicago: Childrens Press, 1974.

An orange calico cat leads a youngster into certain behaviors and selected objects. "Awake," "butterfly," and "cricket" open the sequence. On a white background one large colorful object per page is shown. Upper-and lowercase serif letters in colors are located at the upper corners of the pages with the key word in black serif lowercase underneath. Is a child interested in saying "meow" or "purr-rr" each time that calico cat is found on the pages? There is a final review, in a change of type style from the earlier serif letters: all of the letters in black resemble manuscript. Blue guide lines show the relative height and size of the upper- and lowercase letters. Ages 4–7.

Pattern: Behaviors of calico cat and objects lead to key words and related upper- and lowercase letters.

Cleaver, Elizabeth. *ABC*. Illustrated by the author. New York: Atheneum, 1985.

Cleaver prepares a collage for each letter. In each small illustration are uppercase and lowercase serif letters in black and key objects. Selected objects are placed around each letter. For *X*, one girl models a print of an X ray and holds a card with the words "Merry Xmas," a possible choice for child-adult discussion in the home. On a background of red a zebra for Z breaks through an opening in the collage near an unzipped zipper. Ages 4–6.

Pattern: Capitals with lowercase letters and nouns naming objects are found in each collage.

Duke, Kate. *The Guinea Pig ABC*. Illustrated by the author. New York: Dutton, 1983.

Each large colorful letter of the alphabet is illustrated by the full-page actions of guinea pigs and a capitalized word choice about a guinea pig characteristic. The guineas pigs are *awake, bouncy, clean,* and *dirty.* One pig looks into the mailbox to find it empty; another wears a dragon costume and looks ferocious. And still another spoons ice cream from the dish of an unsuspecting guinea pig to illustrate the word choice "greedy." Ages 4-up.

Pattern: Oversize capitals in color and key words that identify actions of illustrated guinea pigs.

Floyd, Lucy, and Kathryn Lasky. *Agatha's Alphabet.* Illustrated by Dora Leder. New York: Rand McNally, 1975.

Action illustrations are followed with lists of action and object words on the double-page spreads. Verso pages hold the colorful single uppercase letters and face the single lowercase letters that guide the sequence. Is any child ready to arrange the words on one page in alphabetical order by the first letter? There is a short dictionary for a child to turn to on the final pages. Is there a definition that can be passed on to someone else by a child's demonstration of the meaning? By a display of the illustration? By telling the meaning? By a reading of the definition? Ages 6-9.

Pattern: Uppercase and lowercase letters face words labeling objects or actions.

Frederico, Helen. *ABC.* Illustrated by the author. New York: Golden Press, 1963.

Frederico's well-designed book includes objects (needle, nickels, nutcracker) all inserted on large letter-shapes of different colors on white backgrounds. Each noun begins with a capital, the same letter a child sees in the large shape. On the page with an oversize capital *A*, a child sees one bright red apple, two ants, an alligator, anchor, and acorn. The pattern from this one might initiate vocabulary charts cut in the shapes of large capitals. As a child finds illustrations of objects from magazines, posters, catalogs, and newspapers, the pictures are pasted on the appropriate capital for display. Ages 4-5.

Pattern: Capital letters are initial letters in nouns that name alphabetical objects.

Harada, Joyce. *It's the ABC Book.* Illustrated by the author. San Mateo, Calif.: Heian International, 1982.

Pairs of capitals and lowercase letters are found on each page. Illustrations are framed in bright yellow and show animals, objects, and plants whose names begin with the selected letter for the page. A boy or girl may predict and then verify identification by turning to the concluding list of words. Ages 4-up.

Pattern: Illustrations of animals, objects, and plants introduce pairs of guiding letters.

If I Say ABC. Illustrated. Designed and produced by Porter Productions, Inc. New York: Grosset and Dunlap, 1985.

This sturdy accordion-style book begins with behaviors— add, bathe, catch, and drive. At *N* for nap, a child turns the book over and continues the sequence. Small illustrations portray the behaviors of animals and children on orange backgrounds. Ages 2-up.

Pattern: Capitals in colors and key words in bold type are introduced by selected behaviors of children and animals.

Le Tord, Bijou. *Arf Boo Click: An Alphabet of Sounds.* Illustrated by the author. New York: Four Winds, 1981.

A young boy or girl may enjoy chiming in to help make the sounds in this onomatopoeic alphabet book. Here, words represent natural sounds. *A* is for the sound of a sneeze and the arf of a dog. *B* is for the buzz of a bee and the baa of a sheep. *C* is for the cheep of a chick, the cluck of a hen, and the coo of a pigeon. As the pages are turned, there are sounds other than animal sounds to hear and to repeat. What sound will a fire engine make? A ticking clock? A tugboat? An airplane? Car? Some of the sound choices represent sound variations of singular consonants: /Ch/ is heard in "cheep," /Wh/ in "whack," and /Kn/ in "knock." Ages 3–6.

Pattern: Beginning sounds relate to initial symbols of onomatopoeic words.

Munari, Bruno. *Bruno Munari's ABC*. Illustrated by the author. Cleveland: World Publishing Company, 1960.

Recommended. Here are large illustrations with some visual humor. One small fly buzzes in the illustrations. Arriving on the page for *F* along with a flower and a feather, the fly is seen again at *G* for glasses, at *I* for ice cream, and at *Z* for the buzz of the fly. Relative size may be discussed. Is the feather as large as the fish on the page? A California State Department of Education-recommended recreational reading. Ages 5–6.

Pattern: Letter-large object-word arrangement.

My ABC Book. Illustrated by Art Seiden. New York: Wonder House/Grosset and Dunlap, 1980.

Capital letters in different colors show the first letters of key nouns and such objects as airplane, boat, and cat. Some singular nouns in this one are high-frequency words: *dog, elephant, horse, kite, lion, nest, rabbit, and umbrella*. Ages 2–4.

Pattern: Names of familiar objects introduce capital letters.

My Animal ABC. Illustrated by Rene Cloke. New York: Crown Publishers, Inc., 1980.

In addition to animals, several objects whose names begin with the same letter and sound start this alphabet. Full-color illustrations of, for example, a blue airplane with a yellow propeller, a horned antelope, a green apple, are seen on the page with a large black lowercase *A*. Each object is labeled with one- to three-syllable words in black lowercase letters. Ages 3–6.

Pattern: Objects introduce names and beginning sounds and initial letters in words may be matched to a guiding lowercase letter.

Oxenbury, Helen. *Helen Oxenbury's ABC of Things*. Illustrated by the author. New York: Delacorte, 1971.

Recommended. Oversize upper- and lowercase letters are introduced by scenes of objects whose names begin with the appropriate letters in sequence. For *A*, a child sees an ant on an apple and reads the word choices, "ant" and "apple." For *T*, a turkey and two tigers ride a train, and at *Z*, zebras are found in the zoo. Ages 5–8.

Pattern: Upper- and lowercase letters with object and word arrangement.

Polak, Johan. *The True-to-Life Alphabet Book Including Numbers*. Illustrated by the author. New York: Grosset and Dunlap, 1952.

Polak's endpapers show the musical notes and the sequence of the letters in the ABC song. One and sometimes two objects per page introduce the guiding pairs of letters. The pairs are seen both as block letters and as cursive ones. With initial letters in capitals, these word choices are familiar sights—"apple," "ball," "cat"—and are found near each object. Relative size may be discussed. On facing pages a large dog is as large as the elephant. A rabbit is as large as Santa. Vegetables—an onion, cucumber, and radishes—are as large as the wagon that could carry the vegetables. Two final pages offer objects to count from one to ten. Ages 2-up.

Pattern: Shown in block and cursive style, pairs of letters are introduced by large objects and their capitalized names.

Roe, Richard. *Animal ABC*. Illustrated by the author. New York: Random House, 1984.

Roe's blue endpapers introduce the capital letters in sequence and show a child what is to come on the pages. With only two exceptions the double-page spreads offer large animals—alligator, bear, rhinoceros, whale, elephant, giraffe. These animals introduce their names with serif letters in black as well as with pairs of upper- and lowercase serif letters in red. The lowercase letter in red is matched with the lowercase letter in black in the animal's name. A young viewer begins to recognize that color does not affect the shape of the letter or change the letter's name. Ages 2-up.

Pattern: Animals introduce their names and lead to the beginning sounds and initial letters in names.

Rojankovsky, Feodor. *Animals in the Zoo*. Illustrated by the author. New York: Alfred A. Knopf, 1962.

Recommended. Rojankovsky's endpapers lead a child through the turnstile and into the zoo to see the peacock, flamingo, monkeys, hippopotamus, and other animals. Black, brown, and yellow colors are used to highlight the zoo animals in this one. When a child reaches the page for the letter *P*, a pelican is discovered, not the peacock first seen on the endpapers. On the page for *F*, a child finds a fennec (fox) and not the flamingo noticed earlier. For each animal, a child sees oversize capitals and lowercase letters as well as the capitalized key words for the zoo animals. Several of the animals are shown with their young on double-page spreads: dromedary, elephant, giraffe, hippopotamus, kangaroo, lion, seal, wolf, and zebra. The size of the animals in the illustrations makes them easy to see by individual children in a group. Ages 5–8.

Pattern: Guiding letters match initial letters in names of animals.

Rylands, Ljiljana. *The Alphabet Book*. Illustrated by the author. Cambridge, Eng.: Dinosaur Publications, 1978.

Rylands's colorful illustrations on white backgrounds are linked across the double-page spreads. An apple from an apple tree introduces *A*. The bees attracted to the apples on the tree also swarm toward one brown bear for *B*. Objects such as an apple, bear, and clown within the illustrations introduce the key words and the pairs of upper- and lowercase letters. Ages 5-up.

Pattern: Objects and animals linked across illustrations introduce key words and initial letters.

Smollin, Michael J. *The Alligator's ABC*. Illustrated by the author. New York: Random House, 1981.

In Smollin's small illustrations, a child sees one, two, three, or four objects on each sturdy page. *A* is for "alligator," "airplane," and "arrow." All of the objects on a page are grouped together in one nonsense situation. An alligator in an airplane follows the direction of the yellow arrow resting on a cloud. A camel carries a birthday cake with flaming candles. An elephant uses an easel to paint a picture of an egg. Capital letters are in colors. Objects are in full-color on white backgrounds, making the small objects easy to see. Ages 2-up.

Pattern: Objects grouped in nonsense illustrations introduce names and initial capitals.

Stillerman, Robbie. *The ABC Book.* Illustrated by the author. Racine, Wisc.: Western Publishing Company, Inc., 1982.

On Stillerman's pages one object in color introduces each serif capital in white and the accompanying label in black boldface ("pie," "spoon," "umbrella"). Small, thick cardboard pages offer backgrounds in blue, green, yellow, and purple. Ages 2-up.

Pattern: Objects introduce relationship of guiding white serif capital to initial black lowercase letter in object's name.

Szekeres, Cyndy. *ABC.* Illustrated by the author. Racine, Wisc.: Western Publishing Company, Inc., 1983.

As an introduction, all of the capitals and lowercase serif letters in the sequence appear against a faint peach background. For *A*, objects are gathered around a large red apple. While a mouse in an airplane flies over the apple and one large brown ant crawls across its side, one mouse artist paints a picture of the apple and a second mouse chops off pieces of the apple with a mouse-size ax. Pair by pair, the upper- and lowercase letters are located in the upper corners of the pages, to be introduced by various objects collected together in each illustration. One-, two-, three-, and four-syllable nouns (*ant, bubbles, envelope, caterpillar*) in serif lowercase letters in black are near the objects. Two objects include additional explanatory words: *do-it-yourself directions* and *turtleneck sweater.* The number of syllables in each word may be tapped out by the adult and counted together with the child. Ages 3-up.

Pattern: Labeled objects and animals introduce each pair of uppercase and lowercase letters.

Tallon, Robert. *Abcdefghijklmnopqrstuvwxyz in English and Spanish.* Illustrated by the author. London: Lion Press, 1969.

Tallon's key words make an ABC primer, introducing the letters, and are in both English and Spanish. Spanish equivalents for *Ch, Ll,* and *N* are omitted. The English *W* appears, but it is noted in this book that in Spanish, *W* is not used to start a word. For *A* and the word choice *airplane,* one blue airplane tows a large oversize capital *A* through a bright pink sky. English and Spanish words are seen in capitals and in lowercase letters. Two unusual choices are *devil* and *diablo* for *D* and *kiosk* and *kiosco* for *K.* There are some humorous illustrations, accompanying notes, and a bilingual pronunciation guide. Ages 6-up.

Pattern: Objects and labels in English and Spanish introduce the letters.

Wildsmith, Brian. *Brian Wildsmith's ABC.* Illustrated by the author. New York: Franklin Watts, 1963.

Recommended. Since each name is shown twice, once in capitals and once in lowercase letters, these words become predictable ones for a young viewer. On a final page Wildsmith provides the words in a traditional context. Sentences for reading about the objects are simple. With titles such as this one, an adult may read with a young child every day or night and tell the child how well he or she is doing in helping the adult read the book. A California State Department of Education-recommended extended reading. Ages 5–6.

Pattern: Capitals and lowercase letters are introduced by names of objects shown twice, once in capitals and again in lowercase letters.

Letter-object-phrase-sentence

A. B. C. Illustrated by Rose Art Studios. New York: Playmore, Inc., Publishers, n.d.

Doll-like figures pose with animals and objects in full-color scenes on small board pages. Inside, the boy and girl taste ice cream, play a xylophone, and arrange animal figures for a playtime zoo. There are different settings for each illustration. Outside, the children pose by a cat, dog, and hen. Accompanying sentences introduce the capitals and lowercase letters in bright colors. In the sentences the key nouns in bold type are easy to find. They identify the objects in the pictures. Ages 5-up.

Pattern: With capitalization and punctuation, names of animals and objects in bold type in short sentences lead to appropriate upper- and lowercase letters.

Adventures with Letters and Numbers. Illustrated by Walt Disney Studio. New York: Bantam Books, 1985.

Adapted from the Walt Disney Fun-to-Learn Library, this volume includes two sections, "Alphabet A-Z "and "Numbers 1-10." In the alphabet section, Mickey flies in his airplane, spends his money at the market, and sees his favorite animal, a zany zebra at the zoo. There are several original Disney characters—Goofy, Pluto, and Donald Duck. Others are from literature for children: Pooh and Eeyore, Pinocchio and the Blue Fairy, and Peter Pan and Captain Hook. Beneath each pair of block upper- and lowercase letters in black are descriptive sentences about the illustrations. Objects are labeled in the pictures, and their names are seen again in context in the sentences. For example, one full-color, full-page illustration shows Uncle Scrooge at the beach sitting under an umbrella. Beside him is a unicorn. They look at a map of the United States. The unicorn, umbrella, and map of the United States are labeled. These words are seen again in the inserted sentences for *U*. Ages 3-up.

Pattern: Pairs of black block letters, upper- and lowercase, are introduced by Disney objects or characters and their labeled names.

Animal Pals ABC. Illustrated by Henri Parmentier. Los Angeles: Price/Stern/Sloan Publishers, Inc., 1985.

In this board book anthropomorphic animals show the behaviors of humans—e.g., Father Cat picks apples, Poppa Rabbit clicks a photograph with a camera, and Poppa Bear puts gas in a car so the car will run. Block capitals in red are the initial letters in the repeating beginnings: *A* is for——and *B* is for——. Using print appropriate to his or her age, a child may complete a sentence with a word or words of choice. The sentence may be illustrated. Ages 3-4.

Pattern: Block capitals in red begin repetitive openings for short explanatory sentences about anthropomorphic animals.

Brown, Marcia. *All Butterflies: An ABC*. Illustrated by the author. New York: Charles Scribner's Sons, 1974.

Recommended. With a visual arrangement of words, Brown shows how words can link the ABCs. Full-color double-page spreads show the author's woodcuts and the inserted alphabetical words. From *A* in "all" to *Z* in "zoo," each initial letter in a key word carries the sequence forward through the alphabet. There are quiet raccoons, followed by sleepy turtles, and an umbrella shaped as a valentine. A child needs to examine the pages and words closely to see how this is organized. On the concluding page is a review of all of the block upper- and lowercase letters and the key words in the story. After seeing this model, an older child may be interested in writing alphabetical words in phrases and in linking a story together. A California State Department of Education-recommended recreational reading. Ages 5–7.

Pattern: Initial capital letters in key words about animals and their actions are linked across pages.

Chwast, Seymour, and Martin Stephen Moskof. *The Great Big Alphabet Picture Book with Lots of Words*. Illustrated by Richard Hefter. New York: Grosset and Dunlap, 1971.

Animals and objects in full-color illustrations introduce the large white capitals. Each selected capital is accompanied by words that begin with that letter at the foot of the page. Additional lists of words that begin with the letter are seen. Are the words in alphabetical order? If some of the words are rearranged, can an older child arrange the words into alphabetical order? Which child is interested in finding the meaning of "anvil" or one of the other uncommon words? The definition can be presented to someone else in one of several ways: by drawing a picture to illustrate the meaning; by acting out the meaning; by describing the meaning and giving examples; by reading the meaning from a dictionary and using the word in the context of a sentence. Ages 8-up.

Pattern: Names of animals and objects introduce capitals in white.

Crews, Donald. *We Read: A to Z.* Illustrated by the author. New York: Harper and Row, 1967.

Crews's book works directly with vocabulary, making a child realize that in language the same letters are used over and over again to write words. The author reminds a young viewer that all words are made from the twenty-six letters. Concepts that include positions and shapes introduce the words and letters. One pair of upper- and lowercase letters in blue, green, or red announces the concept word and the explanatory phrase. Crews's illustrations of the concepts use double-page spreads and bright colors. *E* is for the equal squares on a black-and-yellow-checkered page. *H* is for horizontal blue and green lines from one side of the page to the other side. *N* is for nothing and shows one blank white page. One unusual word choice is Crews's use of the colon, which leads a child to see that as punctuation it is a signal for more words to come. Each letter, and not the page, is numbered. After reading and discussing the concepts, an adult may read several selected key words and their definitive phrases and ask the child to respond by turning the pages to find the number of the letter for each key word. The numeral one is the locator for *A*. The locator for *B* is the numeral two, and so on. Ages 8-up.

Pattern: Capitals and lowercase letters in colors precede concept words and clarifying phrases.

Frosty the Snowman's ABC. Illustrated by Patricia Schories. New York: Wanderer Books/Simon and Schuster, Inc.,1985.

Categories labeled Holiday Goodies, Trimming the Tree, and Wrapping Presents, are arranged out of the ABC sequence, but there are holiday objects labeled in alphabetical order within each category on the heavy board pages. Some of the goodies found under Holiday Goodies include an apple pie, bread, chestnuts, and a drumstick. With the exception of the final illustration, the elves help Frosty in every one. In the last picture, Frosty leaves, and tips his black top hat in a good-bye signal to the sleeping animals and the elves and leaves. Ages 2-up.

Pattern: With capital serif letters, holiday objects are labeled in the full-color illustrations.

Fujikawa, Gyo. *Gyo Fujikawa's A to Z Picture Book*. Illustrated by the author. New York: Grosset and Dunlap, 1974.

Fujikawa's collection of labeled alphabetical objects appears on black-and-white pages that alternate with full-color ones. Capitals and lowercase serif letters are found in the corners of the large pages. Some alliterative phrases are included. For instance, a child hears that the winter wind can whistle, that dreams can be delicious or disgusting, and that the words "puddle" and "polliwog" begin with the letter *P*. Ages 3–9.

Pattern: With animals, objects, and children at play, labeled objects begin with capitals while lowercase letters are seen in related sentences.

Hargreaves, Roger. *Mr. Happy's ABC's*. Illustrated by the author. Los Angeles: Price/Stern/Sloan, Inc.,1981.

On the board pages of this ABC, Mr. Happy, a yellow personified circle with facial features and hands and feet, appears in each full-color illustration. Two or three colorful objects outlined in black on each page introduce their block labels ("clock," "dog," "envelope") in lowercase letters along with each single guiding letter. At the head of the last two pages is a frieze of all of the lowercase letters. Ages 3-up.

Pattern: Objects outlined in black present names with initial block letters in lowercase.

Lippman, Peter. *One and Only Wacky Wordbook*. Illustrated by the author. Racine, Wisc.: Western Publishing Company, Inc., 1979.

Lippman's contents show serif capitals in colors in alphabetical order. Under each alphabetical category, or heading, are words that are associated with that category. As the title suggests, some of the associations are wacky ones. For example, there are Everyday Disguises, Ugh Pages, and XYZ Truckers. *R* is for "Rex," as in tyrannosaurus rex. The double-page spread for Rex, and other collections, shows many labeled objects in full color. Is an older boy or girl interested in arranging a few names of the objects in alphabetical order? Is an older child ready to consider looking at the second or third letter of a word to get this order? Which dinosaur's name should be written first in a list, aphaneramma or archaeopteryx? Ages 8-up.

Pattern: For each letter there is a wacky topic and labeled objects associated with the topic.

McKie, Roy. *The Alphabet Block Book.* Illustrated by the author. New York: Random House, 1979.

Shaped like a child's wooden alphabet block, this book introduces humorous illustrations and sentences with the format *A* is for———and *B* is for———. One red ladybug rides on top of an alligator's nose, a tiger cat confronts a spotted dog, and a queen in her fur-trimmed robe plays a concert grand piano. Several of the illustrations are linked across the double-page spreads. For an example, at the letters *R*, *S*, and *T*, one lively rabbit (*R*) hops through the snow (*S*) and shows his large front teeth (*T*). Oversize sans serif capitals in bold type begin the sentences. Word choices are capitalized within the sentences. Ending punctuation is seen. The final pages review all of the alphabetical objects and the sans serif capitals. Ages 4–6.

Pattern: With large, introductory capitals in boldface, similar sentences identify capitalized word choices.

Mattiesen, Thomas. *ABC, An Alphabet Book.* Illustrated by the author. New York: Platt and Munk, 1966.

Recommended. Mattiesen presents capitals and lowercase letters in black manuscript. Beneath the letters are the labels for the photographed objects (guitar, telephone, paint) that are shown on the facing pages. Descriptive sentences follow. In this ABC a child realizes that language is used to communicate by speaking and writing in sentences. With word cards to match the key words on the pages, a child can frame each individual key word as it is found and read. An older child may enjoy writing some additional descriptive sentences for photographs or for magazine pictures brought from home. Ages 6-up.

Pattern: Manuscript uppercase and lowercase letters in black identify one-, two-, and three-syllable labels for photographed objects and lead to descriptive sentences.

Merriam, Eve. *Good Night to Annie.* Illustrated by John Wallner. New York: Four Winds, 1980.

In language a child uses courtesy signals, such as a good-night signal, for communication. In this alphabet Annie gets ready for bed, reads her book, and sends a good-night signal to alphabetical animals (inchworm, kittiwake) and selected objects (grass, umbrella trees) and nonliving things (violin, xebec) as they all get ready for bed, too. Met by Annie, each animal in this alphabet book goes to sleep. During this ABC evening a child sees penguins who fold in their flippers, two nightingales nodding, and horses standing still in their barn. An evening farewell goes to dreaming dogs, quiet elephants, and glowing fireflies. These sleepy animals and other objects, introduce the capitals and lowercase serif letters in black. Located in the page corners the capitals are found again in the sentences beneath the illustrations. Capitalization and punctuation are seen. Ages 5–7.

Pattern: Upper- and lowercase letters are found in page corners and again in sentences about animals and objects.

Nolan, Dennis. *Alphabrutes.* Illustrated by the author. Englewood Cliffs, N.J.: Prentice-Hall, 1977.

Recommended. Nolan uses language for fun and nonsense in this ABC. Nolan's collection of friendly green monsters wear shirts decorated with capitals in color. They utter sounds in alphabetical order. The sounds include "Aargh, Blurp," and "Cackle" and are written in bold type within word balloons. Each sound introduces a letter of the alphabet. One by one the curious monsters arrive to stand around a small basket with a pink ribbon tied on the handle. What will be in the basket that offers the final sound for Z? A Junior Literary Guild selection. Ages 4–6.

Pattern: Nonsense sounds in black capitals introduce capitals in colors.

Peppé, Rodney. *The Alphabet Book*. Illustrated by the author. New York: Four Winds, 1968.

Like the language in *All Butterflies: An ABC*, the language in this one is linked alphabetically in its pattern of organization. Each pair of upper- and lowercase letters adds to the sequence across double-page spreads. Along with full-page illustrations are some familiar words in short sentences. Cards with words to match the key words on these pages may be read together with an adult or may be read as an echo after an adult reads. Is a child able to follow the linking pattern for the alphabetic sequence? Ages 4–5.

Pattern: Sequence of familiar words is linked by two letters across every double-page spread.

Rizzo, Fran. *Alphabet*. Illustrated by the author. New York: Modern Promotions Publishers / Unisystems, Inc., 1982.

From a red apple with a bite out of it to a zipper, a child sees one bunny appear in the illustrations. Key words in lowercase letters in black are near the objects. The bunny nibbles a carrot, then spies eggs in a bird's nest, and pulls the string on a yellow yo-yo. Beside each key noun stands uppercase and lowercase letters in black. For a guided activity, a young child may complete a sentence of his or her choice: The bunny wants a————. The child may repeat this same pattern several times and include different nouns to complete each one. Ages 4–5.

Pattern: Upper- and lowercase letters introduce beginning letter and sound for each key object and name.

Singer, Arthur. *Wild Animals from Alligator to Zebra*. Illustrated by the author. New York: Random House, 1973.

Singer uses language and a collection of animals to communicate information in sequence. Singer's collection comprises baby animals and their mothers. Singer points out certain facts for a young listener—e.g., an anteater has a long, sticky tongue; an Alaskan brown bear uses its paws to catch a salmon; and a beaver cuts down trees with its front teeth. Some names that could be unfamiliar ones to some children are *emu, heron, ibex, ibis, lemur,* and *xenops* (bird). For each serif capital in red that begins the names of an animal, there is an accompanying full-color illustration, and sometimes an explanatory sentence. While there are no single letters to identify the alphabetic sequence, the initial letters in the animal names may be followed as a guide. Ages 5-up.

Pattern: Wild animals from alligator to zebra introduce their names through initial capitals in red.

Warburg, Sandol Stoddard. *From Ambledee to Zumbledee: An ABC of Rather Special Bugs.* Illustrated by Walter Lorraine. Boston: Houghton Mifflin, Inc.,1968.

Warburg uses language to name imaginary creatures. What does a child think of on hearing the name Ambledee Bug? Or Mettlebit Bug? Dit Bug? Language and its imaginative uses, such as the naming of imaginary insects, grow as the young listener learns the names of Warburg's imagined bugs. Along with their names, the child hears the words that describe their movements— marching, biting, and pinching. Ages 8-up.

Pattern: For each single letter there is a special imagined bug, one similar to a familiar bug, followed by several explanatory sentences.

Participation

ABC. Illustrated by Hitomi Kuroki. New York: Little Simon and Zokeisha, Tokyo, 1984.

Kuroki's full-color illustrations are on heavy-stock pages. A child finds it easy to participate by chanting lines about children: Christopher loves chocolate, Vanessa loves valentines, and William loves waterfalls. Ages 4–7.

Pattern: ——(letter) my name is ——(name) and I love ——(object).

ABC Book. Cover art by Richard Scarry. Art by Harlow Rockwell. Racine, Wisc.: Western Publishing Company, Inc. 1962.

For each of two letters on a split page, there are four small objects in full color. A large rabbit-shape with movable ears is the back cover for the pages. A child may turn, jiggle, or wiggle the rabbit's ears when a letter or object is recognized. Ages 2-up.

Pattern: Small objects lead to nouns and initial letters in key words.

ABC: Ladybird Teaching Frieze. Illustrated by Lynn N. Grundy. Loughborough, Eng.: Ladybird Books, Ltd., 1980.

In this teaching frieze similar to an accordion-shaped book, each letter in sequence is illustrated with a colorful picture outlined in black. The name of the object is printed clearly in black lowercase letters underneath each item. With the exception of the letter *X* and its final position in the key word "fox," the name of the object begins with the short sound the initial letter represents, and not with the long sound or name of the letter. The frieze brings Grundy's illustrations close to a child for touching and talking about and can be displayed as individual letter cards, as a poster chart, or as a mural arrangement. Ages 3-up.

Pattern: With initial letters in colors, key nouns in lowercase letters label objects.

ABC Zoo. Illustrated by Louise Gordon. New York: Tuffy Books, Inc., 1978.

Gordon's selected animals for this zoo begin with an alligator, bear, camel, and deer. Their accompanying names appear in colors in lowercase letters. Each initial lowercase letter may be matched with the selected uppercase one on the half-page. For each animal, name, and letter that is recognized, the head of the plastic giraffe that backs the pages may be jiggled or turned or wiggled. Gordon's illustrations with half-pages show a capital letter-object-word arrangement. There are two animals per page. A camel stands beside a deer, a kangaroo meets nose to nose with a lion, and a nightingale perches on the antlers of a moose. Capital letters in colors also can be matched with the first letters and the colors of animals' names. All of the ABCs are seen in a final sequence on the last page. Names of selected objects may be dictated by the child and written for the child to see. An adult may model a patterned sentence—e.g., I see a——. If a model is needed, the adult suggests a way to complete the sentence by using the names from some of the book's illustrations. Ages 2–5.

Pattern: Zoo animals and names lead to initial letters.

Allington, Richard L., and Kathleen Krull. *Beginning to Learn About Letters*. Illustrated by Tom Garcia. Milwaukee: Raintree Childrens Books, 1983.

Allington and Krull introduce the letters with a word guessing game. A child is invited to look at a full-color illustration, identify the animals (fish, lion, kangaroo) and the objects (queen, newspaper, yo-yo), and then say the letters that begin the names. These pages offer opportunities to make predictions in object identification. On a following page a child finds key words, capitals, and lowercase serif letters in black. To verify a prediction, the child turns the page for the answer. Beginning with *F* and *L* and ending with *T* and *G*, the letters are out of sequence in the book. There are other participation challenges on the pages. Following arrows for guidance, a child may trace all of the letters, search for all of the capitals forming the shape of a house, and make an individual ABC book by locating pictures from a newspaper or a magazine. Ages 5-up.

Pattern: Initial letter recognition of animal names, predicting, and verifying.

The Alphabet Book. Illustrated by John Strejan. New York: Random House/Children's Television Workshop, n.d.

Beginning with an alligator, bird, cow, and dog, an object pops up on each page. A child identfies the object and associates the name of the object with the selected letter and the sound of the letter. Some objects are hidden and appear only when a tab is pulled on a page. For instance, when one tab is pulled on the page for *W*, the mouth of the whale opens. Inside the mouth, a child sees the swallowed objects for *X* and *Y*—xylophone and yak. Ages 3-up.

Pattern: Object association with selected letter and sound.

The Alphabet Zoo. Illustrated. Dallas:Texas Instruments, Inc., 1982.

In this alphabet zoo a child places a Magic Wand over the zebra bars on the pages and listens to the story about the animals arranged alphabetically at the zoo. Ants perform acrobatics above the alligators, a hammerhead shark has a headache, and a whale wiggles in the water. Several culminating pages invite a review of the letters: matching a part of an animal to the whole animal, relating each animal's name to its beginning letter, matching letters that are similar, writing sentences, putting names of animals in alphabetical order, and matching the animals with their sounds, heard by touching the zebra bars with the wand. Ages 6-up.

Pattern: Guided by upper- and lowercase letters, text appears above zebra bars with key words in red for easy identification. Matching and alphabetical order.

Anno Mitsumasa. *Anno's Magical ABC: An Anamorphic Alphabet.* Illustrated by the author and Masaichiro Anno. New York: Philomel, 1980.

Recommended. In Anno's book a child places a silver cylinder in the middle of each page to turn the distorted image of each of fifty-two full-color paintings of animals (anteater, ant, bee, bear, camel) and objects (doll, elf, faun) into an image with proper porportions. There are twenty-six flower drawings, one in the center of each page for each letter in the two alphabets. Each picture can be a mystery picture. The child looks, determines the name, and pronounces the name of the object. When showing this book to a child, the adult turns the book so the child can see the way the sequence progresses from left to right. The book is turned over again, and beginning with the back cover, a child sees the way the second alphabet progresses. One pattern in the first alphabet presents repetitive phrases that contain lowercase letters—e.g., *a* is for ———. A second repetitive pattern in the second alphabet shows uppercase letters and key nouns. A third pattern for both alphabets is a central circular sketch in the middle of each page. Here a child sees a selected plant whose name begins with the selected letter, e.g., apple, blackberry, and clover. A fourth pattern shows the Japanese characters that represent the names of all of the objects in both alphabets. Last there is the patterned grid needed for drawing one's own images of objects into anamorphic forms. Ages 8-up.

Pattern: Traditional phrases and circular sketches with key objects lead to an uppercase and a lowercase alphabet. Japanese characters for word choices and patterned grid to guide drawings of anamorphic forms are included.

Attwell, Lucie. *Lucie Attwell's ABC 123 Pop-Up Book*. Illustrated by the author. London: Dean's International Publishing, 1969.

Serif capitals in color show in the left margin, and lowercase letters are found in the right margin on each pop-up page. "Acorn," "ball," and "car" introduce the key words. These word choices in bold type are easy to find in the rhyming couplets. A child locates the key objects in each pop-up picture. There are additional objects to count, e.g., one apple, two birds, ten zebras. Ages 3–4.

Pattern: Capitals introduce rhyming couplets with repetitive openings.

Attwell, Lucie. *Lucie Attwell's ABC Pop-Up Book*. Illustrated by the author. London: Deans International Publishing, 1984.

For every pair of upper- and lowercase letters, there is a rhyming couplet about an object in ABC order, e.g., apple, bread, and cake. The pop-up objects may be touched as they are identified. On each double-page spread only one object among several is shown in a pop-up arrangement. Ages 3–4.

Pattern: Couplets with ending rhymes focus on touchable pop-up objects.

Bayer, Jane. *A My Name Is Alice*. Illustrated by Steven Kellogg. New York: E. P. Dutton and Company, Inc.,/Dial Books for Young Readers, 1984.

Recommended. Bayer uses language to express a rhythmic pattern. From a playground game, one the author learned in her elementary school, comes a pattern of names and places and things to sell for each letter of the alphabet. From Kellogg comes a group of zany animals who illustrate the letters. An older child sees some unusual ones—e.g., unau, a two-toed tree mammal, and xigertling, a creature from the planet Xigert. Using this pattern, is any child interested in creating an original name page? Ages 7-up.

Pattern: Key words begin with similar sounds in the following sentence arrangement:——My name is——. My husband's name is——. We live in——. We sell——.

Beginning Sounds Flip Book. Illustrated. St. Paul, Minn.: Trend Enterprises, Inc., 1979.

A child is asked to flip sections of pages and find three pictures of objects whose names begin with the same letter and sound. For example, a child searches for an anteater, apple, and alligator for the letter *A*. When the child has identified correctly the three objects beginning with the same sound and letter, a picture is formed on the back of the three strip sections. For example, on the back of the three sections for *A*, a child sees the black-and-white drawing of an anteater exploring an anthill. Ages 4-7.

Pattern: Initial letters and sounds may be matched to identified names and pictures of objects. Small pictures provide clues.

Besche, Tom. *Professor Breads' Alphabet*. Illustrated by the author. Georgetown, Del.: Besches Bread-N-Butter Productions, Inc., 1980.

A child sings along with the alphabet verses in "The Alphabet," heard on the record that accompanies the book. The verses are repetitive ones. Traditional beginnings open the lines: *A* is for the apple, *B* is for the big bee, and *C* is for the carrot. A boy or girl may identify some of the nonfood items that are included: guitar, light bulb, nickel, quarter, umbrella, villain, whistle, X ray, and yo-yo. This is a book a child may color. Each outlined object in sequence introduces letter pairs. The capitals in sequence are reviewed on a final page and followed by the verses. Ages 2-5.

Pattern: Pairs of letters, objects, key words, and repetitive verses emphasize illustrations.

Bishop, Ann. *A Riddle-iculous Rid-alphabet Book*. Illustrated by Jerry Warshaw. Chicago: Albert Whitman & Company, 1979.

Bishop uses language for the fun of riddling. Beginning with amusements that are animated, bafflers that are buggy, and conundrums that are comic, a child may choose any one of twenty-six categories of riddles, silly questions, and tricks with words. In one section, "Buggy Bafflers," a child responds to questions about starting a lightning bug race and about which ant is the youngest. Answers are found in the colored border at the foot of each page. Ages 6-up.

Pattern: For each letter there are categories of riddles, silly questions, and tricks with words in a question-and-answer format.

Brown, Judith Gwyn. *Alphabet Dreams*. Illustrated by the author. Englewood Cliffs, N.J.: Prentice-Hall, 1976.

Brown uses language to express an alliterative sound and has another version of a familiar playground game. In alphabetical order, words beginning with *A* are selected to complete Brown's arrangement. The words identify a wife's name, a husband's name, where they live, and what they sell. Next, words beginning with *B* are selected, then words with *C*, and so on through the alphabet. Ages 6-up.

Pattern: Rhymes to chant or complete in writing with *A* words, then with *B* words, and others: My name is———. My husband's name is———. We live in———. And we sell———.

Burrows, Roger, project director. *My First ABC Book*. Illustrated. Los Angeles: Price/Stern/Sloan Publishers, Inc./Random House, 1985.

Burrows uses activities to show that many words begin with the same symbol and sound. A child matches letters, tracks a path from capitals to lowercase letters across pages, and traces the shapes of the colorful letters. One microchip sensor called Questron senses right and wrong responses with sounds and lights. Sets of questions or games can be completed. A green light means a child has identified a correct answer whereas a red light and sound mean to try again. Ages 4-5.

Pattern: Capital letters are matched with similar letters in rows, columns, and along game tracks.

Burstein, Chaya. *Hebrew Alphabet Coloring Book*. Illustrated by the author. New York: Dover Publications, Inc., 1986.

From Aleph to Tav, Burstein's book presents twenty-two letters of the Hebrew alphabet and an explanation of pronunciation that follows the Sephardic (Spanish) way used in Israel and in the Middle East. A child sees one Hebrew letter per page with Hebrew words beginning with the letter. For *Aleph* a child sees such objects as an airplane, goose, and tree. Near each word is a black-and-white drawing of the object. Each word is numbered with an English equivalent at the foot of the page. Several patterns are mentioned—e.g., sound changes for certain letters when a dot is taken away or moved in the writing, letters that look different when they are at the end of a word, and vowel signs that are often shown in books for beginning readers. A concluding vocabulary section allows a child to look up a word in English and find out what the word is in Hebrew. A final Hebrew alphabet reads from right to left, beginning on page 32 and ending on page 30. Twenty-two pages for coloring if desired. Ages 5-up.

Pattern: Letter-object-Hebrew/English words.

The Chipmunks' ABC. Interior art by Sandra Berez and Rick Detorie. Cover art by Rick Detorie. New York: Bagdasarian Productions, 1985.

The chipmunks Alvin, Simon, and Theodore introduce the upper- and lowercase serif letters found in the corners of the pages. One chipmunk plays an accordion, another works at a computer, and another strums an electric guitar. A young viewer recognizes that nouns can indicate number. This is a book that can be colored as children see singular ("feather," "house," "jacket") and plural ("acorns," "cymbals," "drums") nouns. Ages 5-up.

Pattern: The chipmunks, with selected objects and plural and singular nouns, introduce upper- and lowercase serif letters.

Coletta, Irene, and Hallie Coletta. *From A to Z: The Collected Letters of Irene and Hallie Coletta*. Illustrated by Hallie Coletta. Englewood Cliffs, N.J.: Prentice-Hall, Inc.,1979.

Recommended. The Collettas demonstrate that in language, picture symbols can communicate meaning. In this rebus approach a child recognizes the pictures. For instance, the numeral two substitutes for the word "too" in one line of a rebus verse. This recognition provides the clues to finish the lines of the rhymes. Ages 6–9.

Pattern: Rebus pictures complete lines in rhymes.

Cremins, Robert. *My Animal ABC*. Illustrated by the author. Los Angeles: Intervisual Communications, Inc., 1983.

Humorous scenes with animals and objects lead a child through the alphabet. A goose delivers a gift, an inchworm shovels a path in the snow to his igloo, and a walrus wears a wig. When a pop-up flap is turned, one small mouse appears somewhere in the scene. For instance, when the tab on the walrus's wig is lifted, the small mouse is perched on top of the walrus's head. Ages 4–6.

Pattern: Capitals or lowercase letters in black are seen as initial letters in key words beneath each scene.

Crowther, Robert. *The Most Amazing Hide-and-Seek Alphabet Book*. Illustrated by the author. New York: Viking, 1978.

Recommended. Small children like the hidden objects in this one. A tab on the page is pulled up or down. Pulling the tab for *A* reveals a brown ape and its name, "ape." When the *B* tab is pulled, a brown bear peers through the letter. Some surprising animals are the koala bear, who slides down a letter stem in *K*; the gray mouse, who runs from leg to leg of the *M*; and the green and yellow snake for S, which unwinds in a spiral across the page. Pairs of uppercase and lowercase letters in black in the page corners may be matched with the large lowercase letters on the pages. Two or three large lowercase letters in black are seen on each page. A child may predict what animal will be seen beneath each letter. Pulling a tab on each letter, a child reveals an animal whose name begins with the selected letter. The names of the animals are seen in lowercase letters. Ages 5–6.

Pattern: Predicting names of animals hidden by large lowercase letters in black.

Debnam, Betty. *Alpha Betty's ABC Fun Book.* Illustrated by the author. New York: Collier Books/Macmillan Publishing Company, Inc., 1982.

A child is invited to find hidden words that begin with a certain letter, to follow the dots from *A* to *Z* to see the outline of an object, to write words that begin with a selected letter into a simple crossword arrangement, and to write in missing letters in selected nouns. Ages 6-up.

Pattern: For each block capital and lowercase letter in black, words and objects are identified.

Demi. *The ABC Song.* Illustrated by Leonard Shortall. New York: A Music Box Book/Random House, Inc., 1985.

Opening the pages of this stocky book, a child finds an airplane, bee, and castle in full color on white backgrounds. The names of the objects are in lowercase block letters. A metal handle makes it easy for a child to start the music box and and listen to the music of the familiar ABC song, language expressed in a musical rhythmic pattern. The last page includes all of the words of the song. Ages 3-5.

Pattern: Lowercase block letter-object-word arrangement.

Demi. *Demi's Find the Animal ABC: An Alphabet Game Book.* Illustrated by the author. New York: Grosset and Dunlap, 1985.

In this alphabet game book a child meets a challenge to find the unicorn, the alligator, or other animal that is associated with pairs of upper- and lowercase letters. Repetitive-question frames begin with the words, " Can you find this——?" A child searches for the animal among many others on each double-page spread. To verify a prediction, the child may turn to the final pages to see the answers in smaller black-and-white illustrated inserts. A large black arrow over each insert identifies the animal to be found. One final challenge appears at the end of the answers. A young viewer is invited to return to the pages and find a cat somewhere in the book. Ages 6-9.

Pattern: Introduced by letter pairs, a selected animal may be found among many animals hidden in illustrations.

Demi. *The Peek-a-Boo ABC*. Illustrated by the author. New York: Random House, 1982.

Opening the first of these sturdy pages, a toddler sees such objects as an ark, barn, and car, along with colorful uppercase and lowercase letters. Each page contains cardboard doors to open. The sides of the ark open to reveal all of the animals waiting inside. A child sees words that begin with similar sounds and symbols. For instance, a red barn door opens to show one large teddy bear, and a colorfully dressed clown smiles as the door of a red car is raised. Is a child ready to say the names of the objects? Colorful upper- and lowercase block letters emphasize initial letters in words near objects. Other cardboard doors open and reveal additional key objects. Ages 3–4.

Pattern: Letter pair-object hidden behind door-word arrangement.

Do-It-Yourself Alphabet Book. Illustrated by Richard Brown. Racine, Wisc.: Western Publishing Comapny, Inc./Children's Television Workshop, 1980.

Grover, from Muppets, Inc., leads a child through this Sesame Street book. For each capital in black there is one object or animal in full color (alligator, box, cat) to introduce it. Beginning with a capital, the noun is printed in black underneath the picture. Grover invites a child to write the letters and to draw pictures of objects that begin with the letters on the accompanying drawing board. Animals and objects and the first letters in their names may be related to the selected block capitals. Ages 3-up.

Pattern: Letter-animal or object-word arrangement.

Doyle, Emma Lyons. *Aloha Alphabet Coloring Book*. Illustrated by John H. Sugimoto. Cover art by Keani. Honolulu: Tong Publishing Company, Ltd., 1958.

For each outlined capital is a similar opening—e.g., A is for ———, and English equivalent of a selected Hawaiian word (*aloha-hello*, *cat-popoki, eel-puhi*) and a black-and-white line drawing. To say the Hawaiian words, a child pronounces *A* as in *father*, *E* as *ay* in *play*, *I* as *ee* in *sweep*, *O* as in *old*, and *U* as *oo* in *moo*. Ages 5-up.

Pattern: Each large outlined capital is introduced by either an English or Hawaiian noun used in context in a sentence.

Elting, Mary, and Michael Folsom. *Q Is for Duck: An Alphabet Guessing Game*. Illustrated by Jack Kent. Boston: Houghton Mifflin Company, 1980.

Colorful serif capitals begin repetitive questions that ask a child to guess why *W* is for "snake," *X* is for "dinosaurs," and *Y* is for "coyote." The phrases are followed by the repeating question, why? Riddles such as these may be entertainment for a child when read aloud. Ages 6-up.

Pattern: Word-association riddles give facts about animals in alphabetical order.

Folsom, Marcia, and Michael Folsom. *Easy As Pie: A Guessing Game of Sayings*. Illustrated by Jack Kent. New York: Houghton Mifflin Company, 1985.

Playing with comparisons such as "easy as pie" and "sly as a fox" may entice a child to make up original ones that are new and different. A child hears some comparisons that refer to animals, others to objects, and still others to the weather. These may be models for some nonsense-comparison writing for an older child who knows the letters, their sequence in the alphabet, and recognizes the key words. Ages 6-up.

Pattern: Predicting. Colorful serif capitals give clues to words needed to complete comparisons.

Forte, Imogene. *From A to Z with Me*. Illustrated by the author. Nashville, Tenn.: Incentive Publications, Inc., 1981.

From *A*, which stands for *almost, all,* and *about,* to *Z*, which stands for *zebra, zipper,* and *Zachariah,* each letter includes an activity that helps a young child become more aware of self and surroundings. For example, at *A*, a child writes a house address. For *B*, a child draws a picture about bumps, bandages, and feeling better after a minor injury. AT *C*, there is space for pictures to be drawn on a clock face to show how a child spends time during the day. Ages 5-up.

Pattern: Illustrated capital letter and a following awareness activity.

Fredman, Alan. *The Gold Star Alphabet Book*. Illustrated by the author. New York: Modern Publishing/Unisystems, Inc./Deans International Publishing, 1981.

Double-page spreads are interspersed with single pages. The colorful illustrations show a green alligator who fills the spread, a sleeping giant who needs two pages to stretch out to take a nap, and a colorful rainbow that arches over both pages of hills to a pot of gold. All of the capital letters are reviewed again on a double-page spread. A final alphabet quiz asks a young viewer to match the pictures with the lowercase letters and to fill in the rest of the words in the blanks. A child may self-check with answers for the quiz. Ages 5-up.

Pattern: Black capitals and lowercase letters guide key nouns that label objects.

Freedman, Alan. *The Computer Coloring Book: It's Not Just a Coloring Book!* Illustrated by Eric Jon Nones. New York: Prentice-Hall, Inc., 1983.

Nones's full-page, black-and-white illustrations are for a child to color. Freedman's words give some of the technical jargon about computers in alphabetical order. From *analog* and *byte* to an *x-y scale* on a graphics table and *zero*, there are informational paragraphs for each word choice, with additional terms and explanations. A reader sees that related information may be arranged alphabetically to aid communication in language. Ages 8-up.

Pattern: Key computer words are capitalized, arranged in alphabetical order, and precede informational paragraphs.

Frompovich, Catherine J. *A Child's ABC's for Nutrition Coloring Book*. Illustrated. Coopersburg, Penn.: C. J. Frompovich Publications, 1978.

An apple helps teeth stay bright and clean, bananas are good for the inside of our bodies, and carrots help keep eyes healthy. For each one of the foods there is a guiding capital and traditional beginning about a nutritious food: *A* is for———and *B* is for———. Descriptive sentences follow and give information about how the food looks and how it helps us nutritionally. The repetitive statements are seen again in a final review of the nutritious foods in this alphabet, along with an invitation to draw a favorite nutritious food. Ages 6-up.

Pattern: Black-and-white line drawings introduce repetitive statements about nutritious foods.

Fujikawa, Gyo. *Gyo Fujikawa's A to Z Book*. Illustrated by the author. New York: Platt and Munk Publishers/Grosset and Dunlap, 1981.

Cloth pages show Fujikawa's capitals and objects for a child to identify. Some illustrations of key objects that might be unusual ones for certain young children are a harp, quintuplets, and a railroad crossing sign. Ages 1–3.

Pattern: Guiding capitals-objects-names arrangement.

Garten, Jan. *The Alphabet Tale*. Illustrated by Muriel Batherman. New York: Random House, 1964.

Recommended. From an alligator to a zebra, there is information about an animal on each page. Several patterns help a child predict the name of a selected animal. The capitals are the initial letters in the names and introduce the verses about the animals. The words in the verses include rhyming sounds. Certain illustrations show only the tails of the animals. After seeing the tail of an animal on one page and the beginning capital in the animal's name, a child predicts the name of the animal, turns to a second page to find the entire animal and verify the prediction. Clues are given about each animal—e.g., one hops in the zoo, another is spotted, and still another roams the forest. The answers rhyme with the ending word in each clue and turn this ABC into a game of words having the same phonogram or ending. The rhyming words may be reviewed as a pattern with a response activity. An adult says two words. If the words rhyme, a child responds with ,yes, they rhyme. If the words do not rhyme, the response becomes, no; no rhyme. The activity continues with the words, Now, here are two more words from the book. Ages 5-8.

Pattern: Information to read, rhyming words to predict, clues to find for predictions, and visual images to confirm predictions.

Geisert, Arthur. *Pigs from A to Z.* Illustrated by the author. Boston: Houghton Mifflin Company, 1986.

In this alphabet Geisert introduces seven little pigs who build a tree house. The letters are seen in detailed full-page etchings and follow the construction of the tree house. Along with each letter, in sequence in each illustration, a viewer will always see the pigs, at least five different forms of the letter, one form of the preceding letter, and one form of the following letter. On the *A* page the little pigs begin the day with Pa Pig. On the *B* page a child will find five *B*s, one *A*, one *C*, and the little pigs in the etching that introduces *B*. Some letter forms are large. The shape of *B* is found in the shape of a large apple core and in the cut of a tree stump. Others are small. One small capital *B* is seen on the weather vane and another found on a nearby leaf. Facing each illustration is a sentence that carries the action forward. The pigs eat apples, chop down a birch tree, and cut countless cords of wood cheerfully. They drag the wood through an eerie forest, float the wood downriver, hoist the wood over a gorge, and then rest with a game of hide-and-seek. Back to work, they find an ideal tree for their tree house, juggle boards, kick over a nail keg, and stop for lunch. The pattern of rest and play, work, rest and play, continues until they return home to Pa and Ma Pig. For a self-check a child may turn to the final pages to see smaller illustrations that provide a key to the hidden letter-shapes in each etching. Sequence is guided by oversize capital serif letters in black and by word choices found in story sentences. Ages 6-up.

Pattern: With traditional sentence beginnings for the sequence (*A* is for———), hidden shapes of featured letter, preceding letter, and following letter are in etchings.

Gordon, Isabel. *The ABC Hunt.* Illustrated by the author. New York: Viking, 1961.

Is a child interested in searching for each letter in the black and white photographs? Several of the photographs emphasize letters in environmental print. Who can find the shape of *A* in a bowl of alphabet soup? Who can see the *Z* in the word "zoo" on the sign at the zoo? The young viewer participates by responding to the visual challenge on each page. Ages 6–9.

Pattern: Within black-and-white photographs, letter shapes are located.

Hall, Nancy Christensen. *Macmillan Fairy Tale Alphabet Book.* Illustrated by John O'Brien. New York: Macmillan Publishing Company, Inc., 1983.

Hall's game of titles is on every page of this ABC. From *Arabian Nights* to *The Teeny-Tiny Woman*, and others, a child is challenged to identify as many literary titles as can be determined from the scenes. For instance, for *G* and *H*, one scene shows a gingerbread house decorated with gumdrops. A horrible hag peers through a window and watches a greedy girl and a hungry hero nibble the icing from the house. Each single letter in the sequence gives a clue to the tale's title. Focusing on one letter for each illustration, labeled objects from the unidentified stories are in each of the scenes. A child mentally gathers the information from the objects in the scenes and identifies the title of the story. Answers are self-checked with a key to the illustrations and the titles at the end of this colorful collection. Ages 8-up.

Pattern: With guiding letters and labeled objects, scenes from familiar fairy tales lead to prediction of unidentified titles.

Hargreaves, Roger. *Alphabet Fun.* Illustrated by the author. Los Angeles: Price/Stern/Sloan Publishers, Inc., 1983.

After an adult identifies the letters and the characters on each page, a child is invited to repeat the names of letters, to trace and write them, and then listen for the sound of the letter in the names of objects shown. From *A* for "ambulance" to *Z* for "zoo," black lines guide a child's writing attempts. There are many concluding activities: finding one letter that is different in a collection of letters, matching one uppercase letter with a lowercase one, or drawing lines to relate a picture of an object to its beginning letter. The child also identifies objects whose names begin with a similar letter, writes in missing letters in the ABC sequence, and answers several riddles. Ages 5-up.

Pattern: Each selected letter is identified, traced, and related to beginning sound in names.

Hayward, Linda. *The Little Engine That Could ABC*. Illustrated by John Nez. New York: Platt and Munk/Grosset and Dunlap, 1986.

Hayward's paperback alphabet book is adapted from the familar story *The Little Engine That Could* (Platt and Munk, 1930) written by Walter (Watty) Piper and illustrated by George and Doris Hauman. *A* is for all "aboard," *B* is for "bears," and *C* for "caboose" as the little blue engine pulls a load of toys from *A* to *Z*. This is a book a child may color. Ages 4-5.

Pattern: Traditonal beginnings for illustrations: *A* is for————, *B* is for————, and *C* is for————.

Hefter, Richard. *ABC Coloring Book*. Illustrated by the author. New York: Dover Publications, 1983.

Hefter includes some familiar and some unfamiliar objects in these black-and-white line drawings. A child is asked to discover and color the objects on each page. One large outlined capital letter is the focus for each collection of objects. Objects whose names begin with a selected letter are arranged in each illustration. For the letter *X* there are as few as five objects, and for *T* as many as thirty-five objects to find. Beneath each collection a number tells a viewer how many objects may be found on the page. To self-check one's observational and identification skills, a list of names of objects is read. The list is printed upside down at the foot of each page. Ages 7-up.

Pattern: After prediction, verification of each object from word list.

Hill, Eric. *Spot's Alphabet*. Illustrated by the author. New York: G. P. Putnam's Sons, 1983.

Hill's endpages introduce the upper- and lowercase letters in the alphabet sequence. A young boy or girl is invited to help color the story of Spot the dog wanting to be an acrobat, balancing a ball, and dressing up as a clown. Full-color objects are interspersed with black-and-white ones for coloring if desired. Each animal (elephant, flamingo, giraffe) and object (nuts, oranges, peaches) introduces its name in black boldface within the sentences. The accompanying block upper- and lowercase letters in black are near the key nouns. These letters may serve as models for a young child's early writing. Ages 3-up.

Pattern: Animals and objects introduce names, capitals, and lowercase letters.

Hoberman, Mary Ann. *Nuts to You and Nuts to Me: An Alphabet of Poems*. Illustrated by Ronni Solbert. New York: Alfred A. Knopf, 1974.

Recommended. For each letter is a verse about such objects as money, a windshield wiper, and a zebra. One unifying feature is the illustrations of ants. Hoberman explains that ants are always all around in this *A* to *Z* book, and for a visual challenge she asks the viewer to look for them as they crawl over, on, and under objects through Solbert's illustrations. Some ants may be found near the ice cream, crawling toward the jam, or walking a circus high wire. Can a young viewer locate the ants on every page? Ages 5-6.

Pattern: With a visual challenge, rhyming verse emphasizes selected letter.

Hughes, Anne, reading consultant. *A Book of Sounds ABC*. Pictures by Toni Goffe. Milwaukee: Raintree Childrens Books, 1979.

Presented to a child in an ABC sequence, the initial sounds of some of these words may take on different sounds when followed by more than one syllable or a blend. A child listens to the sound of *A*, for instance, in such words as "angry" and "alligator." In the full-color illustrations the included nouns are the names of people, places, and things shown in different settings—around a campfire, at a dance, and at the circus. The key nouns are shown in bold, black type in the sentences at the foot of each page. The larger initial letters are shown in black upper- and lowercase in the left-hand and right-hand corners of the page, respectively. There are concluding activities. Alphabet cards can be made for playing a game of ABC dominoes. A collection of three objects includes two whose names begin with the same letter. A child identifies the odd object to play the Odd One Out game. Ages 5-up.

Pattern: Objects, accompanying sentences, and activities introduce nouns and initial letters.

Jones, Kathryn Amanda. *Can You Guess What I Am?* Illustrated by the author. New York: Carlton Press, 1984.

Rhyming couplets are riddles and may be answered by identifying the objects outlined in brown on the pages. Stylized capitals and lowercase letters are in the corners of the pages. A child completes the repetitive opening lines in couplets by identifying a rebus picture—e.g., *N* is for a musical *note* you can hum. Ages 6-up.

Pattern: Capitals and rebus pictures complete lines with ending rhymes.

Katamura, Satoshi. *What's Inside? The Alphabet Book*. Illustrated by the author. New York: Farrar, Straus and Giroux, 1985.

Answering the secret hidden on every page guides a child through the secrets and the sequence of the alphabet. In the full-color paintings, a viewer sees boxes, containers, unusual shapes, and unusual places to explore. The child predicts what hides inside. In the first illustration two lowercase letters, e.g., *a* and *b*, are found in the design of the painting along with something in which the objects are hidden. In the second illustration the hiding places are revealed, and the young child discovers the objects' names. For each pair of linked illustrations, a child sees two lowercase letters, looks at the illustration, and determines where the objects may be hiding and what they might be. The page is turned to verify the prediction. For *W*, a woodpecker, hidden in the foliage of a leafy tree, pecks at the keys on a xylophone. On a nearby yacht one passenger, a zebra, sets sail. In this alphabet, shapes, sizes, and colors of things may be described by the child as a prediction is made. Ages 4-up.

Pattern: Prediction. For each pair of sequential letters, two illustrations are linked.

Kelly, Donna. *ABC Play with Me*. Illustrated by Jim Robison. Racine, Wisc.: Western Publishing Company, 1978.

On each page a young boy or girl is invited to play. Children tumble like acrobats, catch a fast ball in baseball, and dance. Upper- and lowercase letters in black introduce the key words and the descriptive scenes that show children at play. A descriptive sentence follows each scene. A young viewer finds the black capitals and lowercase letters near the key words. Scenes of children playing accompany explanatory text inserted on the pages. Ages 6-up.

Pattern: Play actions and pairs of letters give clues to initial sounds of words.

King, Tony. *The Moving Alphabet Book*. Illustrated by the author. New York: Putnam, 1982.

Every large serif capital in black is surrounded by animals and objects whose names begin with that letter. A child turns a wheel, and a different object labeled with its name appears in each of the windows. Small color photographs are interspersed with drawings of objects in the windows. S shows a snowman, snail, and scarecrow. X is for a spot on a treasure map, a xylophone, and X ray. A repetitive sentence stem occurs on each page. A child reads the traditional lines: "A is for————and B is for————." There is a reference list of all of the objects on two culminating pages of the book. A child says the name of the object and writes the word to study a selected sound or sounds. Is a boy or girl interested in making a personal ABC wheel that moves? Cut from art paper, two wheels are fastened together with a paper brad in the centers. The top wheel has a cutout window. When turned, the second wheel shows the child's ABC drawings through the window. A paper tab may be attached to this wheel for easy turning. The wheels help a young viewer see that everything can be named with language. Ages 5-7.

Pattern: Drawings and photographs of animals and objects lead to names that start with capitals.

The Ladybird Colouring Book of ABC. Illustrations by Roger Hall, Frank Humpris, John Leigh-Pemberton, Bernard Robinson, Henry Wingfield, and Gerald Witcomb. Design and line drawings by Hurlston Design, Ltd. Loughborough, Eng.: Ladybird Books, Ltd., 1977.

One colorful photograph introduces every object for each manuscript lowercase letter in blue. A boy or girl may practice forming each letter on the guidelines. From an apple, buttons, and cow to an X ray of a hand, to a yak and a zebra, there is a simple line drawing for a child to color. An older child may be encouraged to add additional details to the drawings. Two culmination pages offer a review of blue capitals and red lowercase letters with additional guidelines for a child's writing. Ages 5-up.

Pattern: Objects emphasize lowercase letters in blue, related sounds, and lead to writing letters within guidelines.

Learn About ABCs. Book script by Ruth Roberts. Illustrated by Nancy Duell. Newark, N. J.: Peter Pan Industries, 1984.

A is for "aardvark," *B* is for a "box" with a gift in it, and *C* is for a "combo" of animals playing music on drums and trumpet. The lines rhyme and in some cases move across two pages. Some unusual word choices are "genie" for *G* and for *W* for the "W-Whoo" of the wind. For a child's read-along interest, a cassette recording follows the ABC book, word by word. A small workbook includes activities such as tracing capitals and lowercase letters, matching letters, drawing lines from letter to letter in ABC sequence to outline a shape, and locating objects that begin with the same letter. Ages 3-5.

Pattern: Traditional beginnings, such as *A* is for——, and rhyming lines lead to word choices in capitals.

Learning My ABC's. Illustrated by Kathy McCarthy. Chatsworth, Calif.: Superscope, 1981.

In this story about a birthday party, a child sees upper- and lowercase letters at the foot of the pages. Each selected letter is seen again in color in the text. Appropriate objects are seen in the illustrations—e.g., Xavier, a xylophone, and Xanadu are seen on the *X* page. When Sally the sea gull suggests to the other animals that they sing a song, the reader plays an accompanying cassette tape to hear the words and music. A clear acetate sheet and crayons are included for tracing activities. Ages 5-up.

Pattern: Letters in color lead to tracing upper- and lowercase letters.

Leman, Martin. *Comic and Curious Cats*. Words by Angela Carter. Illustrated by Martin Leman. New York: Harmony, 1979.

With words that begin with *A*, Carter names a cat, tells where the cat lives and what it likes to eat. These words begin a word game, one similar to the game presented by Ipcar in *I Love My Anteater with an A*. The game always continues with the next letter in the alphabet sequence. A pattern of difficulty may be initiated by presenting two letters, e.g., *B* and *C*, then naming two cats, two countries they are from, and two foods they like to eat. The pattern increases in difficulty when three letters are considered, e.g., *R. S*, and *T*. The pattern may be adapted from the subject of cats and applied to another topic a child chooses. Ages 7-up.

Pattern: Alliterative word-game pattern names a cat, where the cat lives, and what foods it eats. All nouns begin with the same letter in each verse of the word game.

Lopshire, Robert. *ABC Games*. Illustrated by the author. New York: Thomas Y. Crowell, 1986.

In this alphabet game Lopshire asks a child to select an animal, person, or object associated with an alphabetical object choice. For example, the key letter *A* and the key word "acorn" are found under one golden acorn. On the facing page a child is asked to select one animal who eats acorns from the living things shown on the page. Will a child select the fish, snail, turtle, or squirrel? After seeing *B* for "bird" a child selects a picture of where the bird lives from a series of pictures including a doghouse, an aquarium, a cradle, and a nest. *C* is for "clown," and a child is asked to select an object that the clown might wear. A child sees a telephone, a saw, a wheelbarrow, and a tall yellow hat decorated with pom-poms. Some relationships are subtle ones—e.g., *S* is for "soap," and the question is, which dog needs the soap? After looking at the pictures, a child has to recognize that some dogs are clean and one is dirty and then determine that it makes sense for the dirty dog to use the soap. Other relationships are more obvious. *G* is for "giant," and the challenge is to find the pair of shoes a giant might wear. It is easy to see the oversize pair of giant boots in contrast to the smaller tennis shoes and loafers. Another size relationship is shown for *W*, "wagon." Here a child is asked to determine which living creature can pull the wagon. All of the selections are of approximately the same height or width, and include a panda bear, a horse, an ostrich, and a large blue butterfly.

On another page, determining which items will be eaten by a mouse or a rabbit might generate extra minutes of discussion. While it is true that a child may choose the carrot for the rabbit to eat and the cheese for the mouse, it is possible that another child might consider the lettuce on the hamburger as proper food for a rabbit and see the possibility of a mouse nibbling on the paper pages of a book or the wooden body of the pencil. Other interesting word choices to discuss are *fire, giant, lock, jet,* and *oar*. Ages 3–6.

Pattern: Word associations and relationships in declarative-interrogative arrangement.

Lyon, David E. *The ABC Puzzle Book*. Illustrated by Ralph Stobart. New York: Mulberry Books, n.d.

A child completes the last line in each rhyming line with a predicted rhyming word. An inserted blank line takes the place of the word to be predicted. If *B* is for bear, then *C* is for———. Clues are provided in the illustration, as it shows a brown bear sitting next to a bright red chair. Each large manuscript style letter is oversize when compared to the text and is easy to locate. The final two pages review all of the capitals and the object choices again in sequence. Ages 3 -6.

Pattern: Aided by clues in illustrations, prediction of rhyming words.

Magel, John. *Dr. Moggle's Alphabet Challenge: A Quest for All Ages*. Illustrated by Claudia Del Col. New York: Rand McNally Co., 1985.

In Magel's alphabet are several challenges or quests. First, there are over one thousand objects to identify from the large, detailed, full-color illustrations. Second, there are two hidden words to find, located in a picture and a code in the book. Third, there are inserts of hands, at the foot of each page of rhyming verse, showing the signs for the alphabet used by the deaf or hearing-impaired speakers. Last, there is a story about two searchers who look for more than one thousand words before they reach the last letter, Z. In a dream the narrator and an elf, Mr. Moggle, begin to climb a ladder of knowledge to find the words that will release them from their dream. The scenes shift from page to page. The circus, a frigid pool, nighttime, and a dark storm are some of the background images. Children may identify objects. Some girls and boys may want to discuss their ideas about the rhyming story and illustrations of the dream. Others may take up the challenge of looking for the two hidden words. Who can identify correctly the two hidden words? If the two special words are found, who can explain their meaning or significance? No clues are given. A publisher's note states that to obtain the correct two-word solution, a reader may send a self-addressed, stamped envelope to Dr. Moggle Answer Requests, P.O. Box 76600, Chicago, IL, 60680. Ages 8-up.

Pattern: With secret message in narrative rhyme, names of objects are related to guiding letters.

Moore, Frank J. *The Magic Moving Alphabet Book*. Illustrated. New York: Dover Publications, 1978.

After opening this book, a child sees that when an acetate sheet is pushed up and down slowly, the movement of the sheet creates motion over the pictures on the pages. Two toy tops spin, four airplanes fly, and four diamond crystals sparkle. Repetitive beginnings lead a child to such sentences as *E* is for——and *F* is for——. Four eels wriggle, one bonfire flickers, and a winged griffin seems to fly. Even the shapes of the letters and the key words seem to flicker. Other interesting word choices are kaleido-scope, magnet, and necktie. Ages 4-up.

Pattern: Beginning with single capitals, repetitive beginnings in sentences are read.

Muehl, Lois Baker. *My Name Is———: A Game of Letters and Their Sounds*. Pictures by Aldren A. Watson. New York: Holiday House, 1959.

Here, from Arthur to Zelma, a child is asked to participate in a game using the first letters of names. With words beginning with *A*, a child reads about a character whose name, occupation the character wants or has, objects the character can buy, and what the character can see all begin with *A*. With an airplane, Arthur aims to be an artist and paints such animals as an ape and an antelope. Occupational choices of females are included. Felicia thinks it would be fun to be a farmer, Judy jokes that she would like to be a jeweler for jolly old Santa Claus, while Nancy is a night nurse for animals. Una rides a unicycle in a circus, Virginia wants to be a vet, and Zelma wants to own a zoo. Each character uses his or her initial to state alliterative words to express wishes or to tell a story. Perhaps a young reader will be interested in writing alliterative wishes or a story with words that begin with the first letter of his or her name? Ages 7–8.

Pattern: First letter of child's name begins alliterative pattern in story-sentences.

Murdock, Hy. *Learning the Alphabet*. Illustrated by Terry Burton. Loughborough, Eng.: Ladybird Books, Ltd., 1984.

In this ABC a child hears names of objects that begin with the sounds of the selected letters. An adult may read the included short sentences and ask questions. If time permits, the adult may invite the listener to discuss the shapes and patterns of the letters. Each lowercase letter is introduced in bold, black type as a child is asked to draw additional shapes of the letter. With the selected letter highlighted in color, a simple sentence follows a repetitive pattern—e.g., *A* is for———and *B* is for———. There are accompanying activities such as drawing apples in trees, sketching the number of candles a child would need on his or her birthday cake, and creating happy and sad faces. A child may match initial letters to the names of animals, write lowercase letters next to uppercase letters, and match capitals to selected lowercase letters. Ages 3-up.

Pattern: Letter-key word-activity arrangement.

My ABC Book. Illustrated by Alys Nugent. Racine, Wisc.: Western Publishing Company, 1956.

When the book is opened, the familiar ABC tune is heard. To listen to the music again, a child presses a button on the inside of the front cover. Traditional sentences are read for each large, capital, serif letter and the pictured objects. Each noun for the colorful object ("acorn," "boat," "camel") is capitalized within the sentence—e.g., *I* is for "Island" and *W* is for "Worm." Ages 3–5.

Pattern: Objects, names, and related initial capitals are found in repetitive phrases.

My ABC Book. Illustrated by J. Pavlin and G. Seda. London: Brown Watson, 1985.

Animals and objects pop up when these pages are turned. *F* is for "fire" on the roof of one house, *P* is for "penguins" on an ice floe, and *W* is for one "windmill." Uppercase and lowercase letters in black are scattered across the double-page spreads. Key words are near the animals and objects. The sequence of the letters continues in the upper right-hand corners of the pages. Ages 4–6.

Pattern: Along with key objects, animals and their names are related to upper- and lowercase block letters.

My Pop-Up ABC. Illustrated by Anne Grahame Johnstone. London: Dean and Son Ltd., 1982.

Johnstone's objects in alphabetical order—one bear, a cat, and a doll—pop forward when the pages are opened. A child touches each pop-up object and names it. One snowman, a top, a vixen, and other pop-ups wait to be touched and named. Accompanying key nouns in lowercase letters appear on the page. The lowercase letters are seen twice, once in the pop-up arrangement and again as initial letters preceding the nouns. Key nouns in lowercase letters are read. Ages 3–4.

Pattern: Colorful lowercase letters lead to initial letters in key nouns.

O'Callaghan, Karen. *Join In with Us! Letters: An Action Alphabet.* Illustrated by Eric Rowe. Cambridge, Eng.: Brimax Books, 1982.

One full-page and full-color illustration is paired with the upper- and lowercase letters. The caption shows the placement of the letters by highlighting them in red within the black text. Capitalization and punctuation are shown. Each caption encourages a child to respond in different ways—e.g., by pointing, blowing paper, curling up, and with other actions. Words contain the selected guiding letter are underlined in red. Ages 6–8.

Pattern: Sound-letter relationship found in underlined words in sentences.

Paré, Roger. *The Annick ABC.* Illustrated by the author. Toronto: Annick Press, 1985.

In this alliterative text, initial letters are emphasized. Each pair of black upper- and lowercase letters are introduced by a full-color illustration and a humorous sentence. A boa blows bubbles in the bathtub, a cat in a canoe rides along with a canary, and a dinosaur dances with a dolphin. In each sentence a child finds three or more words that begin with the guiding letter on the page. Each one of the words is found in the picture. Accompanying this book is an included activity set, which consists of a game and two puzzles. On each piece in the game is one of the letters used to spell the words from the book. The two illustrations may be used to make puzzles. Ages 5-up.

Pattern: With capitalization and punctuation short alliterative sentences show key words in boldface type.

Pomaska, Anna. *The Little ABC Coloring Book.* Illustrated by the author. New York: Dover Publications, Inc., 1986.

In this small ABC each capital is illustrated on a verso page along with small pictures of an animal/object whose name begins with the letter. On the recto page is a black-and-white drawing of the object, again, whose capitalized name begins with the guiding letter. Traditional beginnings link across the pages with such words as found in *M* is for "moon," *P* is for "Panda," and *T* is for "tiger." Fifty-two illustrations to color. Ages 4–6.

Pattern: Guiding serif capitals begin traditional beginnings with pattern of *A* is for——and *B* is for——.

Rojas-Lombardi, Felipe. *The A-to-Z No-Cook Cookbook.* Illustrated by Dorothy Ivens. Racine, Wisc.: Western Publishing Company, 1974.

F. Rojas-Lombardi mentions that cooking is one of the best adventures, that it can be done without the use of any harmful utensils, and that keeping one's hands and kitchen clean is important because we eat the food touched while preparing these recipes. Each double page is devoted to recipes guided by one selected letter. For *A*, a child finds the recipes for appetizers and apple salad. For *Z*, a girl or boy can prepare zippy salami bits, cream cheese and salami on crackers, or zodiac treats, peanut butter and jelly on suns, moons, and stars cut from bread. Each guiding letter is formed from outlined shapes of foods. The shape of *A* is formed with outlines of apples, *B* with berries, and *C* with carrots. Comments are highlighted in boxes of full color and mention serving ideas (serve a dinner sandwich with an olive), share facts (vinaigrette dressing is famous with chefs all over the world), and define terms (Xylophone Dips were inspired by thin Italian breadsticks that look like the thin sticks used to play the xylophone). Ages 8-up.

Pattern: With expository writing, each guiding letter is emphasized by selected recipes in alphabetical order.

Schade, Charlene. *Move with Me from A to Z.* Illustrated by Steve Pileggi. San Diego, Calif.: The Wright Group, 1982.

Schade's book encourages a child to learn the letters through play in movements. A young child should enjoy taking turns with someone making movements for the action words. The adult describes the movements for the action words. A child jumps and lands gently like Freddy the frog, runs slowly like Kevin Kiwi, or opens his mouth wide to show his teeth like Henry the hippopotamus. Ages 2-6.

Pattern: For each letter there is an animal character and directions for accompanying actions.

Shreck, Peter K. *First Letters*. Illustrated by Eleanor Wasmuth. New York: Macmillan Publishing Company, Inc., 1982.

In a box at the foot of each page is a key letter and object. A girl or boy recognizes the letter and the object. For instance, *M* is near one monkey. Other objects on the page are seen: a crescent moon, a rabbit magician, and a red motorcycle. In an accompanying envelope are additional cards to be used in sequence. The cards slide back and forth under a cardboard window frame to show the directions and the correct responses. With these cards a child is asked to find the pattern of pictures that begin with selected letters, of key words for the pictures, and to name the letter that begins a chosen word. The separate cards for different letters emphasize the twenty-six letters in the English language alphabet. Ages 6-up.

Pattern: Letter-object-key word arrangement.

Silverman, Maida. *Bunny's ABC Box*. Illustrated by Ellen Blonder. New York: Grosset and Dunlap/The Putnam Publishing Group, 1986.

In this ABC there are die cuts on every page—square holes (shapes) to explore—in this "little poke and look book." A child looks into a bright yellow box along with Bunny. Together they find objects in alphabetical order from ants and apple to zucchini and zebra. Guiding serif letters, capitals and lowercase ones, are presented in bold type. Short story-lines, both declarative and interrogative, show use of capitalization and punctuation. Ages 2–4.

Pattern: Letter-object-word arrangement is supported by brief declarative and interrogative sentences.

Sorensen, Jim. *Sons and Daughters of Mystical Creatures: An ABC Guide*. Illustrated by the author. Mercer Island, Wash.: Peanut Butter Publishing, 1983.

Each one of Sorensen's ABC creatures is a part of a legend or myth. For example, there is the ammit, an Egyptian beast with the forequarters of a crocodile and the hindquarters of a hippopotamus. The basilisk has the body of a rooster and a barbed serpent's tail. The centaur is a creature with the body of a horse and the head and torso of a human. For each creature there is an identifying letter and an explanatory paragraph. Black outlines on white pages offer coloring possibilities. Ages 7-up.

Pattern: Descriptive writing. From ammit to zu, key block letters match initial letters in names of creatures and precede explanatory paragraphs.

Svensson, Borje. *Letters.* Illustrated by the author. New York: Viking, 1981.

Svensson invites a child to play a participation game and look for the hidden letters on the small pages. The rooftop of a house forms the *M*, laundry on the line hangs in the shape of *I* and *J*, and holiday wreaths are in the shapes of *P* and *Q*. Can a child find the *N* in the frame of the gate? The *S* in the shape of the swan's neck? Or the *V* in the tree? Ages 5-6.

Pattern: Objects in the environment form the shapes of letters.

Tallarico, Tony. *Alphabet Flip-Book Game.* Illustrated by the author. New York: Grosset and Dunlap, 1981.

Flipping through the strip pages, a boy or girl matches the patterned parts to see a complete letter of the alphabet. A small picture clue on each strip (mouse, airplane, balloon) is an object whose name begins with the sought-after letter. Once the colorful letter is found, a black-and-white pattern of the same letter is shown on the back side of the strips. Ages 5-up.

Pattern: Shapes of letters and objects completed by turning page strips.

Tillett, Leslie. *Plant and Animal Alphabet Coloring Book.* Illustrated by the author. New York: Dover Publications, Inc., 1980.

In Tillett's book each large letter is decorated with plants and animals whose names begin with that letter. A child colors the objects, identifies as many as possible and checks the identifying names with the charts at the end of the book. For example, the chart for *X* shows such objects as xenopus (frog), xiphophorus (crab), and xiphosura (fish). Ages 7-up.

Pattern: Full-page letters contain plants and objects to color, the names of which begin with the appropriate letter.

Tinies Pop-up Book. Illustrated. London: Dean International Publishing, 1967. Reprint 1984.

Capitals in bright colors are the first letters in the accompanying verses. Key objects (ark, animals, apples) in the verses pop out and can be touched. Some are singular nouns: a "baker" carries "bread" in a "basket." Others are plural: "candles," "flowers," and "oranges." A child in the United States hears about British customs and words—e.g., *E* is for an "egg" for one's tea, *L* is for a "lorry" that carries a load, and *Q* is for a "queen," kind and good. Ages 3–4.

Pattern: With verses, large sans serif capitals are matched with initial letters of singular or plural key words in bold type.

Wall, Elizabeth S. *Computer Alphabet Book.* Illustrated by Julia E. Cousins. Nokomis, Fla.: Bayshore Books, 1979.

For a child who wants to get acquainted with computers, this alphabet connects the letters to definitions of computer terms. *A* is for "address," *B* is for "Basic," and *C* is for "computer." One elf, dressed in blue, serves as a guide through the illustrations. The elf assumes a floppy body position to demonstrate the meaning of the word "floppy," plugs in jacks, and demonstrates the word "run." With this book, a young reader recognizes that an ABC arrangement can help someone locate information quickly in a book. Ages 6-up.

Pattern: Blue capital letters on verso pages introduce key computer words also found in blue. These word choices are followed by explanatory sentences.

Walt Disney's Flash Ahead with ABC's. Illustrated. New York: Simon and Schuster, Inc., 1983.

Short rhyming verses describe objects used by Disney's characters. There is Goofy's automobile, Dumbo's cupcake, and ice cream for Mickey Mouse. Uppercase letters in black introduce the rhymes. On the back side of these flip pages is a second scene showing the object with both uppercase and lowercase letters. A child is invited to name the letters, identify the objects, and listen to the verse again to say the letter. For another reading, a child may listen to the verse this time to say the object's name when it is omitted by the reader. The objects are reviewed again on the final pages where one may point to an object, name it, flip the page over, and find the starting letter for the word that names the picture. Ages 4-up.

Pattern: Objects or letters are named when omitted from selected verses.

Weiss, Ellen. *The Alphabet: The Great Alphabet Play.* Art direction by Robert Pierce. Racine, Wisc.: Western Publishing Company, Inc., 1986.

Weiss's instructions are on tape and guide a child through this participation book with the Sesame Street characters. There is Burt and Ernie, Big Bird, Oscar the Grouch, Herry Monster, and Cookie Monster. A child lifts the reusable vinyl stickers of objects and places them on the scenes in the book. To the music of the ABC Song, Prairie Dawn introduces the play. The alphabet is the star of the show. A signal cues a child to turn the pages. The first letter is *A*, and an airplane is brought on stage by Herry Monster; *A* is for "airplane." Will a child think of an *A* when an airplane flies overhead? *D* is for a "dusty doorknob" contributed by Oscar the Grouch. Big Bird brings an "invention"—an itch scratcher—for the letter *I*. The vinyl stickers may be returned to a backing sheet and stored inside the book. Ages 3–6.

Pattern: With upper- and lowercase letters in black, rhymes are introduced by Sesame Street characters.

Wenk, Dina. *Make Zoup! An Alphabet Book.* Illustrated by John Wallner. New York: Dell Publishing Company, Inc. 1979.

In alphabetical order a child is invited to add the ingredients to an ABC soup. From one artichoke and three beets to one yam and two zucchini squash, each item may be drawn on the page near the large soup kettle. Ages 5-up.

Pattern: Guiding capitals and key ingredients lead to objects for alphabet soup.

Wilks, Mike. *The Ultimate Alphabet.* Illustrated by the author. Designed by Bernard Higton. New York: Henry Holt, 1986.

Mainly for adults, Wilks creates a painting for each of the twenty-six letters He encourages the viewer to read the pictures and pick out the 7,777 words from the pictures. The painting for *X*

shows 30 words, while the painting for S shows 1,229 words. There
are visual references to works of art by other artists. Wilks shows
examples of an anamorphic drawing of an elongated ant on the *A*
page, asks why a banana would be on the *B* page, and makes a
deliberate mistake on the *M* page. What patterns can be put into
perspective on the page for the letter *P*? In an accompanying
workbook, directions are given for entering the ultimate alphabet
competition and for identifying correctly the most words in the
book by April 1, 1988. The winner will receive a prize of $15,000.
Winners' list available.

Pattern: Words depicted in paintings with certain images
representing more than one word.

Wylie, Joanne, and David Wylie. A *Fishy Alphabet Story*. Illustrated by David Graham Wylie. Chicago: Childrens Press, 1983.

The Wylies encourage a child to catch letter fish in alphabetical order. Each fish shows three letters on its scales. After several
fish have been caught, the letters are displayed on one large fish,
the alphabet fish. For a final review there is a fishing game in which
a child identifies a letter on a fish to catch it. Following the review a
list of words in alphabetical order shows a child which words were
introduced in this participation story. Ages 5 -6.

Pattern: With the exception of one fish displaying two letters,
VW, capital letters in groups of three label each fish and are seen
again in a list of words in alphabetical order.

Progressive stories

Banner, Angela. *Ant and Bee: An Alphabetical Story for Tiny Tots*.
Illustrated by Bryan Ward. Los Angeles: Price/Stern/Sloan, 1981.
First published by Edmund Ward, Ltd., 1950.

Banner's small book holds an alphabetical story about an ant
and a bee, and is intended for use by a parent who wishes to read
with a child. Here are small pen-and-ink sketches on white
backgrounds that introduce a brown dog who leads ant and bee
through an ABC story. They meet objects in alphabetical order
along the way. The main narration in this progressive story are the
words in black which are read by the adult. The key words are in
red and are read by the child. If this progressive story is enjoyed,

there are other books about these characters. In *Ant and Bee and the ABC* (Kaye and Ward, Ltd., 1966), Ant and Bee look for their lost hats in twenty-six boxes, labeled with capitals in red. Repetitive sentences, three-letter words, and similar questions are presented for each letter in red. In *More Ant and Bee: Another Alphabetical Story for Tiny Tots* (Kaye and Ward, Ltd., 1981), Ant and Bee travel to Asia on a boat. The story has words of four letters as the ABC choices, ones a child pronounces as the adult reads the words in black. With *More and More Ant and Bee: Another Alphabetical Story* (Kaye and Ward, Ltd.,1981), Ant, Bee, and Kind Dog play with a small girl while her parents are away buying presents. A child reviews all of the words of three and four letters from earlier stories and sees five-letter words in red for the key words.

Pattern: In complete sentences key words in red are read aloud by child, and narrative words in black are read aloud by adult.

Barton, Bryon. *Applebet Story.* Illustrated by the author. New York: Viking Press, 1973.

Using a one-word caption format and black, white, and gray illustrations, Barton presents the adventure of one red apple that is blown about on a windy day. The one-word caption on each page serves as the key word and labels the action. The young viewer may see that a sequence of pictures can tell a story with few words. For the letter *I*, an "Indian" tosses the apple to a "juggler" for the letter *J*. At *K*, a pony "kicks" the apple toward the leader of a nearby band. With his baton the leader of the band hits the apple, and the apple continues on its journey through the alphabetical sequence. If each key word were covered with a word mask, what word would a child contribute for each scene? Ages 4-7.

Pattern: Following the alphabetical sequence, key words lead the action.

Bassett, Scott, and Tammy Bassett. *Artemus and the Alphabet.* Illustrated by Scott Bassett. Spokane, Wash.: Bassett and Brush, 1980.

The Bassetts introduce a child to Artemus, a unique character, who shows a girl or boy the alphabet. A pattern of block letters in black appears in the upper left-hand corner of every page. The words appear with the guiding letter in a selected color. For instance, *B* words contain purple *B*s, *C* words contain yellow *C*s and so on. Each letter leads to several words that begin with that letter on each page. With selected letters emphasized by colors, it is apparent that the same letters are used again and again in language. Some alliteration is heard as Artemus counts cows, marches to music, and pops popcorn. Uppercase and lowercase block letters in black are in corners of colorful bands at tops of pages. Colors of letters in key words match colors of bands. Ages 3–5.

Pattern: With capitals and punctuation ABC sequence progresses through story line.

Black, Floyd. *Alphabet Cat.* Illustrated by Carol Nicklaus. New York: Gingerbread House/ Elsevier-Dutton Publishing Company, Inc., 1979.

To help locate a rat from the Pack Rat Gang, a gang that has captured Catrina the countess, a child looks for the disguised rat in each illustration. As the letters of the alphabet are mentioned in the story, they are shown in black boldface. A child is asked to point to *A* objects, to show the *B* things, or to look at all of the objects that begin with *C*. A second pattern, which shows the passing of time, introduces each episode in this progressive story. Words such as "Turn your back and look what happens" and "I have a funny feeling" are examples of clichés that are recognized readily by an older child. To replace the clichés, what different words can a reader contribute to the story? Ages 7–8.

Pattern: Both capitals and lowercase letters in red appear in the left-hand corner of each illustration and lead to key letters in boldface in the sentences.

Bracken, Carolyn. *Bambi's First ABC Word Book.* Illustrated by the author. Closter, N.J.: Sharon Publications, Inc., 1981.

Living in a five-story tower building, the animals give notice that one room is for rent. Inquiring renters—e.g., a dove, a nightingale, and a rabbit—arrive to see the room. Full-color illustrations alternate with black-and-white ones. The objects in the illustrations are labeled. Their names begin with the one selected letter per page. However, there is no animal named Bambi. Selected letters are shown in red within words in black text throughout the rhyming story. Ages 6–7.

Pattern: With block upper- and lowercase letters in black, ABC progressive story is told in letter-picture-verse arrangement.

Corbett, Scott. *The Mysterious Zetabet*. Illustrated by Jon McIntosh. Boston: Atlantic/Little, Brown, 1979.

In Corbett's story the alphabet is called the Zetabet in Zyxland. It begins with Z and continues through to A. This is the alphabet said backward. To escape from Zyxland, Zachary must ask an unanswerable question of the Zyxlanders. If the Zyxlanders cannot answer the question, then Zachary will be free. What question will a child contribute? Is a child interested in writing a Z story, one in which each sentence contains a word that begins with Z? In writing a story in which each sentence begins with a sequential letter of the alphabet? In writing a story in which imaginary people, places, and things have names? Ages 8-up.

Pattern: With variety of sentence patterns, key words in the story begin with Z.

DeLage, Ida. *ABC Triplets at the Zoo*. Illustrated by Lori Pierson. Champaign, Ill.: Garrard Publishing Company, 1980.

The ABC triplets go to the zoo, where the names of the animals are identified. Each animal's name and its accompanying initial capital is in bold type in the text beneath the illustration. Every word choice is found again in the text at the foot of each page. *U* is "umbrella bird," the bird with an umbrella over his head, *V* is "vulture," who seems to wear nothing on his head, and *W* is "wolf," whose head and body resemble those of a large gray dog. There are other progressive ABC stories by DeLage. In the *ABC Easter Bunny* (Garrard, 1979), the illustrations by Ellen Sloan show the deliveries made in the city and in the country by the Easter Bunny. *ABC Halloween Witch* (Garrard, 1977) is illustrated by Lou Cunette. *S* is for the "spell" that the witch puts on the "toad" (for *T*). The toad becomes a "unicorn" for *U*. In another, Kelly Oechsli illustrates *ABC Pigs Go to Market* (Garrard, 1977). Each item at the market introduces its name. The little pigs want gum, sodas, milk, and ice cream. *Z* is for "zero" at the end of this shopping trip, for Mother Pig has nothing left in her purse. In *ABC Fire Dogs* (Garrard, 1977) the illustrations by Ellen Sloan show *J* is for the "jump" that Lady Dog makes into the net of the fire dogs, *K* is for a "kiss" for each rescuer, and *L* is for the "ladder" to climb as the fire dogs continue to put out the fire. The text, the word choices in boldface capitals, and the guiding capitals in each book are beneath the full-color illustrations. Each key word is seen again in boldface capitals in the text. Ages 6-up.

Pattern: Objects and actions identify their names, and initial letters in word choices shown in boldface capitals. Each choice is found a second time in bold type in text.

Friskey, Margaret. *Indian Two Feet and the ABC Moose Hunt.* Illustrated by John Hawkinson. Chicago: Childrens Press, 1977.

Without using his bow and arrow, Indian Two Feet, a young boy, hunts for his first moose in this simple story in rhyme. A child listens to hear the beginning, middle, and end of the story. *H* is for "hunting" for the moose. *T* is for "trouble" when the canoe tips over and the paddle, arrow, bow, and canoe are lost. *V* is for the "village" where Indian Two Feet returns after the unsuccessful hunt. Ages 5-7.

Pattern: Each sentence begins with a serif capital in black and ends with a rhyming word.

Gág, Wanda. *The ABC Bunny.* Illustrated by the author. Hand-lettered by Howard Gág. Music by Flavia Gág. New York: Coward, McCann and Geoghegan, Inc., 1933.

Recommended. An ABC song about a sleeping bunny who is startled by a crashing red apple introduces and closes this alphabet. There is a refrain of tra-la-la after each alphabetical object is introduced in the sequence of the rhyming story. Oversize serif capitals in red begin each short rhyming line. Large black-and-white illustrations show the bunny as he dashes away and meets such animals as a fat frog, a jaunty bluejay, and a prickly porcupine. A California State Department of Education-recommended extended reading. Ages 5-6.

Pattern: Rhyming words in couplets are followed by refrain and introduce each serfif capital in red in the story with music.

Gantz, David. *The Genie Bear with the Light Brown Hair Word Book*. Illustrated by the author. Garden City, New York: Double-day and Company, Inc., 1982.

From a talking bottle of ketchup comes Genie Bear with the light brown hair to grant Moxy twenty-seven wishes. In double-page spreads, the genie shows Moxy all of the things that begin with *A*, with *B*, and so on. Some alliteration is heard in the labeled objects and in the dialogue found in the word balloons. An alliterative review is found in the endpages. Here a child finds an armadillo who is amused, a badger who is bored, and a cat who enjoys a candy cane. One pattern for the uppercase *X* at the beginning of words is shown with *Xavier, Xerxes*, and *Xenobia*. A second pattern for the lowercase *X* is shown with *excuse, exhale, experience*, and *exhausting*. For *Z*, a special aspect of word play is seen, that of creating and using nonsense names for imaginary creatures. A Zookinshnoz zaps another creature, a Zitzafreeny. A Zorkabong shows a forked tongue, the Zoakabale has twin tails, and the Zapperform wears curly horns. Does any child notice the lack of ending punctuation? What punctuation might be sug-gested? Ages 6–8.

Pattern: With capitals and lowercase serif letters, each double-page spread labels objects and actions. Capitals begin phrases without ending punctuation.

Hargreaves, Roger. *Albert, the Alphabetical Elephant*. Illustrated by the author. New York: Grosset and Dunlap, 1982.

Albert the blue elephant turns his trunk into the shapes of the letters to help a small girl learn the alphabet. The blue shapes are similar to the letters a child uses in manuscript writing. Each letter is followed by an object or an action in the story line. Lowercase serif letters in bold type occur in the sentences of the story for easy identification. The letter *X* stumps Albert and the little girl, so there is no pictured *X* object. Is a child interested in adding an object for *X* to the story? During a second reading, blue pipe cleaners, to simulate the elephant's flexible trunk, may be used by a child to shape the letters as Albert does. Ages 4–6.

Pattern: Lowercase letters formed by elephant's trunk are seen again as serif lowercase letters in boldface in sentences.

Le Sieg, Theo. *Hooper Humperdink? ... Not him!* Illustrated by Charles E. Martin. New York: Random House, 1976.

In Le Sieg's progressive story a child invites some friends in alphabetical order to a party. Hooper Humperdink, a guy not liked, is not invited. Additional items are arranged for the party and described in tall-tale language: a marching band, a bigger table, ten tons of ice cream, and strawberry soda by the tubful. The party is so big and so good that no one should miss it, not even Humperdink. Le Sieg's imagination promotes pictures, visually and in writing. Ages 4–6.

Pattern: In this rhyming story with nonsense words and tall-tale language, friends are invited in alphabetical order to a birthday party.

Leedy, Loreen. *The Dragon ABC Hunt.* Illustrated by the author. New York: Holiday House, 1986.

When ten little blue dragons are bored, Ma Dragon suggests that they go on an alphabetical treasure hunt. From one red apple, one blue ball, and one orange cat to chase, to an X ray, a yellow yo-yo, and a zebra hiding in the grass, the little dragons find all of the items that are needed to complete the hunt. What sound does each letter stand for? Pairs of letters and names of objects are found consistently in the page corners. Can an ending phonogram such as "on" be blended with these beginning sounds? What words can be made? Does it matter that some of the words make sense and that some are nonsense? Will the nonsense words provide words for the small dragons as dragon talk? Can the words be written in word balloons for the dragons? Can another story about the dragons grow from someone's imagination?

One teacher reviewed the sequence of the letters in this book with new words to a familiar tune, "When Johnny Comes Marching Home Again." As the children march around the room, they sing to the music: "When the dragons come marching home again, Hoorah, Hoorah!/When the dragons come marching home again, Hoorah, Hoorah!/When the dragons come marching home again,/they'll know their alphabet to the end./And we'll all say the letters when the dragons come marching home." Then children stop marching and chant the following part of the sequence together: "A, B, C, D, E, F, G,/H, I, J, K, L, M, N, O, P." The marching begins again, with the words of the song repeated. When the children stop marching the second time, the following letter sequence is chanted: "Q, R, S, T, U and V,/W, X, and Y, and Z." The refrain about the dragons is sung for a final time as the children march around the room one last time. Ages 4-6.

Pattern: Opening and closing rhymes introduce dragons, colorful uppercase and lowercase letters, and names of objects.

Lionni, Leo. *The Alphabet Tree*. Illustrated by the author. New York: Pantheon, 1968.

Alphabet letters in an alphabet tree become frightened during a storm and hide from the wind. One word "bug," shaped like a bumblebee, teaches the letters to make words, which makes them strong enough to survive the next wind. One purple caterpillar encourages the words to get together and to make sentences that mean something. Getting together means that the words can write and say things about the wind, the leaves, and the bug. Encouraged to say something important, the letters decide on what to say and travel on the back of the purple caterpillar to show their message to the president. Ages 6-up.

Pattern: Letters form words and words make sentences that can say something important.

McGill, Marci. *The Six Little Possums: A Birthday ABC*. Illustrations by Cyndy Szekeres. Racine, Wisc.: Western Publishing Company, Inc., 1982.

On her birthday, little Peapod the possum goes on a special picnic with her family. In the story, word choices relating to the picnic such as "grass," "hug," and "ice" are introduced. A serif capital in blue appears along with the key word in blue text. The illustrations show the objects mentioned in the text and include these: X marks the spot for the treasure that waits to be found during a hunt in the woods, Y is for "yawns," and Z is for "zippers" on the pajamas of all of the little possums. Ages 4-6.

Pattern: Repetitive words in blue identify objects.

Mack, Stan. *The King's Cat Is Coming!* Illustrated by the author. New York: Pantheon, 1976.

Expecting the king's cat to arrive, the people of the town predict what kind of a cat the king will receive. Here the people describe the cat without telling its name. In each word balloon a characteristic is mentioned and identified with a red capital as the first letter. A drawing of the cat with that characteristic is shown in the illustration, too. A child sees an angry cat and reads "Angry." The words "fat" and "gigantic" show the elegantly dressed cat sitting on the various house tops of the town. Dressed as a court jester, the cat is zany and keeps the people awake. What will the cat be like when it finally arrives? Are there other animals who could have twenty-six characteristics? Could those be dictated by an interested listener? Ages 4–7.

Pattern: With red initial capitals, key words in bold type are clarified by illustrated characteristics of the king's cat.

Mayer, Mercer. *Little Monster's Alphabet Book.* Illustrated by the author. Racine, Wisc.: Golden Press, 1978.

Beginning with a brown, grumpy apple, Little Monster tells about his ABC collection of objects. At the beginning of the short sentences about the objects are serif capitals and lowercase letters in black. In this ABC a child sees that similar beginnings can be used over and over in writing. With two exceptions (*C* and *O*), the letters lead into similar phrases, *A* is a———and *B* is a———. Does a child notice the two exceptions? Is the child able to change the exceptions to fit the patterns? Is a child interested in starting an individual alphabet collection of objects? Ages 4–6.

Pattern: Repetitive beginnings of sentences show initial black serif upper- and lowercase letters.

Mendoza, George. *Alphabet Sheep.* Illustrated by Kathleen Reidy. New York: Grosset and Dunlap, 1982.

Recommended. An old shepherd loses one of his sheep and goes on an alphabetical search. As he searches on the double-page spreads, a child sees capital block letters in black along with the lost sheep in various poses in the corners of the spreads. Key words are in boldface within the sentences. The search begins in the air, in a barn, and in a chicken coop. At Z, the sheep is found fast asleep in a hammock on the shepherd's front porch. The pattern of searching for a lost object can be applied to other situations. What could be lost at the Olympics? At home? In the city? Ages 5–8.

Pattern: Key words in bold type in sentences introduce capitals in black.

Miller, Elizabeth, and Jane Cohen. *Cat and Dog and the ABC's.* Illustrated by Victoria Chess. New York: Franklin Watts, 1981.

While Dog is trying to learn his ABC's from Cat, they eat a delicious Chinese dinner, and one final fortune cookie reveals that Dog will learn his alphabet when he has traveled the world. Dog dreams of alphabetical adventures around the world from Asia and Beirut through Cairo and Denmark to Yugoslavia and Zanzibar. Words that are selected to reinforce each guiding letter are capitalized within the sentences. Pairs of serif capitals and lowercase letters in colors are found consistently in the upper corners of the pages. Beneath each illustration is an alliterative sentence with capitalized key words. Ages 4–8.

Pattern: Upper- and lowercase pairs in color, alliterative sentences, and capitalized word choices.

Miller, Roberta. *Richard Scarry's Chipmunk's ABC*. Illustrated by Richard Scarry. Racine, Wisc.: Western Publishing Company, Inc., 1963.

The chipmunks introduce objects such as ice cream, net, and quilt. They show the actions (jump, swing) and their labels. In the corner of every illustration is a traditional sentence that shows the word choice in bold type along with a beginning capital in color and ending punctuation: Z is for———. In the sentences beneath the illustrations, a word that begins with a similar letter is shown in boldface for easy identification. Ages 4–6.

Pattern: Initial letters of word choices found again in boldface words beneath illustrations of chipmunks.

Richards, Dorothy Fay. *Wise Owl's ABC Book: A Book of Small Creatures*. Illustrated by Helen Endres. Chicago: Childrens Press, 1981.

Wise Owl takes three little owlets for a walk and meets some ABC animals along the way. Each animal is introduced with colorful pairs of upper- and lowercase letters, with a small illustrated insert, and with a repetitive phrase at the foot of the larger illustration. Within the phrases the selected letters and the nouns are in bold type, making each one easy for a child to find. There is a final review for matching the letters and the animal friends who were seen during the walk. Ages 4–5.

Pattern: Colorful capitals match initial capitals of phrases, while names of creatures match boldface words in repetitive phrases.

Scarry, Richard. *Richard Scarry's Find Your ABC's.* Illustrated by the author. New York: Random House, 1973.

Sam and Dudley, two animal detectives, look for the letters in the alphabet. On each full-color page, the objects have their names printed nearby. One letter is featured in red in the names on each page. A child finds some of the letters in a beginning, middle, and ending position in the selected words. In addition, the same letter is shown in black as a capital and as a lowercase letter. A child is asked to help find the letters. After Z, all of the letters of the alphabet are seen in a review painted by Lowly Worm. A child finds out what Sam and Dudley will do with all of the letters that have been discovered. Ages 5–7.

Pattern: On each page a guiding letter in black can be found both as a capital and as a lowercase letter. Labeled objects in full-color illustrations about animal detectives show similar letters in red.

Steiner, Charlotte. *Annie's ABC Kitten: An Alphabetical Story About Annie and Her Pet.* Illustrated by the author. New York: Alfred A. Knopf, 1965.

Steiner joins other authors who emphasize alphabetical word choices and marks her choices in a special way by underlining the key words in the story. Steiner guides the alphabetical sequence about the adventures of this small kitten with these choices for a young reader. This approach may be compared with the methods of other authors: key letters are in red in *Richard Scarry's ABC Word Book* and in *Benji's Book of ABC*, alphabetic word choices are in red which are easy to identify in the black text. For other comparisions there are boldface letters in black in *A for the Ark* and capitalized key words to read in two titles, *All in the Woodland Early* and in *The Sea World Alphabet*. Ages 7–8.

Pattern: Word choices in corners are underlined in sentences about a small girl and her kitten.

Stutzman, Roxy Ann. *The Alphabet Kingdom*. Illustrated by Pat York. Santa Maria, Calif.: Ken Ventrees, 1981.

Designed for students in junior high developmental classes, this story takes place in the Kingdom of Alphabet Land with a king who makes important decisions for his twenty-six alphabet subjects. The king solves *C's* and *G's* problems, creates blends, digraphs, and letter teams. In a nonconsumable paperback format, several activities are included for students to reproduce sounds, say words, and use a dictionary. A teacher supplement is available. Ages 13–14.

Pattern: Phonetic generalizations presented in illustrated story about the Kingdom of Alphabet Land.

Tallon, Robert. *Zag: A Search Through the Alphabet*. Illustrated by the author. New York: Holt, Rinehart and Winston, 1976.

An unidentified narrator receives a call from Zag. The telephone line goes dead and a search begins for Zag. During the search some of the alphabetical characters appear as anthropomorphic foods; exceptions are an Indian, the kite, and the ladder, among others. Finally finding Zag, Zig joins up with Zag and helps to finish a road in a zigzag way, so a parade can march by. Ages 5–6.

Pattern: Capitals introduce an ABC search.

Thayer, Jane. *Timothy and Madame Mouse: A Non-ABC Book*. Illustrated by Don Madden. New York: William Morrow & Company, Inc., 1971.

Beginning with the letters *L* and *M*, the letters are presented out of alphabetical sequence in this one. Timothy Cat, a resident in Mr. Simon's house, is afraid of mice. When a new arrival, Madame Mouse, appears, Timothy finds things to do, activities that keep him from removing Madame Mouse from the premises. Upper-

and lowercase letters are introduced by Timothy's activities and his determination to avoid the mouse. Identification of letters in the author's sequence are followed by tracing shapes and locating letters in sentences on each page. Is a child interested in reviewing letters in a way that is different from the alphabet sequence? Williams and Knafle (1977) suggest an arrangement from easy to difficult for learning ten selected letters: *S, K, O, F, A, U, D, E, H,* and *I*. Ages 6–8.

Pattern: Introduction of capitals and lowercase letters are followed by tracing shapes and locating letters in sentences about a cat afraid of mice.

Warren, Cathy. *Victoria's ABC Adventure*. Illustrated by Patience Brewster. New York: Lothrop, Lee and Shepard, 1984.

One little brown snake, Victoria (named after *V* in the alphabet), attends a cookout and panics the crowd. With the people chasing her, Victoria warns Mama Snake and her twenty-five sister snakes (named for the other letters). The snake family hides from danger under some nearby lettuce leaves. Stretching herself into a long line, Victoria erases every single snake track and saves her family from discovery. Alphabetical words in the text are identified with initial boldface letters. Ages 4–6.

Pattern: In bold type, word choices and lowercase letters are inserted in sequence in sentences about Victoria, the little brown snake.

Whitehead, Pat. *Arnold Plays Baseball*. Illustrated by G. Brian Karas. Mahwah, N.J.: Troll Associates, 1985.

Rainy weather keeps angry Arnold inside and away from his favorite sport, baseball. At *X*, Arnold exclaims when the rain stops. *Y* is "Yippee!" *Z* is zipping up Arnold's jacket before he runs outside to play. Lowercase letters in block manuscript appear on every page. One key word appears above each illustration. In this book, the alphabet progresses for the sake of the story as the plot dictates. Block upper- and lowercase letters are seen in the corners of each page along with one appropriate word choice. Each word choice is found again in the single sentence at the foot of the page.

Other progressive-sequence stories in this 1985 ABC adventure series are published by Troll and written by Whitehead. In

Here Comes Hungry Albert the illustrations by G. Brian Karas give Albert the ape something to eat for every letter. "Doughnuts" (and milk) introduce *Dd*, "ice cream" introduces *Ii*, and *Ll* is for "looking" both ways before Albert crosses a street to buy his ice-cream cone. Friends visit the zoo in Patti Boyd's illustrations for *Let's Go to the Zoo*. The children see some of their favorite animals—one brown gorilla, a wide-mouthed hippo, and a hopping kangaroo, and each child mimics the actions of an animal. Some key words might be difficult ones for certain children to recognize from the illustrations: "idea," "join," and "exactly." These words seem to be difficult ones to illustrate and for a child to recognize. In *Best Halloween Book*, one illustrated by Stephanie Britt, little Annie is frightened by Halloween objects—flying bats, strange cats, barking dogs—but finds that it's she who frightens others when she dresses as a monster with purple batwings.

With read-along kits, there are several titles to consider from the 1986 publications. One read-along selection is *Best Thanksgiving Book* with illustrations by Susan T. Hall in which *A* is for "America," *B* is for "big" and describes the size of the Pilgrims' sailing ship, and *C* is for the "courage" of the Pilgrims in crossing the ocean. Others include the *Best Valentine Book* and *What a Funny Bunny*. Some boys and girls may listen to the *X* words in these books and hear correct sounds but be confused with the "ex" beginnings of some of the words: "exclaims," "extremely," and "excited." Read-along kits for these books include a guide, a paperback, and cassette with music, sound effects, and narration. Ages 3–7.

Pattern: Letter pairs are introduced by key words found above illustrations and again in sentences.

Wild, Robin, and Jocelyn. *The Bears' ABC Book*. Illustrated by the authors. New York: J. B. Lippincott Company, 1977.

Three little bears, Griff, Snuff, and Pawpaw, rummage about and find all sorts of items in alphabetical order. The bears remember to be careful with a sharp axe they find; they have a wobbly ride on a bicycle with one flat tire, run a yo-yo up and down, and try to gallop home on a stuffed toy zebra. Each page is devoted to one letter. The large capitals in faint colors, the text, and the key words with initial lowercase letters in a matching, faint color, always are found beneath the illustrations. Inserted in each picture are word bubbles that show additional dialogue. In the text, will a child notice the pattern of quotations marks around words to show the dialogue of the bears? At the foot of each page, the ending sentence can be completed only by going to the next page to see the next alphabetical word choice. While the key objects are shown in the illustrations, the key words are not always included in the accompanying text beneath the pictures. Objects identify word choices. Colorful capitals match lowercase letters in colors found in key words on the pages. The little bears may help a child listen for certain determiners in the story. Some of the noun determiners in the sentences that a child could listen for are: *this-that, my-our, a, an,* and *the.* When does the child hear these words? The sentences also include capitalization, ending punctuation, and dialogue marked with quotation marks. Ages 4–7.

Pattern: Dialogue in narrative writing with ABC progression.

Winik, J. T., and Lauren Pashuk. *Fun from A to Z.* Illustrated by the authors. Burlington, Ont.: Hayes Publishing Ltd., 1985.

In this rhyming story the authors invite a child to find something hiding in a closet. From the closet, objects appear in alphabetical order: a zooming airplane, falling balloons, and a clown clashing cymbals. Objects introduce their capitalized names in bold type in the rhyming sentences on the colorful pages. Some interesting word choices are, for *R* , a *red rug* for *royalty*; for *T* , *two tubby twins*; and for *V* , *vacuum* cleaner with its sound of *varoom.* Stylized serif capitals in colors are in the upper page corners and are easy to see. Does a child recognize the pattern of rhyming lines that are linked across the pages? A child may have to be close to the book to see this. Ages 5–6.

Pattern: Objects in color identify capitalized names in bold type found in rhyming sentences.

Repetition

ABC Book. Illustrated by Dean Bryant. Chicago: Rand McNally and Company, 1958.

For young children this ABC book begins with one object per page, e.g., apple. Occasionally there are two objects on a page. A child sees a cookie with a duck and an elephant with a fish. None of the objects seem to be related to one another in theme, topic, or category. The endpapers show the capital letters as if cut from colorful fabric. Ages 3–5.

Pattern: Without punctuation, phrases have similar beginnings—e.g., *A* is for——and *B* is for——.

Adams, Pam. *Mr. Lion's I-Spy ABC Book.* Illustrated by the author. Restrop Manor, Eng.: Child's Play, 1975.

A child looks at the picture clues within the holes in the pages, identifies the objects, and predicts the words to read the phrases. Once an object is seen and the page is turned, the opening reveals the object in a second setting. A broken drum becomes repaired in a second scene as a child reads, "*D* is for drum." On one page a child sees a pony. On the next the prancing pony tosses his rider. Does the child see the pattern of the lion's image on every page? Does the child recognize the similar beginning stems under the objects? There is a review of all twenty-six phrases and the key objects (acrobat, bear, clown) on a final page. Ages 4–5.

Pattern: Similar beginnings introduce objects followed by a final review.

Boynton, Sandra. *A Is for Angry: An Animal and Adjective Alphabet.* Illustrated by the author. New York: Workman Publishing Company, 1983.

With Boynton's block capitals, a child meets the animals, their names and the selected adjectives that begin with the guiding letters. For instance, at the letter *B* in bold blue, a reader sees a bashful bear half-hidden behind the letter while a bunny waits nearby. At S, a sleepy snake curls along the shape of the letter, and at Z, a zany zebra hangs upside down from the top of the large green letter. A second ending shows that Z is also for "zoo." It includes a pictorial review of all of the animals and the letters. An additional double-page spread adds another ending when a child sees that Z is also for the sounds of all of the sleeping animals. Ages 4–6.

Pattern: Animals with alphabetical behaviors described with adjectives for guiding letters.

Bruna, Dick. *B Is for Bear: An ABC*. Illustrated by the author. London: Methuen Children's Books, 1972.

Recommended. Dick Bruna's alphabet has lowercase letters in black on verso pages facing bright pictures in bold compositions. Bruna's illustrations—which include a duck, a bunch of blue grapes, and a bright red apple—will attract a young child. In bright colors, the objects are ones a child should enjoy—e.g. a white igloo, a black octopus, and a gray walrus. For each letter, traditional beginnings similar to "A is for ———" are read on a final page. Ages 4-5.

Pattern: For each selected lowercase letter, name of object is followed by predictable words in traditional phrases.

Dean's Picture Fun with the Alphabet. Illustrated by Alan Fredman. London: Dean International Publishing/Hamlyn Publishing Group, Ltd., 1974.

Large pages hold full-color objects such as fish and sausage. The labels are near the objects and introduce the upper- and lowercase letters. The letters are shown in inserts in colors in the page corners. Traditional sentences are the headers for the pages— e.g., *A* is for alphabet, *B* is for butterfly, and *C* is for candle. Capitals begin the sentences, but there is no ending punctuation. An alert child may notice the spelling of "aeroplane," the picture of a valve, and one green vegetable, marrow. For a concluding activity, a child is asked to match a numeral near a pictured object with the initial letter in its name and to write the letters with which the names of selected objects begin. There is an answer page. All of the objects are seen again in different poses on the endpapers. Ages 2-up.

Pattern: Capitalized repetitive beginnings with no ending punctuation.

Falls, Charles B. *ABC Book*. Designed and cut on wood by the author. Garden City, N.Y.: Doubleday and Company, Inc., 1923.

Recommended. Bright colors of blue, green, orange, and yellow will attract a child's eye to these ABC animals. Some of the unusual animals that Falls shows are xiphius (fish), pelican, and orang (short version of orangutan). Falls reviews all of the capital letters again on the endpages. To emphasize the beginning sound in an animal's name, the first consonant sound may be blended with the following vowel sound and repeated two or three times (pe-pe-pelican) by an adult when the word is pronounced. Ages 4–5.

Pattern: Uppercase serif-style letters in black offer short phrases without ending punctuation.

Guthrie, Vee. *Animals from A to Z*. Illustrated by the author. New York: Van Nostrand Reinhold, 1969.

A child will be able to predict the words in the patterned sentences in this ABC book. In Guthrie's sentences a child reads about an illustrated animal and what the animal likes. The alligator likes an apple, a bear likes a ball, and a dinosaur likes a doll. In the first part of the book are manuscript sentences. In the second part another type font is used and there are different settings for the same alphabetical animals. Ages 4–6.

Pattern: Capital manuscript letters in red introduce repetitive sentences:———(name of animal) likes (a, an)———(name of object).

Izawa, Tadasu, and Shigemi Hijikata. *My First Book*. Illustrated. New York: Grosset, 1983.

In addition to the alphabet concept, there are seven other concepts introduced in this one. As two examples, a child may recognize colors and tell time. In the ABC section are the familiar and repetitive phrases: *A* for———and *B* for———. Such objects as apple and boy for the beginning sounds are recognized for their relationships to the displayed symbols. Ages 3–6.

Pattern: With repetitive phrases, beginning sounds of objects are related to displayed letters.

Korr, David. *ABC Toy Chest*. Illustrated by Nancy W. Stevenson. Racine, Wisc.: Western Publishing Company, Inc./Children's Television Workshop, 1981.

Jim Henson's Sesame Street Muppets are seen on the endpapers, and one muppet, Herry, looks for something in a toy chest on the pages. Herry tosses objects out in alphabetical order. First is an accordion, followed by a barbell and a camera. What is Herry looking for in the chest? After each object is tossed aside, a child reads the repetitive phrase: It's not his————. Each object is labeled with the initial capital and the noun in boldface. Each key word is found again in the sentences on each page. Ages 3-up.

Pattern: In bold type, names of toys introduce serif capitals and repetitive sentences.

Kraus, Robert. *Goodnight Little ABC*. Illustrated by Neils Mogens Bodecker. New York: Windmill Books/Simon and Schuster, Inc., 1972.

With this alphabet a child repeats a good-night signal to a variety of animals, and others, with alliterative names in repetitive lines. There is Bertram Bullfinch Basset Hound standing in front of his house, David Daniel Dormouse in his brass bed, and Gregory Guggenheim Guinea Pig standing in front of his mirror. Ages 4-6.

Pattern: Upper- and lowercase serif letters in white introduce alliterative names of animals, repetitive words, and repeating sentence pattern.

My ABC and Counting Book. Illustrated by Rene Cloke. London: Award Publications, 1974.

Large, colorful illustrations of boys and girls playing introduce the letters in this one. A child sees lowercase manuscript letters in bright colors along with children's activities—playing with an airplane, reading books, and driving a toy car. From every illustration one object is identified and matched with a numeral at the foot of the page. For *E*, one child rides a toy elephant on wheels, and another draws a picture of the toy on gray paper. Four small elephants are seen at the foot of the page along with the numeral four. Phrases such as *X* for xylophone, *Y* for yo-yo, and Z for zebra are familiar ones. Ages 3-5.

Pattern: Without punctuation lowercase manuscript letters begin short phrases that present letters and names of objects.

Purvis, Mary Elizabeth. *Animal Alphabet: Wild Animals.* Illustrated by the author. Bonita: Children's Center Publications of California, 1985.

A long-snouted aardvark, the oxlike bison, and an Arabian camel with one hump begin this wild animal alphabet with repetitive couplets. For each one, a child chants along with words of "I see a———and the ———sees me." Line drawings portray the animals on yellow backgrounds. Large upper- and lowercase letters are in black in the upper corners of the pages. After Z there is a page of facts with information about the animals. Facts include the speed of an ostrich (forty mph), the thirst of a camel (twenty-five gallons in ten minutes), and the action of llamas when they are annoyed (spitting). Without a pronunciation guide, a glossary follows for all the names of the animals. Ages 5-up.

Pattern: With repeating couplets wild animals introduce alphabet sequence.

Rhymes and Verses

Animals As Animals

Barnes, Djuna. *Creatures in an Alphabet.* Illustrated by the author. New York: Dial Press, 1982.

In this small book are verses about animals. A child reads about a hummingbird that flies in a single spot, a peacock with its thousand eyes, and a unicorn, a one-horned beast that is seldom seen. There are metaphors, or word pictures, that assign characteristics of living or nonliving things to unlike subjects. Ages Advanced 8-up.

Pattern: Without single letters as guides, each animal's capitalized name is included in rhyming verse.

Cerf, Christopher B. *Pop-Up Alphabet Book.* Illustrated by the author. Designed by Akhito Shirakawa. New York: Random House, n.d.

The reader reviews the alphabet and discovers facts about certain animals. The narwhal is the whale with a horn, a leopard's spots hide him from others, and an otter breaks shells on a stone. When tabs are pulled, the animals pop up from the pages. There is action—e.g., a hippo yawns, a hare turns white for the winter months, and an ibex climbs a mountain. Ages 5–6.

Pattern: Large serif letters introduce rhyming words in couplets about pop-up animals.

Daves, Francis M. *Alpha Bet of Curious Animals.* Illustrated by Jeanie Britt Daves. Decatur, Ga.: Trinity Press, 1976.

From an aardwolf and a blenny (a small fish) to a yak and a zorilla (a striped cat from South Africa), Daves shows animals in alphabetical order. The animals are seen in full-page line drawings and discussed in rhymes. A pronunciation guide is included to help a child say such unfamiliar words as "dugong" (du-gong), a sea cow, "quokka" (kwo-ka), a small wallaby, and "tarsier" (tar see-er), a small lemur monkey. Ages Advanced 8-up.

Pattern: Each key word precedes word pronunciation guide and rhyme for each unusual animal.

Jewell, Nancy. *ABC Cat.* Illustrated by Ann Schweninger. New York: Harper and Row, 1983.

One black-and-white cat goes through a day and shows a child the selected alphabetical words. In turn, a rhyming line is introduced with an *A* word, "awakes," a *B* word, "blinks," and on through the sequence. The cat hurries, jumps, and kneads its claws. A boy or girl may want to repeat words found in the rhymes, such as, " Lick, lick. Click, click. Chomp, chomp," or repeat certain directives such as "Down, cat, down. Go, cat, go!" and "Don't, cat, don't!" Ages 4–6.

Pattern: Words in alphabetical order begin first line of each rhyming verse about a household cat.

Laird, Jean D. *The Alphabet Zoo.* Illustrated by Barbara Howell Furan. Fayetteville, Ga.: Oddo, 1972.

With Furan's full-colored illustrations, a child reads Laird's rhyming lines about the animals seen in a zoo. There are ducks swimming in a cool pool, an elephant with floppy ears, and a fox with a bushy tail. The final pages show an ABC review in rhyme with additional illustrations of the alphabetical animals. Ages 5-7.

Pattern: Inserted in each illustration, oversize guiding capital in black begins each rhyme.

Low, Joseph. *Adam's Book of Odd Creatures*. Illustrated by the author. New York: Atheneum, 1962.

Low's alphabet introduces a child to still more odd creatures. From the alewife and basilisk through the cassowary and the wombat to the yak and zebu, there are twenty-two other animals in watercolors of light red, brown, green, and yellow. The body outlines and features are shown in black strokes. Ages 8-up.

Pattern: Each selected letter is introduced by verse about an odd animal.

Miller, Edna. *Mousekin's ABC*. Illustrated by the author. Englewood Cliffs, N. J.: Prentice-Hall, Inc., 1972.

Mousekin finds acorns, sees a bat and a cottontail rabbit. Other objects that Mousekin finds in the forest and in the surrounding fields during the day and night are introduced. Mousekin hides in a jack-in-the pulpit, perches on the shoulder of a scarecrow, and seeks shelter from the rain under a toadstool with a waterproof hood. One or two verses may be selected and reread or written with blank spaces for selected nouns or verbs, so that the child can contribute a word remembered from the rhymes or another word about Mousekin that comes to mind. The words may be written on paper for future readings. Ages 6-up.

Pattern: Capitals in black begin lines in rhymes.

Newberry, Clare Turlay. *The Kittens' ABC*. Illustrated by the author. New York: Harper and Row, 1964.

Recommended. Newberry's brush drawings in watercolors placed on wet paper show a child twenty-six kittens. Key words are those associated with playful cats e.g., "happy," "nap," and "up." Is any boy or girl ready to recall what was heard in a verse and identify the letters shown? For another activity, an adult reads the rhymes about the kittens and asks a child to listen for words that describe the kittens. The illustrations are shown as the adult reads along. Large stylized capitals in yellow introduce key phrases. Rhyming lines about kittens and their attributes follow the phrases. Ages 4–8.

Pattern: Capitals introduced by rhymes about kittens in verses.

Palazzo, Tony. *A Cat Alphabet: A Tony Palazzo ABC Book.* Illustrated by the author. New York: Duell, Sloan and Pearce, 1966.

A child sees a colorful full-page illustration and a rhyming verse for each of twenty-six cats. Can a child repeat the rhyming words and identify the letters shown? Each large letter is outlined in black. As the selected rhymes end, the adult asks the listeners for their words about cats, and for a further activity, a child may be led into composing some thoughts about kittens or cats, real or imagined. The adult writes a key word, such as "bobcat" or "cheshire cat," on paper and invites suggested words that describe the cat, how it moves and acts, or how the cat might feel. Ages 5–8.

Pattern: Outlined in black, letters of the alphabet are introduced by short verses in rhyme.

Piatti, Celestino. *Celestino Piatti's Animal ABC.* Illustrated by the author. Translated by Jon Reid. New York: Atheneum, 1966.

Recommended. Animals outlined in black are presented in alphabetical order. There are rhyming verses about such animals as a crying alligator, a big brown bear, and some changeable chameleons. Large capitals in black indicate the initial letters in names of animals in alphabetical order and precede the rhyming words. Since some of these animals may be seen at a zoo, an adult takes a small sheet of paper and records a child's thoughts about the zoo, asking, What do you think of when you think of the zoo? The child's thoughts are written on the sheet. The adult demonstrates the responses with a beginning stem: A zoo is——and ——. Ages 4–6.

Pattern: Capitals introduced by alphabetical animals in rhyming verses.

Animals As Humans

Charles, Donald. *Shaggy Dog's Animal Alphabet.* Illustrated by the author. Chicago: Childrens Press, 1979.

One golden shaggy dog in every full-color illustration introduces animals in alphabetical order and accompanying rhymes. The rhymes are linked across the illustrations. *A* is for all of the animals that follow on the pages. First there is a running bear and a curled, sleeping cat, followed later by a jumping kangaroo. The author's words about the bear on one page rhyme with the words on the next about the cat curled in a chair. Stinging yellowjackets and a zebra at the zoo conclude the rhymes. On a final page a child sees all of the upper- and lowercase manuscript letters for a concluding review. The lines of rhyme are the headers across the tops of pages and have repetitive words—e.g., *A* is for——and *B* is for——. Large serif capitals in black introduce each line. Capitalization and punctuation are seen. Ages 3-up.

Pattern: Animals introduce names, initial letters, and related sounds in rhyming lines with capitalization and punctuation.

Digance, Richard. *Animal Alphabet.* Illustrated by Diana Gold. London: Michael Joseph, 1980.

Beginning with Alan the dejected ape a bear who holds a fancy dress party, and the cat who goes to see a movie, here are alphabetical animals with unusual human behaviors in rhymed verses. With a British sense of humor, the author tells of snails and tortoises who introduce the game of cricket to the world, ants who enter the Jungle Olympics, and a kangaroo who goes to the Grand National Race. Names of animals show the alphabetical sequence in titles. There are no single guiding letters. Ages Advanced 8-up.

Pattern: With names in ABC order, animals show human behaviors in rhymed verses.

Digance, Richard. *Another Animal Alphabet.* Illustrated by Diana Gold. London: Michael Joseph, 1982.

From an alligator to a zorilla, more rhymed verses tell about animals and their human behaviors. With additional examples of

British humor, the author introduces the alligator and the crocodile who tan their tums in the sun, the antelope who watches the BBC, Barnaby Boar who was an incredible bore, and Wally the wasp who invites his friend, Win, to the pictures to see "The Sting." Ages advanced 8-up.

Pattern: Without single guiding letters, names of alphabetical animals in boldface titles of rhymed verses lead sequence.

Eichenberg, Fritz. *Ape in a Cape: An Alphabet of Odd Animals.* Illustrated by the author. New York: Harcourt Brace Jovanovich, Inc., 1952.

Recommended. With large red and blue stylized capitals, the captions explain the full-page illustrations. Rhyming words occur within each caption, e.g., *carp* and *harp*, *dove* and *love*, *egret* and *minuet*. A rhyming pair of words can be extended with additional sentences—e.g., This is a carp. This is a harp. This is a carp with a harp. A California State Department of Education-recommended recreational reading. Ages 5–9.

Pattern: Captions with internal rhyming words are preceded by capitals.

Hague, Kathleen. *Alphabears: An ABC Book.* Illustrated by Michael Hague. New York: Holt, Rinehart and Winston, 1984.

Each block serif letter in color is introduced by a teddy bear. Henry loves hot cakes with butter and honey, Pam loves a parade and popcorn, and Elsie explores a jungle. There are rhymes to read in large print and full-color paintings to see. The illustrations include Sarah, the snow-loving bear, Kyle, a kite-flying bear, and John, the bear who loves jam and jelly and sits on a kitchen counter with his paws in the jelly jar. Ages 4-7.

Pattern: In alphabetical order, teddy bears with human behaviors are described in rhymes and introduce letters.

Hillman, Priscilla. *A Merry Mouse Christmas ABC.* Illustrated by the author. Garden City, N. Y.: Doubleday, 1980.

Hillman's rhymes about mice who act like humans introduce objects of Christmas in an alphabetical order. Full-colored illustrations show one mouse dressed up as an angel and one lighting a candle. Another gathers berries to bake in a pie and to string for the holiday tree. A fourth mouse plays a drum all through the house. Ages 6–8.

Pattern: Each letter in black is introduced by rhyming verse.

Johnson, Laura Rinkle. *The Teddy Bear ABC.* Illustrated by Margaret Landers Stanford. La Jolla, Calif.: Green Tiger Press, 1982.

On each page, teddy bears engage in human-like activities— e.g., wearing clothing, carrying umbrellas, and pulling wagons for others to ride. Lines with stylized capitals in black and the constructions *A* is for animals, *B* is for Bears, begin the rhymes in a familiar way. The word choices are capitalized within the lines. Several choices are unusual ones—e.g., *X* stands for the number ten, *V* is for "vexation," and *O* is for "ostrich-tips" to decorate a lady's hat. Rhymed lines explain the use of other objects and the bears' activities. Ages 5–7.

Pattern: Letters and traditional beginnings introduce rhyming lines.

Libbey, Ruth Everding. *Silly Billy's Alphabet.* Illustrated by Gene Holtan. San Carlos, Calif.: Golden Gate Junior Books, 1964.

In Libby's book a young boy Billy watches an animal for every letter of the alphabet. Billy gives a fox his woolly sox. What does Billy see? Billy sees a loon wave at the moon. What does Billy dream? Billy dreams he sees a unicorn who leads a band and plays a horn. Who meets Billy at the zoo? A xenurus escorts him through the zoo. Meeting other animals, Billy sees a mother bear tie a bow in her cub's hair and a cow take a bow. A child is invited to make a rhyme for each one. Ages 5–8.

Pattern: Animals in alphabetical order are introduced in rhymes.

Mazzarella, Mimi. *Alphabatty Animals and Funny Foods: Alphabet and Counting Rhymes.* Illustrated by the author. Cokeysville, Md.: Liberty Publishing Company, 1984.

Mazzarella's rhymes introduce twenty-six animals including alligators who are snappy, a bear who is shy, and cats who are catty. An alert reader who notices that there is no animal name for the letter *X* may be interested in supplying a name for this letter. Several other alphabet books could be examined as references and resources for the word search. Ages 7–8.

Pattern: Serif capitals in black are introduced by rhymes about personified animals.

Oechsli, Kelly. *The Monkeys' ABC Word Book.* Illustrated by the author. Racine, Wisc.: Golden Books/Western Publishing Company,Inc., 1982.

Oechsli's ABC has one to four rhyming lines on each double-page spread. The majority of the lines begin in a repetitive manner, with *A* is for———and *B* is for———. Large capital letters in full-color emphasize the boldface letters in the lines. The setting changes with each double-page spread, and the monkeys engage in activities with objects whose names begin with the key letter. The objects are labeled in the illustrations. Ages 5–6.

Pattern: Traditional beginnings open rhyming lines.

Smith, Robert E., collector. *ABC of Australian Animals.* Illustrated by the collector. Sydney: Agnus and Robertson, 1978.

Rhymes were collected from various sources for this volume. Here are twenty-six Australian animals, beginning with an anteater and ending with the anteater's first cousin, a zaglossus from New Guinea. In the bright, colorful full-page illustrations with the verses inserted, the anteater prepares his dinner for *A*; and a brolgas—a large white storklike bird—dances with other brolgas partners for *B*. At *D*, the tune "Waltzing Matilda" is hummed by a dingo chorus line. Large stylized capitals guide the sequence from the corners of pages. Ages 6–8.

Pattern: In capitals, each animal's name is key word for selected letter and precedes rhyming verse.

Youldon, Gillian. *Alphabet.* Illustrated by James Hodgson. New York: Franklin Watts, n.d.

Using the technique of running words and linking sentences across each double-page spread, Youldon gives the key words in alphabetical order. As a young viewer reads, he or she notices that each word choice begins with its initial lowercase letter in red or in white. On these board pages a child finds several humorous ways that animals wake up other animals. Who drops an apple to wake up the cat? Who throws nuts to wake up the pigs? What does the toad use to wake up the vulture? How does the giraffe wake up the hippopotamus? Ages 5-6.

Pattern: Key words in linking phrases across page spreads show initial letters in red or white for easy identification.

Edward Lear

Lear, Edward. *The Complete Nonsense of Edward Lear.* Illustrated by Edward Lear. New York: Dover Publications, Inc., 1951.

In this section of alphabet books, a reader finds the varied presentations of Edward Lear. In this first title, *The Complete Nonsense of Edward Lear,* Lear's first alphabet is composed of four-line verses for each letter, beginning with A for an ant who built a hillside house and ending with Z for zinc, shiny and bright. The second alphabet is one of words showing the changing of initial consonants. "Pidy, widy, tidy," echo the opening words, "A was once an apple pie." The concluding alphabetic line, "Z was once a piece of zinc," is followed by more rhyming words—"tinky, winky, blinky." The third alphabet is similar in format to the first alphabet, but the subjects of the verses are different—e.g., A is for an ape who stole some tape and Z is for a tamed zebra to ride. In another section, "Twenty-six Nonsense Rhymes and Pictures," there are nonsense rhymes about animals and insects. After hearing about such animals as the confidential cow in an armchair, the dolomphious duck who caught spotted frogs, and the enthusiastic elephant who could ferry himself across the water, a youngster might be interested in drawing an imagined shape of one of the animals. Still other alphabets are in the section of "Laughable Lyrics." In this section the first alphabet, which has the same pattern as the first ABC mentioned, changes some of the subjects again—e.g., A is for an arch under which women sat, while Z stands for a zebra with streaks of black. The second alphabet in this section gives human characteristics to the letters, who speak of tumbling down, fetching a doctor to cure a hurt arm, and putting ice on one's head to make one feel better. Ages 8-up.

Pattern: Nonsense rhyming verses about animals, insects, and objects introduce letters and letter sounds.

Lear, Edward. *Edward Lear's ABC: Alphabet Rhymes for Children.* Illustrated by Carol Pike. Topsfield, Mass.: Salem House Publishers, 1986.

Full-page illustrations in full color show the objects of Lear's "A was once an apple pie" alphabet. A bear searches for honey among buzzing bees, a three-tier cake is decorated with lighted candles, and the little fishy in a dishy is eyed by an observing white cat. Pike includes touches of humor e.g., a woman stands on a stool to escape the little mousey, jumpy-jimpy shrimp jump upright on their tails, and a small kitten plays with the ribbon tail of the flighty kite. Ages 5-up.

Pattern: Rhyming words in nonsense verses about animals and objects.

Lear, Edward. *An Edward Lear Alphabet.* Illustrated by Carol Newsom. New York: Lothrop, Lee and Shepard, 1983.

In full-colored illustrations, a little mouse gets into some silly situations as Lear's verses are read. The mouse watches the bees buzzing around the grizzly bear, who is eating honey. To go fishing, he rides on the back of a large goose. Wearing goggles, flight helmet, and flowing neck scarf, the mouse flies a kite like a glider. A child might notice the contradictions when he or she reads the word "little" in Lear's verses and sees, not small sizes, but the large sizes of the bear, the goose, the hen, and the pump needed to put air into the tires of the oversize bicycle. For each letter a different type font and print style is used. Upper- and lowercase letters in black serve as guides and headings for Lear's verses. Along with internal rhymes there are repetitive beginnings, initial consonant substitutions, and similar endings in key words. Ages 5-6.

Pattern: Internal and ending rhymes model beginnings with similar structure and initial consonant substitution.

Lear, Edward. *The First ABC.* Illustrated by Charles Mozley. Designed by Frank Waters. New York: Franklin Watts, 1972.

Collected from Lear's Nonsense Alphabets, more of Lear's rhymes in verses are seen on the left-hand pages of this one. Additional objects whose names begin with the selected letter are shown in full color on the right-hand pages. From the ape who took white tape to a xylophone, yacht, and zebra, there are four rhyming lines discussing every object. For example, after a child hears about the elephant with two queer little eyes, a child sees other objects whose names begin with *E*: elk, egg, and emu. Ages 5-6.

Pattern: Large upper- and lowercase serif letters in black are repeated in similar beginnings for rhyming verses:———was a———.

Lear, Edward. *Lear Alphabet Penned and Illustrated by Edward Lear.* Illustrated by the author. New York: McGraw-Hill, 1965.

Beginning with *A* and several busy ants who are building their home, the alphabet continues with Lear's original verses from the 1800s. Ages 4-up.

Pattern: Each letter introduces one of Lear's short, rhyming nonsense verses.

Lear, Edward. *A Learical Lexicon: A Magnificent Feest of Boshlobberbosh and Phun from the Vorx of Edward Lear.* Vords selected by Myra Cohn Livingston. Piggchurs by Joseph Low. New York: Atheneum, 1985.

Lear uses words with unconventional spellings, with hidden meanings, with transposed letters, and with natural sounds— onomatopoetic sounds. For example, *rejoice* becomes *erjoice*, *dragon* becomes *dragging*, and *officers* becomes *ossifers*. To begin this one, *A* is for *appy* (*happy*), *B* for *bebothered*, and *C* for *carrotable*. Upper- and lowercase serif letters in black are in the corners of the pages. Key words in bold type are headings. Models are found for unconventional spellings, for using transposed letters, and for onomotopoeia. Ages 8-up.

Pattern: Onomotopoeia, transposed letters in words, and unconventional spellings are seen.

Lear, Edward. *The Nonsense Alphabet.* Illustrated by Art Seiden. New York: Grosset and Dunlap, Inc., 1961.

Apples and an apple pie introduce Lear's "A was once an apple pie" series of internal rhymes. Substituting initial and final consonants for key words, Lear gives a child a series of rhyming words after each repetitive beginning—e.g., "B was once a little bear." A child then reads about a little bear and hears the words *beary, wary, hairy*. A child reads about a little fish, hears the rhyming words of *wishy, squishy, dishy, fishy* and notices the repetitive endings on each rhyming word. Ages 4-up.

Pattern: Repetitive beginnings emphasize sounds of capital serif letters, key words, rhyming words with initial consonant substitutions, and similar endings.

Mother Goose Rhymes

A Book of Children's Rhymes and Verses. Illustrated by Janet and Anne Grahame Johnstone. London: Dean and Son, Ltd., n.d.

In one section colorful lowercase serif letters begin still another version of *A Apple Pie*. In a second section both uppercase and lowercase letters introduce verses about subjects in alphabetical order. Parallel to this presentation are the names of boys and girls, from Andrew and Belinda to Yves and Zoe with accompanying verses about them. Ages 4-5.

Pattern: Alphabetical sentence stems, alliteration, and repetitive beginning sentences for verses about children's names are included.

Anglund, Joan Walsh. *In a Pumpkin Shell: A Mother Goose ABC*. Illustrated by the author. New York: Harcourt, Brace and World, 1968.

Recommended. Each verse is preceded by a serif capital letter and by a key word selected from the Mother Goose verse. The key noun from each verse begins with the appropriate letter. For instance, "apple" is the word choice from "If I were an apple," the word "Dog" is chosen from "Old Mother Hubbard," and "clock" is selected from " Hickory Dickory Dock." Does a young listener want to hear a favorite verse again? After the child points one out, the pen-and-ink drawings may be displayed as the rhyme is read or recited, and the child invited to say the rhyme along with the adult. An adult may help to maintain the rhythm by tapping on a table or lightly beating on an overturned plastic dish. Ages 4-6.

Pattern: Twenty-six Mother Goose verses follow large serif capitals and selected word choices from verses.

Burgess, George W. *The Adventures of A, Apple Pie Who Was Cut to Pieces and Eaten By Twenty-six Ladies and Gentlemen with Whom All Little People Ought to Be Acquainted.* Illustrated. Reprint circa 1835. New York: Dover Publications, Inc.,1973.

Capitals in black are beneath each colored illustration. On the facing verso page are the lowercase letters and accompanying phrases about how the pie was sliced, dreamed of, and eaten. Perhaps this model might be used to write parallel phrases about favorite foods. Phrases about an apple pie such as *B* biting it, *D* dreaming of it, and *E* eating it can serve as models for a child's writing about a favorite pizza or dessert pie. Ages 7–8.

Pattern: Alphabetical phrases are in sequence about children's behaviors toward an apple pie.

Craft, Kinuko. *Mother Goose ABC*. Illustrated by the author. New York: Platt and Munk, 1977.

Beginning with "A diller, a dollar" and "Baa, baa, black sheep" and ending with "X,Y and Z, the cat's in the cupboard...." these Mother Goose rhymes all begin with a word that represents the selected letter of the alphabet. Like the verses from *In a Pumpkin Shell*, the verses in this one are in alphabetical order. Unlike Anglund's arrangement, where the key words come from anywhere in the verses, Craft's verses all begin with alphabetical word choices. Large serif letters in blue begin key words in verses and lead to examples of language patterns. *A* is for "A diller, a dollar," *B* is for "Baa, baa, black sheep," and *C* is for "Curly Locks, Curly Locks." Different patterns are found. A repetitive patterning of language is seen in "There Was a Crooked Man." In "Fiddle-de-dee" a child hears some natural sounds in onomotopoeic words. A riddle is asked in "Humpty Dumpty" and in "Elizabeth, Elspeth, Betsy, and Bess," while "Rub-a-dub-dub" leads a child to enjoy nonsense. Ages 4–6.

Pattern: Onomatopeia, repetition, riddles, and rhymes are included.

Crane, Walter. *An Alphabet of Old Friends and The Absurd ABC.* Illustrated by the author. New York: Metropolitan Museum of Art, 1981.

Crane's illustrations for *The Absurd ABC* have bright colors of white, red, and yellow, and are shown on black backgrounds. The endpapers present serif capitals in sequence. Letters introduce familiar verses or familiar rhymes as models for chanting. A child might compare the verses in *The Absurd ABC* with Crane's *An Alphabet of Old Friends.* The letter *J* stands for "Jack Sprat" in Crane's first alphabet but stands for "poor Jack and also for Jill" in his second alphabet. The verses also may be compared with those in another Mother Goose alphabet book to discover if similar characters introduce the letters. For example, "Humpty Dumpty" who had a great fall in Craft's book is met again under the letter *H* in Crane's book, as the one who "resig'n his seat on the wall." Ages 6-7.

Pattern: Rhymes and rhythms, emphasize short-story pictures in verses.

Delacre, Lulu. *A. B. C. Rhymes.* Illustrated by the author. New York: Simon and Schuster, Inc., 1984.

Delacre's ABC is another version of the familiar *A Apple Pie* rhyme. In this one, portly pigs gather around an apple pie, eat it, fight for it, and inspect it. This rhyme is followed by some novel characters, such as Allspice *A*, Brother *B*, and Cousin *C*. Alliteration in rhyming phrases occurs again in the names of characters that personify letters of the alphabet. Ages 4-5.

Pattern: Alliteration and personification emphasize rhyme.

Delaunay, Sonia, compiler. *Sonia Delaunay Alphabet.* Illustrated by Sonia Delaunay. New York: Crowell, 1972.

Using the letters as basic forms, Delaunay creates a bright painting for each letter. To accompany the painting a short rhyme from traditional and classical children's literature is presented. *L* is for "Ladybird, Ladybird, Fly Away Home," *O* is for "One Old Ox Opening Oysters," and " *T* is for Thomas a' Tattamus." Ages 4-8.

Pattern: Guiding letters in black are introduced by initial key words in rhymes.

Greenaway, Kate. *A Apple Pie: An Old Fashioned Alphabet Book.* Illustrated by Kate Greenaway. New York: Merrimack Publishing Corporation, Distributor.

Recommended. This alphabet rhyme goes back to an earlier English in which the letter *I* and the letter *J* were used as one letter. No letter *I* is included in this version. Children are seen in the sketches that center around a large apple pie. One child bites it, another cuts it, and still another jumps for it. Ages 4–7.

Pattern: Without punctuation, phrases with key words about an apple pie introduce large serif capitals.

Pearson, Tracey Campbell. *A Apple Pie.* Illustrated by the author. New York: Dial, 1986.

This ABC folds out to show some slapstick, large type in text, active children, and an apple pie. The pie makes its journey down a long table that stretches across the pages for a length of 18 feet. *T* trod on the pie (a child stomps in the pie pan), *U* upsets it (one boy dumps pieces of pie on another's head) and *Y*, who receives the empty pie pan, yearns for it. Will the alphabetical pie party begin again? At *Z*, Zealous, arrives from the kitchen with another pie. Ages 3–7.

Pattern: Capital letters introduced by phrases about an apple pie.

Vogel, Malvina G., ed. *The Big Book of Mother Goose.* Illustrated by Jesse Spicer Zerner. Stories by Michael J. Pellowski. New York: Playmore, Inc./Waldman Publishing Corporation, 1980.

Beginning with "A is for apple pie" and ending with "Yankee Doodle," there are 140 rhymes in ABC order by titles in bold type. There are no rhymes for *U*, *V*, *X*, and *Z*. Ages 4–6.

Pattern: Rhyme, rhythm, and repetition are found in traditional selections.

Other Rhymes and Verses

Chase, Catherine. *An Alphabet Book.* Illustrated by June Goldsborough. New York: Dandelion Press, Inc., 1979.

Seeing spicy gingerbread for the letter *G* or a sweet cookie for *C* may entice a child to turn the page and to read the next rhyming

couplet. Large, colorful block letters are inserted over the illustrations that show a variety of objects. Ages 5-6.

Pattern: Repetitive sentences begin lines with rhyming words
linked across two pages.

Curry, Peter. *Peter Curry's ABC*. Illustrated by the author. Los
Angeles: Price/Stern/Sloan, 1981.

Curry offers rhymes that link across two pages. For the
sequence of *A* through *G*, a child hears words about a variety of
objects: an anchor is dropped that causes a boat to stop, a duck
sounds a quack while an egg starts to crack, and after seeing a
forest where trees grow, we see a gate through which one can go.
Text is inserted over bright illustrations. Ages 5-6.

Pattern: Lowercase letter-object-rhyme arrangement.

Davis, E. K. *My Alphabet*. Illustrated by Pat Stewart. Racine,
Wisc.: Western Publishing Company, Inc., 1981.

Full-color illustrations of such objects as one bright red apple,
a bed for sleeping at night, and a crunchy carrot introduce lines
that rhyme across two pages. The large serif capitals are in colors
and begin the traditional openings of *A* is for————and *B* is for
————. On the final page along with the yo-yo and the zebra is an
invitation to say the entire alphabet. Which illustrations show
animals? Which show foods? Which objects are seen in the house?
Which ones can be found outside of the house? Ages 5–up.

Pattern: Objects in illustrations lead to initial letters and
sounds.

Dulac, Edmund. *Lyrics Pathetic and Humorous from A to Z*.
Illustrated by the author. New York: Warne, 1908.

Including *L* for a lorn little lass, *M* for a merry milkmaid, and
N for a neat necromancer, these limericks introduce a personality
for every letter. Some words may catch the imaginations of
youngsters—e.g., the kingdom of Ultramarine, a witch of the
wood with a wonderful hood, and an ugly sardine. Ages 7-up.

Pattern: For each limerick, serif capitals in colors introduce personalities and such traditional beginnings as *H* was a———, *I* was an ———, and *J* was a———.

Fletcher, Helen Jill. *Picture Book ABC*. Illustrated by Jennie Williams. New York: Platt and Munk, 1978.

A pair of colorful upper- and lowercase letters lead to a repetitive beginning in the couplet about an alligator and Noah's ark, a butterfly, and bulldogs that bark. The couplet is linked across two doube-page spreads. This same arrangement two spreads (four pages) is followed through the ABCs with other objects—a camel and cats, a dinosaur and ducks, and a giraffe and grapes. Does a young reader recognize the pattern of the rhymes which read across two double-page spreads? Ages 4-6.

Pattern: In rhyming couplets linked over two spreads, block letters reinforce initial letters in key words in repetitive beginnings.

Izawa, Tadasu. *Fun with the Alphabet*. Illustrated by the author. New York: Simon and Schuster, Inc., 1981.

Izawa's rhymes introduce the letters of the alphabet. Puppets pose in pictures. An engine pulls a flatcar; this short train carries gaily decorated letters. A girl drives a toy car through the center of the letter *H*, and one boy flies an airplane through the letter *D*. Both children attach balloons to the last four letters of the alphabet to watch them float away into a blue sky. Ages 4-6.

Pattern: Rhyming words in verses.

Kennedy, X. (Charles) J. *Did Adam Name the Vinegaroon?* Illustrated by Heidi Johanna Selig. Boston: Godine, 1982.

Kennedy makes use of uncommon creatures in this ABC bestiary. A child is introduced to a Minotaur from the days of King Minos, an ounce (spotted cat from Tibet), and a pangolin (armored anteater). A pronunciation guide is included for two animals whose names might be unfamiliar ones: the archeopteryx (ark ee OP ter icks), a bird from the age of the dinosaurs, and the xiphosuran (zif a SOOR an), a horseshoe crab. Ages 8-up.

Pattern: Initial letter in each uncommon creature's name at head of rhyming verse guides sequence.

Kuskin, Karla. *Abcdefghijklmnopqrstuvwxyz*. Illustrated by the author. New York: Harper and Row, 1963.

In Kuskin's book each of the letters stands for a word such as "ants," "bulldogs," and "courts." Each of these words in turn likes a friend named in a short rhyme. "Ants" like plants and are seen climbing all over the leaves and stems and petals of flowers. "Bulldogs" like wool dogs and circle a stuffed, woolly toy dog. "Courts" like sports such as tennis. Here, players hold their racquets up to serve tennis balls across the center nets on the two pictured courts. Some word-friends may be difficult ones for a young girl or boy to understand as they hear that "foals" like knolls, "hawkers" like gawkers, and "Utes" like buttes. Each guiding capital letter is seen in a different type font and shows a creative use of print. Ages 8-up.

Pattern: Repetition, similar word order, and rhyming words found in two-line verse.

Lane, Harriet. *ABC and Counting*. Illustrated. London: Dean International Publishing /Hamlyn Publishing Group, Ltd., 1975.

Rhyming verses about *A* is for apple through *N* is for news up to *Z* is for zebra crossing are read for each pair of upper- and lowercase letters. In each page corner the lowercase letter is the larger letter in color. With the oversize presentation for the lowercase letters, this book offers an opportunity to emphasize the letters as lowercase letters. Full-page illustrations show some interesting word choices for a young viewer. There is a *dragon's curls of flame, a tree house,* and a *round-about* (merry-go-round, carousel). A manuscript letter in color matches the first letter of every key word that appears in bold type in the verse. The front endpapers hold the alphabet in lowercase block letters and appropriate objects, while the back endpapers show a review of all of the lowercase serif letters. Ages 5-up.

Pattern: Scenes in full-color illustrations introduce key words, repetitive sentence stems, rhyming words, and appropriate lowercase letters.

A Little ABC Book. Illustrated. New York: Wanderer Books/ Simon and Schuster, Inc., 1980.

No more than two objects are seen on each small page. Each object is identified by one serif capital in black. Rhyming lines are found at the foot of the pages. In this collection a child sees animals. One cat is ill and visits a veterinarian; a green elephant has a long, funny nose; and a black-and-white panda sleeps on a quilt. There are also musical instruments. One golden harp plays music for dancing, a trumpet toots, and a violin rests in a red wagon. There are ways to travel. An airplane flies, one bicycle rolls by, and a wagon delivers the violin. Ages 2-up.

Pattern: With rhyming lines, each object in color introduces its name, beginning letter, and related sound.

Longanecker, Georgia Alexander. *Howdy Out There! Phonics Fun*. Brewster, Wash: Longanecker Publications, 1977.

Longanecker's book emphasizes sounds. From ant and ape to yellow dog and zebra, there are rhymes about each one. Here are objects for the sounds of the consonant letters, vowels, digraphs, and diphthongs. Several selected key words present sounds different from the names of the letters: *igloo* (I), *oil* and *out* (OI and OU), *brook* and *poodle* (OO), *shell* (SH), *there* and *thimble* (TH), *under, unicorn,* and *urban* (U). Ages 6-7 up.

Pattern: Rhyming verses seen about selected objects whose initial letters and medial letters reflect sounds different from those of single letters.

Lowe, Edith May. *Alphabet Picture Book A to Z*. Illustrated by Elsie Darien. New York: Follett, 1966.

Lowe identifes objects and their names in capitals in these rhyming lines. Darien's objects are shown in delicate, full-color drawings. Even though a child reads that X is a letter that almost never begins a word, some descriptions are included for the letter X. Lowe mentions that a golden xylophone has a tinkling, bell-like tone. Ages 5-7.

Pattern: Names of alphabetical objects are shown in capital letters in verses.

McGinn, Maureen. *I Used to Be an Artichoke*. Illustrated by Anita Norman. St. Louis: Concordia, 1973.

McGinn and Norman integrate large, stylized serif capitals into the illustrations and guide the sequence of the artichoke's changes from a butterfly to a crayon to a dandelion to other transformations through the alphabet. The names of the changes are in bold type within the rhyming verses. The last line of each verse shows the last word deleted, a riddle requiring the reader to determine the next change for the artichoke. Turning the page, a child verifies a prediction and sees the capitalized word that completes the verse. Ages 7–9.

Pattern: Rhyming words may be predicted in verses to complete lines before turning pages to verify predictions.

Moncure, Jane Belk. *Magic Monsters Act the Alphabet*. Illustrated by Helen Endres. Elgin, Ill.: The Child's World,1980.

Moncure's rhymes present the actions of monsters alphabetically. With these rhymes, a child is invited to see what each monster can do and then perform the action for each letter along with such monsters as a creepy crocodile, a dancing dragon, and one green elephant. There are acrobatics, bubbles to blow, and some clowning around to do. The final page shows a review frieze of the alphabet in lowercase letters. The frieze serves as an upper part of the stage frame seen above the final curtain in this monsters' ABC act. Ages 3-up.

Pattern: With upper- and lowercase letters in colorful inserts, full-color illustrations of monsters introduce their names and rhyming lines.

My ABC of Nursery Rhymes. Illustrated. Great Britain: Derrydale Books/Crown Publishers, 1974.

Full-colored illustrations show all of the selections in these twenty-six selected rhymes. The letters are illustrated with objects the names of which begin with that particular letter. The letter *B* attracts black-and-yellow bumblebees, *C* holds the face of a cat, and one duck steps through the center of the letter *D*. The first word in each rhyme is the key word for the alphabetical sequence. Ending rhymes are heard. Ages 4–6.

Pattern: Illustrated letters precede initial key words in rhymes.

Smith, William Jay. *Puptents and Pebbles: A Nonsense ABC.* Illustrated by the author. Boston: Little, Brown, 1959.

Smith's book is an experience with the nonsense of words. Here are uppercase letters in black to illustrate the first letters in the nonsense sentences. To illustrate the nonsense words are such objects as an alpaca, bats, and cabbages to see. Ages 4–6.

Pattern: Nonsense is introduced with capitals and key nouns.

Storm, Myrtle. *ABC's Now and Then.* Illustrated by Barbara Whitworth. Laramie, Wyo.: Fort Laramie Historical Association, 1984.

Today objects presenting the letters in the alphabet are different from the objects in Grandfather's day. In rhymes that compare the objects of these two periods, we read that *A* used to mean apple, but today, *A* is for astronaut. While *B* was for bed in Grandfather's day, *B* is now for bubblegum. *C* is for the computers of today, and not the cats of Grandfather's day. Each child sees a letter in three styles—e.g., as an outlined capital, as a capital in bold style, and as a lowercase letter in outline style. Sketches of the objects from both time periods illuminate all of the outlined letters. Some interesting word choices for today's alphabet are "video games," "movies," and "jogging." Ages 7-up.

Pattern: With capitalization and punctuation, verses in rhyme compare objects from two time periods and lead to letters shown in different styles.

Word Associations

Being Entertained

Barker, Cicely Mary. *A Flower Fairy Alphabet.* Illustrated by the author. London: Blackie and Son, Ltd., 1978.

The titles of books in this word association section reflect different ways that children might be entertained. Some boys and girls may entertain themselves by exploring origami, playing with dolls and games, visiting a circus, or with imaginative thoughts of small creatures who live in a fairy world. Reflecting one aspect of a possible flower fairy world is this book by Barker. Barker's faint colors decorate the serif capitals that are found in the corners of the illustrations. Each picture shows an imaginative fairy, one who looks like a tiny child, for each selected flower. In rhyming verses, a child reads about one sentinel fairy who stands as a lookout near the woodland bronze-leaved bugle; about a fairy piper, ragged robin, who plays for fairy dancing at night in a garden, and about the fairy for the lavender mallow who sells mallow seeds as fairy cheeses to fairy housewives. Each flower in the book is included on a final chart that lists its botanical name and natural order e.g. lily of the valley, *Convallaria majalis, Liliaceae*. These flowers may be seen again, with a smaller, accordion-page format, but without the final chart, in Barker's later edition, *The Flower Fairies Miniature ABC* (Philomel/Putnam, 1981). Ages 9-up.

Pattern: Serif capitals are identified by flowers and rhyming verses that describe characteristics of flowers.

Chardiet, Bernice. *C Is for Circus*. Illustrated by Brinton Turkle. New York: Walker and Company, 1971.

Recommended. Clusters of words about the circus, some with alliteration, are found in these colorful events. Chardiet describes comic clowns, flipping flyers, terrible tigers doing tricks, and a boxing kangaroo. Several of the rhythmic clusters are linked across to the following pages. This linking leads a young reader into completing a thought by turning a page. On the X page a young circus visitor hopes for a performer's good luck and safekeeping. She keeps her fingers crossed, or x'd, for good luck to help a high-wire performer land safely on the ground. Some rhyming occurs within the lines—e.g., some monkeys are jigging as they jump from the show rigging. Other monkeys are vaulting and somersaulting. A child notices the rhythm of the words as the acrobats enter the arena, the brass band begins to play, and poodles in tutus dance a ballet. If this proves interesting, invite the child to dictate some of the happenings as the adult writes words. The child watches the writing. The story is reread. Is a boy or girl interested in pointing to known words? If the viewer wishes to illustrate a circus activity, the picture may be kept along with the dictation in the child's story folder to be discussed again at another time. During future rereadings the words known by the listener may be underlined again and again. Ages 5-up.

Pattern: With oversize serif capitals in colors, circus performers are introduced with rhythmic words, alliteration, and some internal rhymes in lines.

Cooney, Barbara. *A Garland of Games and Other Diversions: An Alphabet Book*. Illustrated by the author. New York: Holt, Rinehart and Winston, 1969.

Cooney's playful activities entertain a child and give information about the entertainment of children over two hundred years ago. Some of the games are familiar ones, such as playing with dolls, dancing, and using string to make a design called a cat's cradle. Mud pies are baked, marbles are shot within a drawn ring, and the words of "Here We Go Round the Mulberry Bush" are sung. Is making a book entitled "My ABC of Games" of interest? What present-day activities might be included? What games are seen in Cooney's ABC that are still played today? Ages 6-9.

Pattern: With rhyme, games and other activities are introduced in alphabetical sequence.

Dreamer, Sue. *Circus ABC*. Illustrated by the author. Boston: Little, Brown and Company, 1985.

In Dreamer's small, sturdy book of board pages, one suitable for a toddler's collection, a child sees performers and animals at the circus. From acrobats to chimpanzees playing a xylophone and doing tricks with a yo-yo, illustrations for each ABC letter are identified. Words are associated with the circus and the activities, e.g., "ringmaster," "unicycle," and "wirewalker." The Initial letter in each key word is illustrated—e.g., the G in the word "giraffes" shows the dark brown spots seen on a giraffe's hide. Ages 2-4.

Pattern: Performers introduce word associations about a circus with guiding illustrated letters.

Manson, Beverlie. *The Fairies' Alphabet Book*. Illustrated by the author. Garden City, N.Y.: Doubleday, 1982.

Serif capitals in black lead similar beginnings of rhythmic words about bands of fairies who look like playful young people. From Apple Fairies, Butterfly Fairies, and Candy Fairies to Zoo Fairies, the sentences describe such activities as harvesting apples, teaching other fairies to fly, and building houses out of candy. Ages 7-up.

Pattern: Initial sounds of alphabetical names of fairies begin descriptive sentences and introduce related sounds of large serif capitals in black.

Parish, Peggy. *A Beastly Circus*. Illustrated by Peter Parnall. New York: Simon and Schuster, Inc., 1969.

Complete sentences with alliteration are found in this one. Some of the words may contribute to a child's journal as personal selections for reading or writing. For instance, at *M*, a writer may discuss and copy any or all of the words for the M page in an individual dictionary or journal. There are words to choose from such as *malted, masked, messily, milk, minks, mischievous,* and *mix*—all of which are illustrated in Parnall's drawings. Younger children may want to dictate the words of their choice and watch an adult write what is said. After reading about this beastly circus, an older child may ask or answer short comprehension questions that begin with one of the words from the pattern of who, what, where, when, or how. Each alliterative act in this circus lends itself to the questions: Who mixed the malted milk? What was mixed messily? When were the malted milks mixed messily by the masked minks? Where were the minks messily mixing the malted milks? How did the masked minks mix the malted milks? Ages 5-7.

Pattern: With alliterative sentences each illustrated page presents an animal, its behaviors, and its contributions to a humorous beastly circus.

Sarasas, Claude. *The ABC's of Origami: Paper Folding for Children*. Illustrated by the author. Originally published in Japan in 1951. Rutland, Vt.: Tuttle Co., Inc., 1964.

Sarasas gives directions to show how Origami may be accomplished. There are diagrams for folding paper into twenty-six objects beginning with albatross and ending with zebra. Each alphabetic heading is in English, French, and Japanese. Colorful illustrations are included which show the finished objects. Ages Advanced 8-up.

Pattern: Expository writing. Named in English, French, and Japanese, each object can be made from following directions and carefully folding paper.

Sedgwick, Paulita. *Circus ABC*. Illustrated by the author. New York: Holt, Rinehart and Winston, 1978.

To open Sedgwick's circus, the Alphabet Man asks a child to find ABC words. Upper- and lowercase manuscript letters in black are located in the corners of the circus scenes. Alliterative words appear below each illustration about such acts as the amazing armadillo acrobats, a big brown bear band, and a clown calliope. On a final page is a souvenir program that lists alphabetically all of the words again in columns with guiding letters shown in red. Visually there is an added challenge: can a child find the alphabet man on every page? Ages 5-up.

Pattern: Beginning sounds and initial letters in alliterative words below circus scenes reinforce sounds of lower- and upper case letters in black. Alphabetical word order in columns.

Tudor, Tasha. *A Is for Annabelle*. Illustrated by the author. New York: Walck, 1954.

Recommended. Inside Tudor's garlands of flowers, which form frames, the black serif capitals lead to similar beginning stems. The stems tell about Grandmother's doll, Annabelle, and the doll's attire—e.g., *B* for her ——, *C* for her ——. A child is introduced to the doll's articles of clothing, among them a cloak, fan, and shawl. Some of the words may represent items unfamiliar to some children: *kerchief, muff, nosegay, overskirt, parasol, veil,* and *tippet*. Since these words are words used when Grandmother (more likely Great Grandmother of today's generation) was little and played with her doll, a child will need adult help, with a dictionary definition. Will a boy or girl find evidence that clothing and language changes? If *nosegay* is not found, can *bouquet* be located? Is a young child able to help an adult find some of these words in a dictionary for a beginning reader? Can any be found in a dictionary for an older reader? Which ones? Ages 5-up.

Pattern: Serif capitals in black begin similar opening stems for rhyming lines linked across double-page spreads.

City and Ways We Travel

Alexander, Anne. *ABC of Cars and Trucks*. Illustrated by Niñon. Garden City, N. Y.: Doubleday and Company, Inc., 1956.

The topic of the city and ways of traveling link the letters in these alphabets. This alphabet book of the fifties features pictures by Niñon. On each illustrated page one car or truck is sketched in shades of black, green, and red. Serif capitals begin each sentence. *A* is for auto trailer, *B* is for bulldozer, and *C* for a cement mixer. There are rhyming lines on each page. Each key word is shown in capitals in bold type for easy identification. Through the primary grades when research about transportation is sometimes required of a young student, an alphabet book such as this serves as a reference book about the transportation of the time period. Some of these sentences might serve as models and launch a series of statements about a child's personal experiences with cars and trucks. Would a child be interested in bringing this more-than-thirty-year-old collection up-to-date with the cars and trucks that are seen today? There are transportation vehicles now that are not seen or included in Alexander's ABC. For certain letters, a boy or girl might select such vehicles as these:

ambulances	golf carts
armored cars	highway striping trucks
artmobiles	paramedic vehicles
bookmobiles	parcel post trucks
diesel trucks	recreation vans
elongated buses	small shuttles

Ages 6–9.

Pattern: Cars and trucks and rhyming lines with similar openings lead to capitalized key words in bold type and to serif capitals in colors.

Bond, Susan. *Ride with Me Through ABC*. Illustrated by Horst Lemke. New York: Scroll Press, Inc., 1965.

Bond's colorful alphabet book features paintings by Horst Lemke, twice recipient of the international award for children's books, the Hans Christian Anderson medal. Lemke paints automobiles, boats, Chinese junks, and a "Dauntless Captain." Accompanying each illustration oversize serif capitals in black begin each rhyming line. A child might enjoy preparing his or her own list of transportation words after reading Bond's lines. Some words may catch a child's imagination as there are helicopters that look like dragonflies, motorcycles that whiz, and tractors that plod. Each rhyme begins with oversize serif capitals in black. Beginning capitalization and ending punctuation are seen in sentences. Ages 4–7.

Pattern: Ways of travel lead to alphabetical word choices in rhyming lines.

Deasey, Michael. *City ABC's*. Illustrated by Robert Perron. New York: Walker and Co., 1974.

Black-and-white photographs of places and objects in a city present such key words as "manhole cover" and "overpass." Some poetic lines are seen and heard when a child reads about *bridges* that can *stretch* in *giant steps*, a *dump* where *shovels heap clumps into trucks*, and an *escalator* that *glides through a store*. There are additional word choices to talk about. *Water* can touch you, *open gates let you play*, and a *newsstand* shows bursting *headlines* and spreading *news*. Questions may be asked. Why would a "quiet zone" be a "whisper" zone? How would an *umbrella snare some air*? What are the *X-forms* that help *hold bridges together*? Similar beginnings open each three-line verse: *A* is for———and *B* is for ———. An interested student might develop an individual list of words and sentences about city life to read to others after reviewing these photographs of New York, Philadelphia, Chicago, New Orleans, and San Francisco. Ages 5–8.

Pattern: With rhymes and similar beginnings, photographs identify objects in a city.

Fife, Dale. *Adam's ABC*. Illustrated by Don Robertson. New York: Coward, McCann, 1972.

Recommended. Fife gives word choices that should appeal to some children. Three boys, Adam, Arthur, and Albert, live in the same apartment house and show what they like to do at home, at school, and after school. There are times of fun as Adam plays with his dog, Charlie; buys licorice sticks at the candy store; and pets a mewing kitten on the school playground. There are also quiet times. For one example, it is dusk and Adam and his father walk along the river, see the shadows of trees, and then run to avoid a sudden rain. Objects of black are on every page. An elephant of ebony introduces *E*, the fire escape stands for *F*, and iron grating is for *G*. One simile, a word picture, emphasizes that the river in the city is like a thin black ribbon. Is any child interested in writing word pictures for an individual alphabet with special images that have particular appeal? The word pictures can be cut apart, rearranged, and reread in different sequences. These sentences can be rewritten for future additional reading. If the alphabet rearrangements are kept in a booklet, the lines are available for future rereadings. Ages 8-up.

Pattern: Images of black introduce word choices in the alphabet and lead to letters in sequence.

Grant, Sandy. *Hey, Look at Me: A City ABC*. Illustrated by Larry Mulvehill. New York: Bradbury, 1973.

The illustrations are black-and-white photographs by Mulvehill and accompany Grant's captions of words ending in "ing." Beginning with "adding" and "blowing," these word choices emphasize the actions. Ages 4–6.

Pattern: Alphabetical actions in black-and-white photographs are identified and recognized in "ing" word choices.

Grossbart, Francine. *A Big City*. Illustrated by the author. New York: Harper and Row, 1966.

Recommended. In Grossbart's book a child sees silhouettes on colored pages for the shapes of such city objects as antennas, buildings, and cars. Large capitals indicate the initial letters in the capitalized names of the objects: *Doors, Elephant, Fire escape,*

Garbage can, Hydrant. Since there is one simple object per page and plenty of surrounding space, the objects are clear and distinguishable for a young child. These objects and word choices could serve as sentence starters. Considering alphabetical order, a child might add something personal about personal experiences in a city to write an individualized ABC. Ages 6–8.

Pattern: Identification of oversize capitals and initial sounds of nouns are introduced by city objects. Beginnings with similar patterns of *A is for*———*and B is for*———*are seen.*

Holl, Adelaide. *ABC of Cars, Trucks, and Machines.* Illustrated by William Dugan. New York: American Heritage Press, 1970.

Dugan's full-color illustrations alternate with bright red-and-white ones to show a collection of trucks and machines. Trucks that dump loads, carry groceries, deliver newspapers, and haul objects are seen. Others to identify include a bulldozer, a crane, a cement mixer. Does any viewer notice that all of the cars, trucks, and machines have animal drivers? A bear drives a mail truck, a goat steers a tractor, and one pig delivers the bakery's goods. Some letters are represented by a pair of capitals in color and a pair of four-line verses. On one page for *G*, for example, the oversize capital in three dimension leads a verse about grocery trucks delivering food in bunches for lunches, and the smaller block capital begins information about a garbage truck that clashes and crashes. Unfamiliar words for certain children may include the "hansom," a coach for riding through the park; the "king's coach," accompanied by coachmen; and the "zone truck," one that carries the workmen and their orange cones that signal "work ahead" to motorists. Ages 4–7.

Pattern: Alternating lines about cars, trucks, and machines end in rhyming words.

Illsey, Velma. *M Is for Moving.* Illustrated by the author. New York: Walck, 1966.

Illsey's alphabet presents one occurrence of a child's life—moving day. With words that rhyme, the narrator tells about the day from a child's point of view. Each event of the day introduces a word choice about moving and introduces a capital letter.

Leftovers for lunch introduce the letter *L*. Mess and moving are for *M*. The letter *T* stands for tying up boxes. *X* is a spot x-ed on a map to show where the family is going. *Z* is for being off with a zoom, the sound of the family's car following the moving van. This pattern may be adapted for another series of events in a child's environment. Simple sentences dictated by a child may be read, cut apart, and the words rearranged for other readings. Ages 5–7.

Pattern: With rhyming text, each event on moving day introduces one capital.

Isadora, Rachel. *City Seen from A to Z*. Illustrated by the author. New York: Greenwillow, 1983.

The textured appearance of Isadora's black-and-white ABC illustrations of New York might encourage a child to touch some textured letters. *A* is for art, a large painting of children on the side of a brick building, *B* is for a beach ball, and *C* is for a car wash. After reviewing the book with a young reader, letters may be cut by an adult from a highly textured fabric such as corduroy or velvet or from sandpaper. As each letter is touched, the adult pronounces its name. To transfer to a page of print, a child frames with two fingers all of the individual letters that are the same as one letter given aloud by the adult. If a child is ready to touch all of the letters in a total word, the fabric or sandpaper letters may be arranged to spell a selected word. Ages 4–7.

Pattern: Block letters in beige introduce nouns that identify city sights and objects.

Little, Mary E. *ABC for the Library*. Illustrated by the author. New York: Atheneum, 1975.

ABC for the Library takes children to the library for a story hour. Letters are represented by objects in the library and by activities that should appeal to certain children. For example, *F* is for a fairy tale, *J* is for jokes in a joke book, and *Z* is for a visitor zooming down the sidewalk after leaving the library. Ages 6–8.

Pattern: Rhyming lines about the library introduce oversize capital letters, and the concept of enjoying a library visit at the same time.

Lobel, Arnold. *On Market Street*. Illustrated by Anita Lobel. New York: Greenwillow, 1981.

Recommended. On this imaginary shopping trip one small child travels to Market Street and finds that, just as shown in seventeenth-century French trade engravings, Anita Lobel's paintings of the shopkeepers show each shopkeeper composed of the items that each one sells. For each letter from *A* for apples and *Z* for zippers, Lobel creates these figures. For example, there is a woman composed of noodles for the letter *N*. With the exception of the woman's face and hands, the woman is made from a variety of noodles or other pasta forms. Some children will contribute the names for the noodles when they see this illustration. Lasagna noodles make the lady's headdress. Linguine forms the curls of her hair. The lady's long dress is decorated with spaghetti and manicotti. Other shops and shopkeepers are visited as the pages are turned. Oranges, quilts, ribbons, and shoes are just some of the objects used to compose the other shopkeepers. After *Z*, and a shopkeeper made of zippers, all of the purchases are given by the young shopper to a patient waiting friend, one large white cat. Ages 5-up.

Pattern: Introducing word choices and guiding serif capitals, this gives an opportunity for reader involvement and contribution.

McGinley, Phyllis. *All Around the Town*. Illustrated by Helen Stone. New York: J. B. Lippincott Company, 1948.

Recommended. In lively rhyming lines, oversize initials announce that *B* is for "Bus," a bouncing one. *R* is for "Restaurant," a special place to eat, where waiters rush with plates of food and run to hold a diner's chair. *E* is for "Escalator," something that gives you an elegant ride, and *S* is for "Subway." Some comparisons in word pictures are heard. McGinley refers to the subway as a snorting dragon, because it roars with a dragon's sound, and to a jaywalker as a sort of human jeep. Silence walks the city in velvet shoes and umbrellas are like many-colored mushrooms, while a taxi answers to a whistle like a collie. Other interesting word choices are "kindergarten" and "letter-box." The rhyming verses with traditional beginnings of "*A* is for——" offer these metaphorical descriptions of the city, and Stone's illustrations, full-color ones alternating with brown-and-white, project some of the sights. Ages 4-up.

Pattern: Introducing large serif capitals in color, rhyming lines with traditional beginnings present word choices and figurative language about sights and sounds in a city.

Mendoza, George. *The Alphabet Boat: A Seagoing Alphabet Book*. Illustrated by Lawrence Di Fiori. New York: McGraw-Hill, American Heritage Press, 1972.

Mendoza's ABC concentrates on objects about boats and the sea. Brown upper-and lowercase letters and Di Fiori's full-color illustrations face pages with poetic text about the objects. *A* is for anchor, *B* for a bird, and *C* for captain. Joining the boy and girl on the boat is a tiger-striped cat. Responding to a visual challenge, can a child find the cat in every illustration? Terms such as *dinghy, east wind, west wind,* and *galley* are mentioned. After seeing this book some children may be interested in tactile experiences that allow them to write letters in water or in another medium. Pouring water, salt, or sand into a plastic lid, a clean plastic food tray, or a plastic-coated paper plate, a child interacts with different tactile sensations while writing selected letters or words. Ages 5–7.

Pattern: Poetic text about boats and the sea introduces each upper- and lowercase letter in brown.

Moak, Allan. *A Big City ABC*. Illustrated by the author. Montreal: Tundra Books, 1984.

Moak's paintings, filled with detail and color, make Toronto an interesting city for children, showing things a child should like. *C* is for Casa Loma, a 98-room medieval castle with towers and secret passages. *E* is for excavation, construction work that is always interesting for a child to watch in a city. *R* is for the skating rink that is right in front of Toronto's city hall. Each painting is captioned with a traditional sentence that is introduced by a lowercase letter in the pattern of " *A* is for———." However, there is no beginning capitalization or ending punctuation. On the final pages of the alphabet is a review of the word choices. The lowercase letters in bold type in the sentences make the letters easy to identify. Each is followed by an informative paragraph that identifies the place in each painting. Ages 6-up.

Pattern: Paintings of Toronto introduce traditional sentences as captions and follow bold lowercase letters in sequence. Descriptive writing.

Moore, Lou. *I Live in the City ABC*. Illustrated by Tom O'Sullivan. Racine, Wisc.: Western Publishing Company, Inc., 1969.

In this small book Moore uses letters to begin each sentence about city life told from a child's point of view. Some of the choices will be interesting to a child who lives in the country as well as to one living in the city. For instance, *X* is a mark to use for a game of tic-tac-toe. *U* is for hiding under a table and *T* is for tiptoe, a way of standing to make a child feel tall. Ages 5–7.

Pattern: Illustrations and word choices about a child's activities introduce guiding letters.

Poulin, Stephanie. *Ah! Belle Cité!* Illustrated by the author. Montreal: Tundra Books, 1985.

Poulin's paintings show selected places in Montreal with one-word captions in both English and French. For each letter there is additional information and painting at the end of the book. Some of the captions might serve a youngster as patterns for labeling places in the city in which the child lives. Ages 6-up.

Pattern: Followed by descriptive writing, one-word captions in English and French label paintings of Montreal in alphabetical order.

Rosario, Idalia. *Idalia's Project ABC/Proyecto ABC: An Urban Alphabet Book in English and Spanish*. Illustrated by the author. New York: Holt, Rinehart and Winston, 1981.

Rosario's book may be useful for inner-city awareness. Children play in the water spouting from fire hydrants, look through a peephole before opening an apartment door, and ride the elevator in the housing development. The key words are discussed both in English and Spanish. The key choices, such as *bricks, cement,* and *graffiti,* are introduced by English sentences in black and Spanish sentences in red. Since the Spanish alphabet has three more symbol-sound relationships than the English alphabet, the letters *CH, LL,* and *N* are included. Each is presented in an introductory sentence. *Ch* is for *chimenea, chimney. Ll* is introduced by *lluvia, rain. Nñ* stands for *ñame, yams.* An English explanation for each relationship follows in parentheses. A California State Department of Education-recommended reading in literature. Ages 5–8.

Pattern: In English and Spanish text, word choices and letters in sequence are introduced by housing project life.

Rosenblum, Richard. *The Airplane ABC.* Illustrated by the author. New York: Atheneum, 1986.

Rosenblum's sentences about flying can be turned into word associations that an older child can use for an airplane trivia game of questions. Who held many flying records and disappeared during an attempt to fly around the world? (*E* is for Earhart). Who flew his airplane, the Winnie Mae, around the world on two separate record-breaking flights? Who was the first navy flying ace of World War II? More information might be gathered by a child to expand upon the limited entries. Questions may be asked: Why is each event important in the history of flying? When and where did the event take place? Some of these ABC sentences may support a young reader's use of nouns or introduce a child to pronouns as referents. For certain word choices, the pronoun and the word needed as the referent for the pronoun are always on the same page of this ABC. However, a child needs to read two sentences, ones related by the pronoun, to find the referent that is appropriate. Ages 7–8.

Pattern: Informative sentences about flying include pronouns as referents to nouns found in previous sentences.

Ruben, Patricia. *Apples to Zippers: An Alphabet Book.* Illustrated by the author. Garden City, N. Y.: Doubleday and Company, Inc., 1976.

Recommended. Patricia Ruben's ABC has black-and-white photographs of scenes in the city. There are interesting associations for each letter. For *A*, a child recognizes several objects—apple, accordion, and airplane. For *B*, there is a bicycle, a balloon, and a brother. Among Ruben's black-and-white photographs, certain young viewers return often to the photographs of the puppy wearing a party hat, the close-up of a child winking, and the photograph taken from a view near the floor which shows the legs of performing children during a ballet. Other children, places, and things are seen. Clusters of alliterative words are read on each doublepage spread. For instance, on the *W* page, one alliterative word cluster identifies the photographs of wink, window, and wishbone. Terms for the parts of a child's body are included on other pages: arm, belly button, eyes, ears, elbows, freckles, foot, and tongue. Oversize pairs of serif letters in black are found in the corners of the pages. Ages 5–7.

Pattern: Visual associations in city scenes of children, places, and things, are labeled with alliterative key words and guided by pairs of serif letters.

Shuttlesworth, Dorothy. *ABC of Buses.* Illustrated by Leonard Shortall. Garden City, N. Y.: Doubleday, 1965.

In Shuttlesworth's alphabet there is the fun of traveling by bus. Among all of the buses that take a child somewhere, perhaps the most fun is a bus trip to the place the child wants to be. A child hears the rhymes about buses going somewhere—to school, across the country, to the airport—and about the fun of rolling along on the wheels of the buses at a rate faster than the passengers can walk. Information about buses is given through the couplets. A young listener hears that brakes make a bus stop, that the gear shift affects its speed, and that the instrument panel is needed to show how much fuel is in the bus. Ages 4–7.

Pattern: Four-line rhyming verses about buses, their destinations, and ways they help passengers, introduce letters.

Staats, Sara Rader. *Big City ABC.* Illustrated by Robert Keys. New York: Follett, 1968.

Staats includes action words, four-line verses, and illustrations in this small ABC. For example, the illustration for *R* shows a child enjoying roller-skating. The words, "roller skates," are the key words. An accompanying verse about playing on wheels all over the city sidewalks introduces the letter *R*. Ages 4–6.

Pattern: Four-line verses about actions of life in the city introduce capitals.

Stevenson, James. *Grandpa's Great City Tour: An Alphabet Book.* Illustrated by the author. New York: Greenwillow, 1983.

With an alligator for a pilot, Grandpa takes Louie and Mary Ann on an ABC tour of the city on Alligator Airlines. Since none of the alphabetical objects are labeled, what does a child recognize and talk about in each double-page spread? Something serious? Something silly? At *B*, Grandpa plays a banjo, Louie plays baseball on the top deck of a sightseeing boat, and Mary Ann holds a balloon and eats a banana. Black upper- and lowercase serif letters are separated by commas and found in the corners of the pages. On a final page, as the airplane flies into the distance, all of the capitals are shown on twenty-six colorful ballons. The lowercase letters are seen on the side of one tall building. Ages 6–8.

Pattern: Objects on a city tour whose names begin with sounds of selected letters lead to serif capitals and lowercase letters in black.

Walters, Marguerite. *The City-Country ABC: My Alphabet Walk in the Country and My Alphabet Ride in the City.* Illustrated by Ib Ohlsson. New York: Doubleday, 1966.

In this turnabout book Walters's text may lead a child to an increasing awareness of the differences between a city setting and a country setting. In Ohlsson's illustrations, a child sees a country setting in an early summer morning in one-half of the book, and then turns the book upside down to see a country setting during another early summer morning in the second half. Alliterative words are emphasized in the poetic prose: in the city are grillwork fences and great glass blocks; in the country are gardens and a great green grasshopper in the growing grass. The selected letters, some shown in color, are seen as capitals in the lines. During the summer walk in the country setting, a child sees the guiding letter S and reads about six scampering squirrels on a sassafras tree. During the ride in the city, the unseen narrator also enjoys a summer morning, and the emphasis on sounds continues with different sounds of *C* heard in a clattery, churning, cement mixer. Internal rhymes are noticed as flashing and dashing describe a city fire engine. Attention is drawn to the shapes of letters in the objects around us. For example, in the country the shape of *X* is seen in some crisscrossed branches, and the shape of *Y* is found in a forked stick. In the city there is an invitation to look around to see *X* at the point where two paths cross. Ages 4–6.

Pattern: Alliterative words emphasize letters in sequence in two settings, the city and the country. Also, chances to see letters in the environment are afforded.

Conservation and Ecology

Asimov, Isaac. *ABC's of the Ocean.* Photographs and illustrations. New York: Walker and Company, 1970.

Conservation and ecology are the topics that link the alphabets in this section. Asimov's book is useful for information about the ecology of the ocean. Two oceanographic terms for each letter of the alphabet are defined. One illustration accompanies each letter. For each letter there are word blanks where the child can collect and write his or her own ocean words and definitions. A pronunciation guide is included for words that might be difficult ones, e.g., *xiphorsurus, xiphius, tsunami, salina, phytoplankton,* and *ichthyologist.* Serif capitals in color introduce such capitalized key words as *Buoy* for *B*, *Continental shelf* for *C*, and *Echo sounding* for *E*. Lowercase letters in color introduce additional key words for each letter: *bore* for *B*, *current* for *C*, and *ebb tide* for *E*. Ages 7-up.

Pattern: Two terms associated with the ocean are defined in informational paragraphs for each letter of the alphabet.

Friedman, Judi. *The ABC of a Summer Pond.* Illustrated by the author. Photographs by John Dommers. St. Petersburg, Fla.: Johnny Reads, Inc., 1975.

Friedman's book may increase a child's awareness of life in a pond. This alphabet has words that name and illustrate life in and around a pond. Ants, a silver bass, a small crayfish, and other living things are seen in photographs with ample text. In front of the title page, a young reader sees the pond along with an empty beaver house. Here additional sketches of the pond are included so the viewer can see what the pond looks like from above, from inside, and from underneath. Through the pages are suggested activities that encourage a child to look, listen, and touch. Facing the illustrations are inserts with questions. Is a child interested in making a home for some pond animals? In naming the pond animals that are seen in a review on the endpaper? In creating an original sequence of animals in alphabetical order? In reading any of the additional books that are found in the bibliography about pond life? Ages 7-9.

Pattern: Descriptive writing. Each pond animal, the beginning sound of its name, and related questions, are guided by letters in sequence.

Green, Ivah. *Conservation from A to Z*. Illustrated with photographs. Fayetteville, Ga.: Oddo, 1968.

Green's theme of conservation awareness ties this alphabet together. Though there are no single letters to guide the sequence, this one has words that introduce the letters with their initial capitals. From *A* and "Agriculture" to *Z* and two capitalized words that typify the practices of conservation workers, "Zeal" and "Zest," a reader reviews the use and conservation of the natural living resources of the earth. Black-and-white photographs are inserted on pages with ample text about conservation and ways it is practiced. Word choices include the "beaver," a wildlife benefactor, the "owls," whose prey is mainly the rats and mice who destroy food, and the "quail," who eat weed seeds and feed upon insects that harm food crops. Specific conservation terms such as "contour," "erosion," and "humus," are defined and explained. Ages 8-9.

Pattern: Expository writing. Needs of conservation and ways conservation is practiced are accompanied with black-and-white photographs and key terms that guide the alphabetical sequence.

Gwynne, Fred. *Ick's ABC*. Illustrated by the author. New York: Windmill Books, Inc., 1971.

Gwynne concentrates on causes of pollution and on the attitudes toward the environment. With a created creature of ecology named Ick, every illustration reflects Gwynne's short captions. Helpful attitudes are seen as trash is recycled, presticides are avoided, and trash is collected and disposed of in a proper way. Ages 6-9.

Pattern: Illustrations and text about pollution introduce guiding capitals.

McConnell, Keith A. *The SeAlphabet Encyclopedia Coloring Book*. Illustrated by the author. Owings Mills, Md.: Stemmer House, 1982.

Sea animals that may interest older children are in this one. Some sea animals have "wings" that give blows to their enemies, and others have appendages that look like lures to attract prey. Still others have bodies that adapt to their environment and camouflage them from enemies. Each verso page contains an alphabetical listing of sea animals and informative paragraphs about each one. Recto pages show drawings of sea animals along with an outlined capital letter. Ages advanced 8-up.

Pattern: Descriptive writing. From African pompano and albacore to zebra angelfish and zebra shark, each sea animal is described, identified by number, and located in black-and-white drawings.

Miles, Miska. *Apricot ABC*. Illustrated by Peter Parnall. Boston: Atlantic Monthly Press/Little, Brown and Company, 1969.

Recommended. One ripe, yellow apricot falls from a tree and startles a bee. Caterpillars, crickets, and other insects come to look. The insects see a hen of enormous size with big yellow feet. The hen pecks at the fruit and eats it down to the apricot seed, while the insects hide. As the days pass, the warm sun, a cover of dirt, and cool rains help the apricot seed grow into another apricot tree. Since the letters are arranged in the foliage, a child's visual discrimination skills are required to locate the sequence. Can a child locate the letters? Is a child ready to pronounce the letters in order without assistance? For a guided class activity to move an older child toward descriptive words about nature, a teacher displays a small branch from an apricot (or peach, pear, plum) tree. The teacher invites a child to swish the small branch back and forth gently over the glass plate of an overhead projector. With the light of the projector turned on, the shape of the branch, the apricots, and its leaves are magnififed as it is shown on the white screen. As the branch moves, children are invited to think of a word or of several words that express their thoughts about the branch, the fruits, its leaves, or the movement. Ages 5–8.

Pattern: Rhyming verses about growth cycle of apricot tree emphasize key words and serif capital letters in green.

Milgrom, Harry. *ABC of Ecology.* Illustrations by Donald Crews. New York: Macmillan, 1972.

Milgrom gives boys and girls a key word about ecology for each letter of the alphabet. Along with the black-and-white photographs by Crews, each one relates to something in the environment. A child is asked to think of some ways to stop pollution. *I* is for "ideas," the thoughts from a child about ways to help fight the effects of pollution. *L* is for "litterbugs." *Z* is for "zero hour," the time to do something to stop pollution in the environment. On the final pages are notes for each word choice to aid parents and teachers. More information about the concepts is given along with the suggested activities. For another activity, consider showing I-can-elaborate patterns (I.C.E. Breakers) in open-ended sentences to help an older child mentally break into the topic of ecology. I.C.E. Breakers are introduced to an older child for oral responses or for written composition and may be completed before further reading. The I.C.E. Breakers for Milgrom's book could include patterned beginnings for sentences such as a) I think ecology is———; b) If I were in charge of ecology, the first thing I would do about it is———; c) If I were going to talk about ecology, I would include these ideas:———. Ages 7–9.

Pattern: Expository writing. With guiding capitals, ecology concepts are emphasized with black-and-white photographs and text.

Country and Farm

Azarian, Mary. *A Farmer's Alphabet*. Illustrated by the author. Boston: David R. Godine Publisher, 1981.

Recommended. The alphabets in this part present some aspect of country or farm life. This first alphabet by Azarian features rural behaviors that still occur in such areas as Vermont and other New England states. Oversize capitals in red guide the sequence. In Azarian's woodcuts maple syrup introduces *M*, a stove for *S*, and a neighbor for *N*. Ages 5-up.

Pattern: Guided by upper- and lowercase letters in red, single key words identify behaviors and objects shown in black-and-white woodcuts.

Booth, Mary. *Jolly Days*. Illustrated. Priaterdam, Ire.: William Walker and Sons, Limited. n.d.

Available in Ireland, *Jolly Days* includes "The Floral Alphabet," one also known as "The Alphabet of the Flowers." Here flowers are personified. For example, the Dahlia is stately and tall and nods her proud head, William's first name is Sweet, and the Tulips are like guardsmen in their bright jackets. A second ABC section has traditional sentences such as *A* stands for apron, *B* is for broom, and *C* for the cook, along with rhyming lines. *E* is for eating, something one does every day, and *F* is for the role of the fairy in a play. The closing section presents the story of "The Sleeping Beauty" told in rhyme by Arthur Mansbridge. Ages: 5-up.

Pattern: Traditional repetitive beginnings with ending rhymes.

Burton, Robin. *Aaron Awoke: An Alphabet Story*. Illustrated by the author. New York: Harper and Row, 1982.

Burton's alphabet has a topical theme, progresses as a story, and also asks a child to visually interact with the artist's work. As Aaron works, plays, and entertains friends during this day on the farm, a child hunts for objects in the illustrations that begin with each new letter in the alphabet sequence. Does a child see the painting of an airplane on the page for *A*? The birds flying outside an open window for *B*? The cactus in the planter for *C*? The small hidden drawings in the illustrations can be found again on the endpapers. However, to keep the objects in an alphabetical sequence on the endpapers, a child needs to move his or her eyes from right to left to identify apple, bird, cat, and the other objects in ABC sequence. Ages 4–6.

Pattern: With no ending punctuation, each alliterative phrase begins with a capital to continue the narrative writing with ABC progression.

Cameron, Elizabeth. *A Floral ABC.* Illustrated by the author. New York: William Morrow and Company, Inc., 1983.

Cameron writes this book to interest her grandchildren in the flowers and nature around them. Cameron urges them to go out and look for flowers, to bring them back, identify them, and to preserve them. For each flower's illustration on a recto page, Cameron writes information and a verse on each decorated verso page about the selected English flower. Cameron states *A* is for anemone (*Anemone nemorosa*), once known as the wind flower. She mentions that in mythology, Anemone was loved by Zephyr, god of the west. Jealous goddess Flora, who loved Zephyr, turned Anemone into the little wind flower one sees today, a flower that is said to represent those forsaken and forlorn. Another plant of special interest is the ivy (*Madera helix*), believed to have magical powers when accompanied by holly. These two would drive demons and goblins away from cows and keep them from turning the milk and butter sour. *Z* is for zigzag clover, once called claver. A four-leafed clover, believed to have miraculous powers, was thought to be a lucky symbol. It brought a person luck and protected one from danger. Ages advanced 8-up.

Pattern: Descriptive writing, folklore, verses, and block letters in inserts on verso pages face illustrations of flowers.

Cameron, Elizabeth. *A Wildflower Alphabet.* Illustrated by the author. New York: William Morrow and Company, 1984.

Cameron identifies twenty-six flowers, ones native to Scotland. *A* is for avens, a member of the rose family, *B* is for bluebell, and *C* is for campion, whose scent attracts moths at night. There is interesting lore about some of the flowers—e.g., the dandelion is known as the children's clock because the number of puffs that it takes for a child to blow away the seed heads gives the child the hour. The word "heather" comes from a Teutonic word for a wasteland heath, a home for people once referred to as heathens. The marsh marigold, or king cup, is known also as the mayflower. This flower was prominent on one festival day, May Day, as a protection from the witches and fairies who were believed to be around during festive celebrations. Ages advanced 8-up.

Pattern: For the introduction of each letter, a hand-lettered description of a flower found in Scotland, its name, where it grows, what it is used for, and folklore about it faces the illustration.

Cleary, Beverly. *The Hullabaloo ABC.* Illustrated by Earl Thollander. Berkeley: Parnassus, 1964.

Thollander's double-page spreads link Cleary's rhyming lines in this ABC. The lines emphasize the sounds heard during one day as two children play on a farm. A young listener enjoys hearing the natural sounds as words and may predict the rhyming words to come at the end of each line. For example, after hearing the rooster's crow and seeing a playful child clatter down the farmhouse stairs, a young viewer might predict the rhyming word for crow in the line "away we———." Some rhyming words will be familiar ones: *bell-well, pig-big,* and *rose-nose.* Others may be unfamiliar: *bray-neigh, stall-bawl,* and *there-repair.* Large serif capitals in black introduce traditional opening phrases, such as *X* for *Exclaim, Y* for *Yodel,* and *Z* for *Zoom.* Key words are in bold type and make their initial letters easy to identify and to match with the single letters in sequence. As a guided activity, an adult may turn this alphabet into a sound participation ABC. A young child is asked to listen and to think up a sound that he or she associates with each alphabetical happening in the alphabet story. The sounds may be listed next to the titles of the happenings:

crow of rooster: cock-a-doodle-doo

ringing of bell: ding-dong

echo from well: hello-hello

buzzing of bee: buzz, buzz

running down steps: clatter, clatter

beating on washtub: drum, drum, drum

wings of near birds: flutter, flutter

bray of donkey: hee-haw

As parts of the alphabet story are reread, the adult stops when one of these happenings occurs. The listening child contributes the sound agreed upon for the rereading. Ages 4–6.

Pattern: Guided by single serif capitals, activities on the farm include natural sounds, onomotopoeia, in rhyming couplets and introduce key words in bold type.

Kinkaid, Eric, and Lucy Kinkaid. *Benji's Book of ABC*. Illustrated by the authors. London: Brimax Books, 1980.

Each scene about the boy Benji on these sturdy board pages is emphasized with additional illustrations of the key objects for the alphabet letters. From apple and bee to yellow and zebra, there are colorful upper- and lowercase block letters and a traditional sentence to introduce each one of the word choices. Beneath every introduction is an inserted illustration of another scene of Benji and the objects. Below the insert are lines with rhyming words that take a child through the alphabet. The rhyming lines are linked across two pages. The key word for *X* is an unusual choice: *X* marks the spot where one worm disappears into the ground. All of the word choices in the introductory beginnings and in the rhyming lines are in red to contrast with the rest of the text in black. Ages 5–7.

Pattern: Rhyming lines in black and Illustrations of word choices introduce key words in red.

Miller, Jane. *Farm Alphabet Book*. London: J. M. Dent and Sons, Ltd., 1981.

Recommended. Miller's clear photographs in full color are helpful in developing farm awareness. This alphabet has backgrounds of black with isolated key words in white. Each photograph in color shows individual farm animals, such as a bull, calf, and donkey, and identifies the key word. Each word choice leads to the explanatory text in white. Pairs of oversize letters, also in white, guide the presentation from apple to zipper. Ages 4–8.

Pattern: With capitalization and ending punctuation for sentences in white, color photographs and word choices introduce capitals and lowercase letters.

Watson, Clyde. *Applebet: An ABC*. Illustrated by Wendy Watson. New York: Farrar, Straus and Giroux, 1982.

When the apples are red and ripe, a farmer and Bet, her daughter, take them to the country fair. Their adventures during the day introduce key words and the single letters. At the fair, a *juggler* tosses oranges in the air for *J*, *kites* are shaped like birds, bats, and dragons for *K*, and a *lollipop*, *licorice*, and *lime* all stand for *L*. Along with the single letters, the author includes some interesting letter-team choices: *CH* for *cherry*, *QU* for *quarrel*, *SH* for *sh-h*, *TH* for *thief*, and *WH* for *whisper*. Two other choices recognize the soft sounds of two letters: soft *C* is for *cider* and soft *G* for *gentleman*. *Z* is for a *zigzag*, the shape of the country road, that leads back home again. A review of the illustrations can provide another visual challenge: can one red apple be found somewhere in every illustration? Some of the words in this ABC are found on the preprimer level of George Mason's Sight Word Recognition List: a, can, for, go , in, is, it, of, the, you. Ages 4–7.

Pattern: With key words in bold type to guide rhyming story, single capitals in red introduce traditional beginnings such as *A* is for——and *B* is for——.

Whitehead, Pat. *Let's Go to the Farm*. Illustrated by Ethel Gold. Mahwah, N.J.: Troll Associates, 1985.

In Ethel Gold's illustrations for *Let's Go to the Farm*, a small girl and boy visit a farm to see the animals and to hear the sounds the animals make. *M* is for the moo of a calf, *N* for the neigh of a colt, and *O* for the oink of a piglet. Ages 3–7.

Patttern: Block capitals and lowercase letters in corners with key words seen twice, once above illustrations and again in the sentences below.

Incredible Animals

Kingdon, Jill. *The ABC Dinosaur Book*. Illustrated by Seymour Fleishman. Chicago: Childrens Press, 1982.

For every large, sylized letter in color, there is a dinosaur word choice in bold type, a pronunciation guide, and a descriptive paragraph. Based on the available information gained from skeletons and natural history, the large colorful pictures are the author's opinions of what the dinosaurs looked like when they were alive. With these illustrations a viewer sees the stegosaurus, with two rows of bony triangles going down the backbone; the nodosaurus, which looked like a large turtle with its shell of bony plates; and the diplodocus, one of the longest dinosaurs, with a length equivalent to three transit buses. Ages 10-up.

Pattern: Dinosaurs and descriptive paragraphs introduce oversize sylized letters in colors.

Robinson, Howard F., editorial director. *Incredible Animals A to Z*. Judith E. Zatsick, art editor. Washington D.C.: National Wildlife Federation/Ranger Rick Magazine, 1985.

Oversize capitals in colors on each page are introduced by choices of unusual animals, informative paragraphs, and full-color photographs. There is a blue-feathered cassowary, with its thick, bony helmet; a close-up of a stag beetle, with its staglike antlers that are really jaws; and zebra look-alikes—the zebra butterfly, the zebra angelfish, and the zebra finch. A helpful index is included. Ages 10-up.

Pattern: Unusual animals with names in bold type and informative text are introduced by oversize capitals in colors.

Whitehead, Pat. *Dinosaur Alphabet Book*. Illustrated by Joel Snyder. Mahwah, N.J.: Troll Associates, 1985.

This alphabet book and its illustrations present a beginning introduction to the characteristics of dinosaurs. In the corners of the pages, capitals and lowercase letters appear along with appropriate word choices such as "allosaurus," "big," and "claws." Beneath the full-colored illustrations are short, simple sentences that give information: some dinosaurs were meat eaters and others were plant eaters; some lived on land and others in the water; there were many kinds of prehistoric animals. Ages 3–7.

Pattern: Pairs of letters and word choices are followed by single sentences.

Wilson, Ron. *100 Dinosaurs from A to Z.* Illustrated by Cecilia Fitzsimons. New York: Grosset and Dunlap/The Putnam Publishing Group, 1986.

Descriptions of some of the most popular dinosaurs are listed alphabetically from the familiar allosaurus to the final entry, zephyrosaurus. The descriptions are followed by information about each dinosaur's weight, length, location, and its time period in dinosaur history. Full-color illustrations accompany the information. With these illustrations, a child sees the illustrator's projection of what the dinosaurs were like. Some unusual features are the thumb spikes of the iguanodon; the porcupinelike, spiny projections of the kentrosaurus; and the distinctive hatchet-shaped head crest of the lambeosaurus. A similar pattern of writing may be found for each descriptive information about the dinosaurs, making it easy for a reader to compare information. First the meaning of the name of each dinosaur is discussed—e.g., "velociraptor" means "swift plunderer." The group to which the dinosaur belongs is identified. The velociraptor belonged to the dromaeosaurids—the running lizards. Then the walking, running, eating behaviors, and body characteristics of each dinosaur are mentioned. On a final page is a chart of dinosaur history that lists the time periods in the Mesozoic and Cenozoic eras. Ages 10-up.

Pattern: Dinosaurs and descriptive paragraphs follow the alphabetical sequence.

Names and Occupations

ABC. Illustrated by Hitomi Kuroki. New York: Simon and Schuster, Inc., 1984.

With this book, and the others in this part of the bibliography, the theme of names and occupations is used to present the alphabet. For example, Kuroki's illustrations in *ABC*, a tall, thin book, introduce a child to boys and girls through their names. Aaron loves apples, Bridget loves blowing bubbles, and Christopher loves chocolate. A child may enjoy completing this alphabetical pattern about some of his or her friends. Ages 6–8.

Pattern: Capital letters are introduced in sequence by the pattern———(name) loves———(object).

ABC. London: Ramboro Books, n.d.

The sturdy cardboard pages of this ABC show the names of twenty-six children in alphabetical order in scenes of work and play. In the garden young Alice waters flowers with a watering can, Bob plants yellow daffodils, and Charles turns over the soil with a spade. In the kitchen Debby and Edna have a tea party with cookies and cake for their invited guest, a teddy bear. Ages 4–6.

Pattern: Guided by colorful initial letters in sequence, children's names are in block manuscript print in black.

Ackerman, Karen. *Flannery Row: An Alphabet Rhyme.* Illustrated by Karen Ann Weinhaus. New York: Atlantic/Little, 1986.

On Flannery Row lives Commander Ahab Flannery, his wife, and their twenty-six children. To say good-bye quickly when the commander goes to sea, they all alphabetize and arrange themselves from *A* to *Z*. The rhymes include the names from Ahab and Blanche to Yancey and Zack. There is a variety of details to look for in the illustrations. The children are found in the illustration just above the letter that begins their individual names in the text. Each child's clothing reflects the color of the letter that begins his or her name. Some houses along Flannery Row receive one bottle of milk each, whereas the Flannery house receives ten bottles of milk from the delivery wagon. Inside, a young viewer sees that each Flannery child has a special alphabetical peg for hanging up hat or coat. Twenty-six pairs of shoes rest on the long shelf above the coats. Saying a final good-bye, they all gather together in alphabetical order and then, in a concluding scene, rearrange themselves on the dock after Captain Ahab sails away. The endpapers show cameo-shaped illustrations of the children. Ages 4–6.

Pattern: Narrative writing in ABC progression.

Boxer, Devorah. *26 Ways to Be Somebody Else.* Illustrated by the author. New York: Pantheon, 1968.

Beginning with an acrobat for *A*, some boys and girls will enjoy Boxer's review of ways to be someone else. Word choices include the personalities of Napoleon and William Tell, and others, and are on verso pages that face the black-and-white illustrations. Ages 6–8.

Pattern: Word associations. Each black-and-white illustration identifies one of twenty-six ways to be somebody else and introduces a word choice that leads to a guiding capital letter.

Ewen, Doris, and Mary Ewen. *An ABC of Children's Names.* Illustrated. La Jolla, Calif.: Green Tiger Press, 1980.

This reprint of an early twentieth century alphabet presents a child, a verse about the child's behavior, and an illustration for each capital. The behaviors reflect earlier times—e.g., blowing out a candle before jumping into bed, making a duster for nurse, having milk and bread for supper, and reading a book entitled *Matilda's Golden Deed.* This ABC may have limited appeal to today's child. However, some of the names are alliterative ones and may serve as beginning sentence starters for present-day behaviors. On the *C* page, cross Charlie is not allowed to eat the bath soap, for it will make him ill. Katharine is kind and gives away the white and brown eggs that her hens lay each day. Willful Willie does not want to go to bed. Does a boy or girl know someone who reminds them of a cross Charlie, a kind Katharine, or a Willful Willie? Are there alliterative words to write about their behavior? Is there an interest in drawing an illustration about someone who is cross or not cross? Kind? Pleasant to be around? For a review, the stylized lowercase letters are seen on the endpapers. Ages 6–7.

Pattern: Verses introduce children whose names begin with the guiding letters.

Farber, Norma. *I Found Them in the Yellow Pages.* Illustrated by Marc Brown. New York: Little, Brown and Company/Atlantic Monthly Press, 1973.

Farber's alphabet book contains occupations found in the yellow pages. Acrobats are for *A*, bakers for *B*, and clowns for *C*. With these entries and others, this ABC builds an awarensss of vocations. There are occupations from dog walkers and hula dancers to pickle packers and zookeepers. Each occupation introduces the capitalized word choices and the block capitals. After reviewing these choices, could the word choices be arranged into a rhythmic chant of alphabetical occupations? If needed, several favorite occupations could be included for a single letter:

acrobat, baker, chimney sweep, clown, dog walker, earth mover, electrician,———.

Since each occupation and full-page illustration looks as if it had been designed as an ad for the yellow pages, a child may turn to the local yellow pages and compare what is found there with the illustrations in Farber's book. How many of the occupations shown in the book's black line drawings can be seen in the yellow pages? After a child sees the samples on these pages, a child may want to imagine an occupation to aspire to and make a yellow-page ad for that occupation. Another child may create an original set of yellow pages. For discussion, a girl or boy might respond to the question, Why do grown-ups work and do what they do? Ages 5-up.

Pattern: With word associations, each black line drawing on a yellow background introduces an occupation, a word choice, and one oversize, block serif capital.

Johnson, Jean. *Firefighters A to Z*. Photographs by the author. New York: Walker and Company, 1985.

Johnson's book is useful for occupation awareness. In Johnson's alphabet, large black-and-white photographs are accompanied by a brief text. The boots of a firefighter introduce *B*, and the emergencies to which the firefighter respond introduce *E*. One dalmatian, the firefighter's mascot, is named Xavier and introduces *X*. There is added information, illustrations, and text for teachers at the close of the alphabet presentation. Ages 6-9.

Pattern: In expository writing, word associations about firefighters are discussed. Each black-and-white photograph emphasizes the selected key word whose initial letter guides the sequence.

Johnson, Jean. *Police Officers A to Z*. Photographs by the author. New York: Walker and Company, 1986.

Johnson's ABC about police officers also is useful for occupation awarenesss. Each aspect in this alphabet is related to a police officer and associated duties and is guided by a letter in the sequence. Words that start with capital letters are the topics for the black-and-white illustrations and for the explanatory sentences that follow. *Accident, Badge, Crime, Dispatcher,* and other choices, are on white pages with framed pictures. Women are seen in various roles—e.g., as a dispatcher using a computer, as a

fingerprint expert, and as an officer who carries a weapon. After Z
is a section entitled " More about Police Officers." Here additional
words and pictures are included to foster discussions with the child
about the value and importance of the police officers in the
community. Ages 6-9.

Pattern: Expository writing. Each large block capital in gray
and each initial letter in a key word in bold type is accompanied by
sentences associated with role of a police officer.

Kahn, Ruth E. *My Daddy's ABC's*. Illustrated by Celeste K. Foster.
Minneapolis: T. S. Denison, n.d.

Written with repetitive beginning segments of "My Daddy is
———," these alphabet verses use occupations and rhyming words
to present the sequence. *A* is for accountant, *B* is for baker, *C* is for
clown, and *D* is for doctor. Illustrations about the occupations held
by fathers introduce each letter, including a doctor, engineer,
farmer, and grocer. Is a boy or girl interested in naming or writing
additional occupations for the letters? Ages 5-7.

Pattern: With illustrations and repetitive beginning segments,
patterned words in rhyme are read in verses about working roles of
fathers.

Lillie, Patricia. *One Very, Very Quiet Afternoon*. Illustrated by the
author. New York: Greenwillow, 1986.

On a quiet afternoon Annabelle Barbara Cavendish decides to
have a tea party outside. One teddy bear is her guest. Daniel Ezra
Fiddleson literally drops in from an overhanging tree branch.
Miranda Naomi Ortez makes mud pies. Peter Quentin Ryan
throws the pies. As the afternoon goes on, more and more of the
children get involved in the not-very-quiet activities. A final page
repeats all of the rhythmic names of the children. If a child does not
appreciate the pen-and-ink line drawings with touches of orange,
an adult should consider reading aloud only the text with its
unusual names of children. With this arrangement a young child
can focus on listening to the rhythm in such names as Gabrielle
Hillary Ives, Jeremy Kenneth Lombardi, and Vincent Wallace
Xanadu. Ages 4-6.

Pattern: Narrative writing in ABC progression with rhythmic
names of children.

Smith, Donald. *Adam, the Astronaut: A Name and Occupation Alphabet Book*. Illustrated by the author. London: Hamish Hamilton Children's Books, 1983.

Smith presents names of people and the jobs they perform for this alphabet. Adam is an astronaut, Betty is a beekeeper, and Charlie is a clown. Certain occupations that may be unusual ones for children to see are the kennelmaid, the undertaker, and the xylophonist. Edward is an electrician, Gary is a golfer, and Michael is a magician. The end pages review again all of the names and the jobs in the ABC sequence. Ages 4–5.

Pattern: Large upper- and lowercase letters in black are introduced by each character and a phrase that emphasizes an alphabetical name and occupation:———(name), the———(occupation).

Tallon, Robert. *Rotten Kidphabets*. Illustrated by the author. New York: Holt, Rinehart and Winston, 1975.

Children, their alliterative names, and their illustrated behaviors introduce block capitals. For S, selfish Sam holds all of the objects, while other children are without. Sam has the bat, the ball, the books, and the boxes. At Z, Zachary, another kidphabet, is introduced. Standing on a rooftop and dressed in a version of a Superman costume with a Z on his chest, Zachary becomes a Zu Zu Nut. Ages 6-up.

Pattern: Alliterative names of children and their behaviors introduce initial letters and related sounds.

Townsend, Jessie G., collector. *Annie, Bridget, Charlie: An ABC for Children of Rhyme*. Illustrated by Jan Pienkowski. New York: Pantheon, 1967.

Illustrations of children, their alphabetical names in sequence, and their attributes lead to the large outlined capitals on the verso pages. Apt Annie, bad Bridget, and curious Charlie begin the sequence. The traditional words open the lines, with *A* is for——— and *B* is for———. Rhyming words are heard, e.g., "Charlie," "barley," "snarly." Ages 5–7.

Pattern: Rhyming verses about children with alliterative names and behaviors introduce oversize capitals in colors.

Special Faces and Places

ABC's in Arabic. Illustrated. Troy, N.Y.: International Book Centre, 1984.

Special people or special places identified by their names in the titles connect the alphabets in the books that follow in this section. In this first title, the reading format is right-to-left. Questions introduce the first set of objects. For example, brown-and-white eggs appear above a caption of flowing Arabic characters. These words, when pronounced by a person speaking English, sound similar to "Kam baidatan?" This means "How many eggs?" A second picture of pencils has a caption of "Kam galaman?" which means "How many pencils?" Introducing the sequence are *A* is for arnab, rabbit, and *B* is for bakaka, a cow; and tamron, a date fruit, is for *T*, the third letter in the Arabic alphabet. In addition to other animals, a viewer sees a fox, a camel, and a pigeon. There are some high-frequency nouns, in both singular and plural forms:
cow, head, tree, rocket, plane, letter, pencil, hand, balloons, cars, apples, books. Invite a child to use the plural form of the noun in a response to the question, How many——? All of the objects are shown in full color. In a band in color at the foot of each page is the symbol for the letter and the key word in Arabic for the object. Ages 6-up.

Pattern: In a right-to-left format, objects in full color are labeled in Arabic.

Anastasio, Dina. *The Romper Room Book of ABC's.* Illustrated by Nancy Stevenson. New York: Doubleday and Company, Inc., 1985.

Fans of the Romper Room television show will recognize some of the familiar characters who join this story and prepare for Up-Up's birthday party. *A* is for the apron, the one Granny Cat wears, and *Z* is for the birthday gift, a zebra with a red bow on its tail. The end pages show a simple maze for a child to follow. The child puts a finger on the letter *A* and then follows the letters in sequence until the *Z* is reached. Ages 4-6.

Pattern: Names of objects capitalized in sentences introduce large capital serif letters in yellow.

Bond, Jean Carey. *A Is for Africa*. Illustrated with photographs. New York: Franklin Watts, Inc., 1969.

For older children Bond's facts and photographs form an alphabet to introduce a child to selected information about the Africa of the sixties, information with which to compare the current Africa. *A* is for Africa, the second largest continent in the world, and *Z* is for Zanzibar, a group of islands that are part of the nation of Tanzania in East Africa. Color photographs alternate with black-and-white ones and show Africans at work and Africans' possessions. For example, there is the large leather-and-straw hat of a Bolgatanga farmer, a golden Ashanti pendant, and a statue of Ethiopia's national symbol, the Lion of Judah. The initial letters in the key words guide the alphabetical presentation. Ages 8-up.

Pattern: With descriptive writing, photographs of Africa illustrate ample text about key words.

Bridwell, Norman. *Clifford's ABC*. Illustrated by the author. New York: Scholastic, Inc.,1983.

Clifford, the big red dog, and Emily Elizabeth appear on each page, with additional objects and scenes. Colorful upper- and lowercase serif letters are in the corners. All objects are labeled in lowercase serif letters. A young child should enjoy finding Clifford on every page. Relative size is not shown; Clifford is as big as a house, taller than an igloo, and larger than an elephant. Relative size and other concepts of related terms are enjoyed by some older children through hyperboles. The pattern of hyperboles and their use may be introduced through Clifford, since he is the biggest and reddest dog in all of the books about dogs for children. For instance, Clifford is so large that a house is tiny compared to him. Invite a child to try to improve on that hyperbole by giving another final clause about relative size—e.g., Clifford is so large that——. Some hyperbolic beginnings that relate to Clifford's ABC include: 1) Clifford sits near the igloo for *I*. Clifford is so cold that——; 2) Clifford towers above an elephant for *E*. Clifford is so tall that ——; 3) Clifford eats sausages for S. Clifford is so hungry that ——; and 4) Clifford sleeps with the sound of Zzzzz. Clifford is so sleepy that——. The labeled pictures support a child's independent writing of hyperbole patterns at home or in a classroom writing center. Ages 4-7.

Pattern: Each large lowercase serif letter matches initial letters in noun choices with Clifford, the big red dog.

Clifton, Lucille. *The Black B C's*. Illustrated by Don Miller. New York: Dutton, 1970.

Clifton concentrates on such respected black people as Harriet Tubman, Sojourner Truth, Martin Luther King, Jr., and others who have contributed to America. Miller's paintings face pages that have lines of text about the personalities and their different aspects: athletic, brave, inventive, and inspirational. Ages 7-up.

Pattern: Descriptive writing. For each description of a black American, there is an illustration and a guiding key name.

Cowell, Phyllis Fair. *The Care Bears: The Baby Hugs Bear and Baby Tugs Bear Alphabet Book*. Illustrated by Tom Cooke. American Greetings Corporation, 1984. .

Sliding down a rainbow to earth, the bears find the letters of the alphabet everywhere. Some of the shapes of the letters are seen clearly in the shapes of the objects in the illustrations and are easy to find. For instance, clouds form an uppercase *A* in manuscript. The letter *B* decorates balloons. One *C* is the logo on the shirt of a garden scarecrow. Hidden in some of the shapes, other letters may be difficult ones for a young child to locate. For instance, the *L* has to be found in the border of a picnic cloth, one *M* hides in the stitching of a mailman's bag, and *N* is formed by the the outline of a rope. Ages 4-5.

Pattern: Narrative writing. Block capital letters in various colors are found in illustrations and guide the alphabetic sequence in the story. Practice in puzzle solving.

Davis, Jim. *Garfield A to Z Zoo*. Illustrated by Mike Fentz and Dave Kuhn. New York: Random House, 1984.

While walking to the zoo, Garfield is startled by a grak bird, hits his head, becomes unconscious, and dreams of imaginary zoo animals. From Aquawalker, an animal who teaches swamp surfing; and purple Bob, who operates a day-care center for plants; to the dotted Yuhguk, who doesn't understand much; and the Zuni Bird, who likes giggling on the telephone, these animals show a child the creative possibilities of language. Small illustrated dream-clouds show the animals and their names over Garfield's head on the pages. Ages 5–7.

Pattern: Nonsense zoo animals with names beginning with guiding letter in red.

Feelings, Muriel. *Jambo Means Hello: Swahili Alphabet Book.* Illustrated by Tom Feelings. New York: Dial, 1974.

Recommended. This ABC by the Feelingses is an experience with Swahili words. There is clear text and strong paintings, impressively created with black ink, white tempera, and linseed oil. Descriptive sentences introduce the key words in English and Swahili. Stylized capitals in black are found in the left-hand corners of the double-page spreads. Helpful pronounciation guides are included for the words. For example, *G*, pronounced as in "gave," is heard in *ngoma* (n GO mah), meaning "drum" and "dance" or a "party." *R*, pronounced by rolling the tongue like rolling the *R* in Spanish, is heard in *karibu*, (kah REE boo), which means "welcome." Swahili has two less sounds than the English language. In the sequence does a child notice that there is no page for *Q* and for *X*? After hearing the descriptive sentences, can a student select a word that fits the meaning of the context when a key word is deleted or masked? A California State Department of Education-recommended extended reading. Ages 8-up.

Pattern: Descriptive writing introduces Swahili words, English equivalents, and stylized capitals.

Feeney, Stephanie. *A Is for Aloha.* Illustrated by Hella Hammid. Designed by Einar Vinje. Honolulu: University of Hawaii Press, 1980.

Black-and-white photographs of people, places, and happenings in Hawaii shows scenes of what life is like in the islands. Inserts of green in the photographs emphasize each word choice in white and introduce the capitals and lowercase letters in black. Upper-

and lowercase letters in black are identified and may be matched with the first letter in each key word. A culminating feature includes information about Hawaii: May Day is called Lei Day; a gecko is a small gray lizard that makes a strange chirping noise; and *Tutu* is the Hawaiian word for grandmother or grandfather. An adult guide for discussing this book with young children is included. Some specific suggestions include talking about the pictures, encouraging practice in letter recognition, and learning the sounds of the letters. Ages 4–6.

Pattern: People, objects, and places associated with Hawaii lead to key words with capitals and lowercase letters as guides.

Freire de Matos, Isabel. *ABC de Puerto Rico.* Illustrated by the author. Selections by Ruben del Rosario. Sharon, Conn.: Antonio Martorell, 1968.

Oversize serif capitals are inserted into illustrations and introduced by word choices from *A* is for *agua*, to Z,for *zumbador* and *zapatero*. *N* is for *noche*, a key word found in a dark evening scene with one owl perched on the top of the letter in the moonlight. The center bar in the letter *H* forms a hammock to illustrate the key choice, *hamaca. E* is for *estrella*, one star, where blue *E*s radiate around a center point to form the rays of a star, and *I* is for *isla*, "island," where the letters are shown at the edge of the island surrounded by the blue water. Instructions are found on the final pages. Here attention is drawn to the letters *K, LL, V, W, X, Y,* and *Z*. There are pronunciation hints. A California State Department of Education-recommended recreational reading. Ages 5–8.

Pattern: Letter-object-sentence arrangement.

Gruelle, Johnny. *Raggedy Ann and Andy's Alphabet and Numbers.* Illustrated by the author. Indianapolis: Bobbs-Merrill Company, Inc., 1972.

In the first section, "Raggedy Ann's Alphabet," serif capitals from *A* to *Z* are in colors and introduced by small full-color illustrations and accompanying rhymes. A short story that emphasizes the selected letter is included before another letter is reviewed in sequence. For example, after *B*, a story with *B* words is read, then *C* and *D* words are inserted for a child to hear or to read, followed by a story about crickets and dwarfs. Then the letter sequence begins again with *E*. Other stories feature creatures such as elves, fairies, grasshoppers, and humming birds. Ages 6-up.

Pattern: With narrative writing and rhyming lines about Raggedy Ann and Andy, capitalized names of objects introduce serif capitals in color.

Harrison, Ted. *A Northern Alphabet*. Illustrated by the author. Plattsburgh, N.Y.: Tundra Books, 1982.

From *A* to *Z* with words about people, places, animals, and objects of the North, Harrison creates an ABC book with alliterative sentences that could serve as story starters. Every full-color picture shows the person, an activity, and additional objects associated with the key letter. For instance, there is alliteration in the words about one man who wears a red parka and walks past a white paddlewheeler. For *P*, one pan, pail, pipe, and puddle are seen. As a child sees the man walking toward the paddlewheeler, what response might be given to the words "What do you think this man does next?" A young viewer sees that each page is bordered with names of places in the North. Where are such places as Prince of Wales island, Point Barrow, and Porcupine River? Is there a pattern to be discovered in the arrangement of the words in the border? After a short sentence is read, does a child recognize how many words in the sentence begin with the selected letter? Ages 5-up.

Pattern: Introducing capitals and lowercase letters, alliterative words in bold type form narrative sentences about life north of the fifty-fifth parallel.

Holly Hobbie's Book of ABC's. Illustrated by Holly Hobbie. Chicago: Childrens Press, 1978.

Illustrations showing activities such as baking apple pies, wearing a bonnet tied with a bow, or baking cakes and cookies introduce traditional openings. With block capitals in bright pink, the pattern for the openings is similar to *C is for candy*. In contrast to the capitals the block lowercase letters are in bright blue. Within the rhyme on each page, the selected letter is identified in bold type each time it appears in a word. For example, on the *C* page a child sees the letter in several words: *candy, rich, chocolate, cake, cherry,* and *cookies.* Other word choices include *P* is for *prayers,* *S* is for *smiles,* and *R* is for *rainbows.* A careful reader notes that on the page for *X,* the *X* in excellent is referred to as a middle letter. Is any child confused by this message? Does the child understand that the colors do not affect the process of matching the uppercase letters to the lowercase letters? Ages 5-up.

Pattern: Rhyming verses about Holly Hobbie and illustrations of key objects lead to upper- and lowercase letters in color.

Hughes, Shirley. *Lucy and Tom's ABC's.* Illustrated by the author. New York: Viking Kestrel, 1986.

Lucy and her smaller brother, Tom, introduce the alphabet as they meet the people and visit the places that are a part of their daily experiences. In the full-color illustrations, a child finds several details to hold his or her interest, ones that lead the reader back to Lucy and Tom for a second viewing in this ABC book or in one of the author's other titles about these children. Ages 2-6.

Pattern: Letters introduced through children's daily experiences with people and places.

Hyman, Jane. *The Gumby Book of Letters.* Illustrated with photographs. New York: Doubleday and Company, Inc.,1986.

Hyman's book of letters shows a pair of uppercase and lowercase letters on each page and introduces a child to the sounds of the letters in the alphabet. The sounds are represented by objects in the color photographs of television scenes featuring Gumby, the little green blob. To begin this alphabet presentation, Gumby and Pokey, the clay horse, land on a planet in space where *A* is for astronauts. Gumby and Pokey talk about their past adventures. They reminisce. *B* is for the book in which Gumby first found Pokey. *D* is for a dinosaur they once saw, and *E* is for an elephant they found in a jungle on Earth. Endpapers show all of the uppercase and lowercase letters in blue in sequence. Ages 3-6.

Pattern: In blue, upper-and lowercase letters along with initial letters of key words are introduced by photographs and story about Gumby and Pokey.

Jefferds, Vincent. *Disney's Elegant ABC Book.* Illustrated. New York: Simon and Schuster, Inc., 1983.

Capitals in color introduce the colorful traditional arrangements of the beginning lines in these verses about Disney's movies—e.g., *B* is for Bambi, *C* is for Cinderella, and *D* is for Dumbo. Some of Disney's original characters are here, too: Goofy portrays an artist for *A*, Donald Duck stands for *D*, and *J* is for Jaq, the small mouse who helped Cinderella. Famous story characters such as Eeyore and Pinocchio are easy to recognize. Does any child see a break in the pattern of the repetitive beginning lines shown in blue or green text? Where is the beginning line in color to help identify *B*? For *D*? For *L*? In a final section additional verses for a child give directions for writing certain capitals in manuscript in this order: *O, E, J, S, H, A, M, V, Y,* and *K.* Ages 3-up.

Pattern: With rhyming verse colorful single capitals are identified again as first letters in repetitive phrases.

Kahn, Peggy. *The Care Bears' Book of ABC.* Illustrated by Carolyn Bracken. New York: Random House, 1983.

Serif letters introduce the rhymes about the bears. A child identifies the characteristic of rhyme in the words that are heard and predicts the next word. For instance, a child sees an airplane flying in the sky beside one bear floating along with balloons. Will a child rhyme *sky* with *fly*? Other rhyming words to see and hear are *bakes-cakes, green-jellybean,* and *bright-night.* Ages 3–5.

Pattern: Rhymes follow large serif letters in colors.

Kahn, Peggy. *The Wuzzles' Alphabet Book.* Illustrated by Bobbi Barto. New York: Random House, 1986.

The Wuzzles are a group of colorful animals. This group includes yellow Butterbear, blue Hoppopotamus, purple Eleroo, and pink Rhinokey. The Wuzzles balance apples, play ball, and eat carrots and cabbage. Some interesting word choices are *S* is for a "snuzzle," a hug given by a Wuzzle, *K* for "kids," and *J* for "junk." The junk includes a broken toy, a wheeless bicycle, and a piece of string. Colorful letters, upper- and lowercase, are the headings for the rhymes. Each selected letter is seen again in bold type in the lines. The endpapers contain a review of the sequence with capitals and lowercase serif letters in colors. Ages 4–5.

Pattern: Rhyming lines about Wuzzles emphasize serif letters in colors.

Kraus, Robert. *The Old Fashioned Raggedy Ann and Andy ABC Book*. Illustrated by Johnny Gruelle. New York: Windmill Books/ Simon and Schuster, Inc., 1981.

Small full-color illustrations feature Raggedy Ann and Andy and selected objects in this ABC. The dolls, Ann and Andy, dance, snooze, and meet such creatures as Fred the frog, Spot the puppy, and Willie the wooden boy. All of the object choices, including ice cream, kitty, and moon, introduce key words and rhyming lines on every page. Capitalization and punctuation are seen. The initial serif capital letter in each word choice is seen in bright blue and may be matched with the initial serif capital in the key word found again within a rhyming line. Ages 5-up.

Pattern: Rhyming lines present capitalized key words shown as objects posing with Raggedy Ann and Andy.

Lucero, Faustina H. *Little Indians' ABC*. Illustrated by Jeanne Pearson. Fayetteville, Ga.: Oddo Publishing, Inc., 1974.

In addition to introducing the alphabet to children, this title presents illustrations of authentic clothing, utensils, and living quarters of children from thirteen Indian tribes. From *A* for a Chippewa boy's arrow to *Z* for a Navaho boy's zia (sun) design, there is a serif capital-object-word arrangement. For instance, one Apache girl carries an urn, while another braids yucca. A Zuni Pueblo girl collects gourds; another paints pottery. A key to the Indian tribes is found on a final page. Ages 5–7.

Pattern: Letter-object-word arrangement.

Mayers, Florence Cassen. *ABC, Museum of Fine Arts, Boston*. Illustrated. Boston: Museum of Fine Arts/Harry N. Abrams, Inc.,1986.

In this alphabet are color plates of objects from Boston Museum's Fine Arts collection. This tall, thin book allows older children to get acquainted with selected items in the museum's collection and allows a younger child to review letters with the different fine arts objects in this ABC collection. Furniture, paintings, and artifacts are included. Each letter is shown as a capital and as a lowercase letter in color: *A* is for armchair. *B* is for the boy in blue in the painting called *The Torn Hat* by Thomas Sully. *C* is for *Cats*; one black cat and one tricolor cat rest together in a hand-colored lithograph by Theophile Alexandre Steinlen. At *M*, there is a golden mummy case to introduce the guiding letters in red. Explanatory and informative sentences are at the foot of each page. Ages 6-up.

Pattern: Objects from the Boston Musuem's collection of fine arts introduce key words, informative sentences, and oversize pairs of upper-and lowercase letters in color.

Mayers, Florence Cassen. *ABC, Museum of Modern Art, New York*. Sheila Franklin, ed. Illustrated. New York: Museum of Modern Art/Harry N. Abrams,Inc., 1986.

In this ABC book modern art is brought to the child. Some of the works of modern art that Mayers includes are a shiny, red automobile by Pinin Farina, a bronze goat by Pablo Picasso, *Campbell's Soup* (oil silkscreened on canvas) by Andy Warhol, and *Two Cheeseburgers with Everything* (burlap, plaster, and enamel) by Claes Oldenburg. Mayers recommends this book as a first art book, a novel way to learn the ABCs, and as a guide for a child on a visit to the museum. Ages 5-up.

Pattern: Objects from New York museum's modern art collection introduce key words and informative sentences for each pair of oversize capitals and lowercase letters.

Mendoza, George. *Norman Rockwell's Americana ABC*. Illustrated. New York: Harry N. Abrams, Inc., 1975.

Mendoza's ABC is an review of Rockwell's paintings, with reproductions of Rockwell's original oil paintings along with Mendoza's text. Each painting reflects a key word that begins with the selected letter. From *New Kids in the Neighborhood*, a painting created for a *Look Magazine* illustration, "neighbor" becomes the key word in red and is emphasized with an oversize lowercase *N* in red. In other paintings,a boy looking out to sea introduces *B*, a group singing carols at Christmas illustrate *C*, and

D shows a young girl dancing. Reflecting Americana verbally as well as visually in these scenes, the titles of Rockwell's paintings become important and are included in a final list along with the dates of their publication for *The Saturday Evening Post*, for *Look*, the Department of the Interior, and other publishers. When Rockwell's paintings and Mendoza's words are seen a second time in a review, can a student recall one of Mendoza's carefully selected word choices in color from its poetic context? Can a student recall a key word when all letters but the initial letter in the word are covered with a word mask or replaced by dashes? Ages 8-up.

Pattern: Oversize lowercase letters and key words in color are introduced in sequence with Rockwell's paintings and Mendoza's poetry.

Meynier, Gil. *Mexico A-Z*. Illustrated by Carlos Mérida. New York: Franklin Watts, 1966.

Mérida, one of Mexico's distinguished abstract artists, opens a youngster's eyes to the visual aspect of Mexican folkways with several illustrations. The rhyming text by Meynier enhances a young reader's alphabetic introduction to Mexico. *D* is for dance. This dance is the Ribbon Dance, and children weave in and out the way Indians danced it long ago. *P* is for a decorated piata filled with candy and toys. Once broken, the piata releases its contents, and boys and girls rush to collect their favorite treats. *M* is for the market where customers buy meats, fish, green vegetables, lilies, and sugar candy. Traditional beginnings of phrases start with such openings as *A* is for amigo and *B* is for bravo. Like Tallon's *ABC in English and Spanish*, this ABC points out that *W* is not used often as a Mexican sound. Unlike *Idalia's Project ABC/Idalia's Proyecto ABC: An Urban Alphabet Book in English and Spanish* by Rosario, there is no mention of the sounds for *Ch*, *Ll*, and *N*. Ages 5-up.

Pattern: Mérida's scenes of Mexico introduce Meynier's rhyming text, similar beginnings, key words, and capitals in color.

Milne, Alan Alexander. *Pooh's Alphabet Book*. Illustrated by E. H. Shepard. New York: E. P. Dutton, 1975.

Recommended. Word choices in color from quotations found in the Pooh books introduce the letters of the alphabet. Serif capitals in color are located in the corners of verso pages. These quotations all begin with capitalized key words in color: "Animal," "Bear," and "Company." The words feature examples of Pooh's behavior. Pooh "eats" Eeyore's birthday present, likes talking to "Rabbit" who uses short, easy words, and has the "idea" to look carefully into the Heffalump trap to see if there really is one. For an activity in developing transitional cues for oral storytelling about Pooh, an adult rereads some of the quotations, shows several words and phrases from the Pooh books on bear-shaped flash cards, and suggests that the child help compose a story about Pooh by using some of the words and phrases on the cards to keep the story going. Ages 4-up.

Pattern: With quotations about Pooh and his friends, capitalized key words in color introduce serif capitals in color and examples of narrative writing.

Moss, Jeffrey. *Oscar-the-Grouch's Alphabet of Trash.* Illustrated by Sal Murdocca. Racine, Wisc.: Western Publishing Company, Inc./Children's Television Workshop, 1977.

Oscar-the-Grouch, one of Jim Henson's Sesame Street Muppets, shows a collection of objects from his trash can and the nearby surroundings. Similar beginnings announce that *B* is for ———, *C* is for———, and continue through the alphabet. For *E*, Oscar puts eggshells in his bed to have a crummy sleep. For *I*, he makes an icky ice-cream topping of sardines and pickles, and for *P*, sleeps, not with a teddy bear, but with a prickly, patched-up porcupine. Ages 4-up.

Pattern: With capitalization and punctuation, traditional sentences about Oscar-the-Grouch show selected capitalized key nouns and guiding serif capitals.

The Muppet Babies' ABC. Illustrated by Sue Venning. New York: Random House, 1984.

Young admirers of the Muppets will not care if there is no story in this ABC. On each page is a Muppet and a selected word that together introduce each letter. *U* is for Baby Piggy's "umbrella," *V* is for valentines, and *W* is for "water lily," a resting place for

Baby Kermit. Can a child recognize Gonzo and some of the other Muppets? All of the Muppets are small and look young on these pages. Ages 2–4.

Pattern: Capitals are introduced by key words in alphabetical order, which label the objects near the baby Muppets.

Murdocca, Sal. *Grover's Own Alphabet*. Illustrated. Racine, Wisc.: Western Publishing Company, Inc./Children's Television Workshop, 1978.

Grover, another of Jim Henson's Sesame Street Muppets, is the central character in this ABC. With the help of other objects, Grover creates body postures that make the shapes of the letters. Bending his elbow just at the right angle, Grover forms a capital *E* by sitting on the trunk of an elephant. He juggles jam to make a *J* and uses his reflection in a full-length mirror to help himself form the capital *M*. After posturing for the letter *Z*, Grover lies flat on the ground and reminds a young reader that this posture is not a letter—just a tired Grover resting. Explanatory sentences are found at the foot of the pages. Ages 3-up.

Pattern: With narrative writing in ABC progression, Grover's different body postures form letter shapes that match block capitals in colors.

Musgrove, Margaret. *Ashanti to Zulu: African Traditions*. Illustrated by Leo and Diane Dillon. New York: Dial, 1976.

Recommended. Musgrove's words are an informational introduction to different tribes of Africa. Some of the customs and ceremonies of each tribe are presented. In each framed illustration by Leo and Diane Dillon, there is an object unique to the tribe, a regional animal, a family (man, woman, and child), and their home. In the frames, an alert viewer will see the design of the Kano knot, which is explained in the introduction as symbolizing searching without end. A California State Department of Education-recommended core reading. Ages 8-up.

Pattern: Guided by letter sequence, information about twenty-six African tribes introduces tribal names as word choices for descriptive writing.

Ogg, Oscar. *The Twenty Six Letters*. Revised edition. New York: Thomas Y. Crowell Company, 1971.

In this informative book the author traces early humans, their tools, and culture—particularly the development of writing. From the cave drawings in Northern Spain to linotype techniques, Ogg gives an older child several anecdotes and drawings about the twenty-six letters, which should hold a reader's interest. Ages 9-up.

Pattern: Descriptive writing provides anecdotes about the twenty-six letters in our alphabet.

Parker, Nancy Winslow. *The United Nations from A to Z*. Illustrated by the author. New York: Dodd, Mead, 1985.

Parker gives youngsters a straightforward information book arranged with the letters at the foot of each page. *A* is for "Atlantic Charter" and "ambassador." Does an alert older child notice that the term "Atlantic Charter" appears before "ambassador"? The flags of Japan, Kenya, Qatar, and other nations appear in the illustrations. Is any child interested in verifying the information shown by the flags by locating one or more of these flags in another resource and then determining if the symbols, designs, colors, are accurate ones? People are also included. For example, there is Eleanor Roosevelt, one of the important forces behind the United Nations as it was being formed, and John D. Rockefeller, the man who provided the land upon which the buildings of the United Nations stand. In addition, the International Court of Justice, the World Bank, and the World Health Organization, along with several other UN organizations, are discussed. Activities supported by the United Nations International Children's Emergency Fund—the Educational, Scientific and Cultural Organization and the International Telecommunication Union—are presented. Ages 9-12.

Pattern: Descriptive paragraphs about selected people, organizations, and activities of the United Nations are guided by letters in colored inserts in lower corners of pages.

A Peaceable Kingdom: The Shaker Abecedarius. Illustrations by Alice and Martin Provensen. Afterword by Richard Meran Barsam. New York: Viking Press, 1976.

Recommended. Alice and Martin Provensen's presentation has a rhythmic text of twenty-six lines. This ABC is a rhymed verse from the Shaker Manifesto, 1882, and is illustrated. There is a rhythm to the words, a pattern to the lines in the rhyme, and an alphabetical sequence from the first to the last animal. From *alligator* and *beetle*, through *camel* and *chameleon* and *mockingbird*, to *zebra*, there are more than one hundred names of real and fanciful animals to repeat. Some of the nouns may be unfamiliar ones to certain children: *dromedary* (a camel with one hump), *anaconda* (long snake that resembles a python), *pickerel* (fish), *ichneumon* (member of weasel family), and *basilisk* (lizardlike creature with upright scales on back). Is an older child interested in these multisyllable words that rhyme? Can the nouns be sung to the tune of the familiar ABC Song? Can a child find and pronounce a selected two-, three-, or four-syllable word? Indicate the number of syllables in the selected word? A California State Department of Education-recommended extended reading. Ages 8-up.

Pattern: Every rhyming line of this twenty-six line ABC verse begins with a large serif capital in black that introduces name of the first animal to be recited.

Petersham, Maud, and Miska Petersham. *An American ABC*. Illustrated by the authors. New York: Macmillan, 1941.

Recommended. Guided by the alphabetic sequence, illustrated scenes about America's past begin with *A* is for America, *B* is for the Liberty Bell, and *C* is for Christopher Columbus, and initiate this book about America. Each subsequent scene on a recto page faces one page of informative text. Descriptive sentences about certain personalities from history mention Simon Bolivar, Daniel Boone, Henry Hudson, Abraham Lincoln, and George Washington. Although It is possible that some of the text may have limited appeal to today's reader, the full-page illustrations by these award-winning artists should hold the attention of a young researcher. Ages 9-12.

Pattern: Alphabetical collection of scenes and informative text from the history of America is guided by oversize capitals in colors.

Peyo. *The Smurf ABC Book*. Illustrated by the author. New York: Random House, 1983.

Selected activities of the blue Smurfs include reading a book, growing flowers, and using a hammer. Short single sentences on each page introduce the objects, their names, and the letters. With the exception of Azrael, the cat, and Gargamel, the wizard, the objects are inanimate ones. For a review on a final double-page spread, Papa Smurf points to the serif capitals in color. Each object, first seen in a previous illustration, is seen again as it stands beside each reviewed letter. For instance, a young viewer sees that the cat who chases Clumsy Smurf on a previous page can be found again beside the letter *C* in the review chart. Ages 2-up.

Pattern: Key nouns are seen twice, once in the short sentences about Smurfs beneath illustrations and again beside capitals and lowercase letters in corners of pages.

Polansky, Leslie, and Susan Torrence. *The Oregon Alphabet Book.* Illustrated by Susan Torrence. Eugene, Ore.: T. P. Publishing, 1983.

Alliterative patterns of names, places, and activities from Oregon are read in this ABC. For each letter, a reader finds a pattern of words that locate a place, name a character, and identify an occupation or action. In Ashland, Adrian, an actress, stands on the stage of the amphitheater. In Beaverton, Betty, a baker, bakes brown bear cookies. In Coraville, Charlie cooks clam chowder. Some sentences may turn into tongue twisters as they tell about chubby Charlie Chadwick, Hilda Hilton, a hiker, and jumping Jack Jasper. Will a child be interested in saying a tongue twister based on one of the alliterative sentences in this ABC? After repeating the tongue twister, is a child interested in writing alliterative sentences about his or her state, county, or city? Stylized upper-and lowercase letters are found consistently in the corners of the full-color illustrations. The final pages include a review of the letters and a map of Oregon with twenty-six alphabetical places identified. Ages 6-up.

Pattern: Alliterative words in descriptive patterned sentences about Oregon introduce upper- and lowercase letters.

Polansky, Leslie, and Susan Torrence. *The Washington Alphabet Book.* Illustrated by Susan Torrence. Eugene, Ore.: T. P. Publishing, 1983.

The illustrations by Susan Torrence in this ABC feature another alliterative text by Leslie Polansky. The text gives a short episodic and alphabetic happening for each letter. *A* is Arnold Arbuckle, an Aberdeen angler. To admire some ancient angelfish, Arnold stops his rowboat and adjusts the anchor. On the *O* page a rowboat full of pink pigs play musical instruments. The pigs are an "orchestra of oinkers" led by Odessa Osinsky. In a zoo at Zillah, Zazu uses a bow and some arrows made of zucchini to zoom zucchini to a zebu. A final alphabet, with both upper- and lowercase letters, provides a concluding review. The culminating illustration is a map of the state of Washington with all of the alphabetical cities that were mentioned in the episodes identifed. Ages 6-up.

Pattern: Each letter of the alphabet is introduced by a full-color illustration and alliterative words in descriptive patterned text about Washington.

Price, Barbara Pradal. *Ancient Egypt from A to Z.* Illustrated by Paulita Sedgwick. New York: Bobbs-Merrill, 1971.

Price's book is useful for an overview of Egypt in ancient times. From the artists and architects of these historical times to Zoser, a Third Dynasty pharaoh who built the first step-pyramid in layers, this ABC has words that reflect different aspects of ancient Egypt. For each letter there are Egyptian equivalents of the alphabet, or symbols, at the heads of pages. Knowledge of the English sounds for the alphabet help a child match them to the Egyptian symbols and to the patterns found in the Egyptian hieroglyphs in the book. Is a reader interested in searching for certain symbols and then writing his or her own name in Egyptian hieroglyphs? Word choices such as "Pyramids," "Queens," and "Religion," are shown in hieroglyphs. In the informative text on each page, more hieroglyphs are inserted to translate certain words. As a reader recognizes the English sounds for the Egyptian symbols, the Egyptian words may be pronounced. Accompanying illustrations are based on findings from monuments, papyrus scripts, and tombs. Ages 10-up.

Pattern: With descriptive writing, each letter of the alphabet is introduced by an aspect of ancient Egypt discussed in informative text.

Rice, James. *Cajun Alphabet*. Illustrated by the author. Gretna, La.: Pelican Publishing Company, 1976.

Gaston, a green-nosed alligator, gives a child a Cajun French lesson with verses and colored sketches. With his alphabet book held upside down, Gaston begins to read and surprises some children as they find they know some of the words in Cajun French. Does a child recognize armadillo and bayou ? More than one hundred words and phrases about such objects as a zapote, a hard wooden shoe, Jean Laffite's map, and yammes present information about Cajun society, language, and culture. Ages advanced 8-up.

Pattern: Traditional phrases of *A* is for————and *B* is for———— begin rhyming lines that give meanings to Cajun French key words.

Rice, James. *Cowboy Alphabet: For Grown Ups and Young 'Uns Too*. Illustrated by the author. Austin, Tex.: Shoal Creek Publishers, 1977.

For the older child who is interested in what can be seen and done in life in the West, Rice selects key words associated with cowboys and cowgirls. Large block letters in color are centered on the pages and introduce such words as a "bronc," a "dogie," and a "greenhorn." Also in color, small serif letters begin the sentences that describe each word choice: a horse who can shake the kinks out of you (bronc); a four-legged animal that can be stubborn (dogie); and a new cowboy with little know-how (greenhorn). Ages Advanced 8-up.

Pattern: Similar beginning phrases such as *A* is for————and *B* is for————lead to descriptive sentences about life in the West.

Reed, Giles, compiler. *Learn the Alphabet With the Munch Bunch*. Illustrated by Angela Mitson. New York: Rand McNally and Company, 1981.

Mitson's full-color illustrations show Billy Blackberry, Olly Onion, Pedro Orange, and the other Munch Bunch characters in different settings. A child sees Reed's variety of objects on each page along with the selected letter. At the beach, can a young viewer find the bucket, boat, basket or ball? Concluding pages include key words for *ch, sh,* and *th.* With these last three choices, a listener hears that sometimes consonants are blended together to represent a sound different from any of the single letters. A review of all of the upper- and lowercase letters in the alphabet is seen on a final page. Ages 2-up.

Pattern: Objects introduce names, capitals, and lowercase letters in bright blue on each page.

Sloan, Alan, Incorporated, and Sea World Press. *The Sea World Alphabet Book.* New York: Harcourt Brace Jovanovich, 1980.

Information about marine life from alligators and beluga to yellowtail and zooplankton is found in this ABC. Capitals and lowercase letters in colors are seen on every page and guide the sequence of each rhyming couplet. Similar beginnings lead into the rhyming lines with *C* is for——and *D* is for——. Full-color photographs illustrate the descriptive text. The reader discovers that coral is a group of tiny sea skeletons, a hermit crab has no shell, and a manatee likes to eat weeds. Each word choice is identified in the lines in bold type, making the words easy to see. In this book, a pattern of rhyme presents words and meanings to a young child in the context of couplets. For example, only one sentence is needed to mention "slithery snakes" as a way of defining the key word for *E,* "eels." Additional animals are described in context—e.g., flamingos have long necks and bent bills, while gulls, the birds with sad-sounding cries, can float on the waves. Ages 4–9.

Pattern: Rhyming lines with repetitive beginnings and word choices in bold type introduce block capitals and lowercase letters in colors.

Sloane, Eric. *ABC Book of Early Americana: A Sketchbook of Antiguities and American Firsts.* Illustrated by the author. New York: Doubleday and Company, Inc., 1963.

If a child respects the skills of dedicated craftsmen and craftswomen, the reader will appreciate Sloane's work with its penciled sketches, hand-lettered ABCs, and the descriptions of early American realia. Beginning with the almanac and ending with a zigzag fence, all of the sketched choices are pleasing to the eye: hex sign, johnny cake, niddy-noddy, and quill pen. After seeing Sloane's hand-lettered alphabet, is a child interested in creating an original hand-lettered alphabet for an ABC of modern America? An ABC of the eighties? An ABC of the nineties? Ages 8-up.

Pattern: Descriptive writing about early American objects and pencil sketches introduce a hand-lettered alphabet.

Tasker, James. *African Treehouse*. Illustrated by Kathleen Elgin. New York: Harvey House, 1973.

Tasker's pronunciation guide from aardvark (ARD' vark) to zebras (ZEE' bras) introduces the African animals. Each double-page spread is devoted to drawings and verses about the animals. A child gains information read about the koodoo, with large curling horns; the nyala, a blue-gray antelope, and the quagga, a zebralike animal with some gray stripes. Ages 6–8.

Pattern: For each African animal one repetitive sentence introduces a rhyming verse and presents the animal's name as a key word in boldface capitals.

Travers, P. L. *Mary Poppins from A to Z*. Illustrated by Mary Shephard. New York: Harcourt, Brace and World, Inc., 1962.

For older children is Travers's book, an alphabet with short stories about the Banks family. With Shephard's full-page sketches, the illustrations are as pleasant as the text. The short stories emphasize the letters in sequence by capitalizing the selected letter wherever it is found in a one-page story. For example, *A* is for Annabel and *A* is for words such as" Airing," "Asking" and "Against," ones found capitalized within the sentences. Does the child notice this capitalization pattern? On the *T* page everything is "Topsy-Turvy." Mary Poppins "Twirls" through the air like a "Turning Top" and lands on her head. The children turn "Topsy-Turvy," too. This ABC story and the others have additional stylized capitals at the heads of the pages. Each story has a familiar beginning segment: *B* is for——and *C* is for——. Ages 7–9.

Pattern: Narrative writing of one-page stories and full-page sketches are guided by stylized capitals in sequence.

Travers, P. L. *Mary Poppins in the Kitchen: A Cookery Book with a Story.* Illustrated by Mary Shephard. New York: Harcourt Brace Jovanovich, 1975.

For this ABC presentation, Travers collaborates with Mary Shephard, the illustrator of the original story, and with Maurice Moore-Betty, a culinary consultant. In this one, Mary Poppins teaches the Banks children how to prepare three meals a day and how to be safe in the kitchen. Admiral Boom and other familiar characters appear throughout the cookbook story to help and keep the story line progressing. Beginning with angel cake for *A* and finishing with zodiac cake for *Z*, all of the recipes are ones that a child can easily prepare. Ages 6-up.

Pattern: With recipes arranged from *A* to *Z*, expository writing has an ABC progression within narrative frame.

Weinberg, Lawrence. *Learn with E. T.: The ABC's.* Illustrated by Jody Wheeler. New York: Simon and Schuster, Inc., 1982.

Weinberg's alphabet has upper- and lowercase letters and illustrative words at the foot of each page. Small framed pictures show E. T. in each scene. *A* is for alien and *Z* is for zooming home. Each time the selected letter appears in a word, the letter is underlined. As one example using *Aa,* a young viewer sees that *A* is the capital letter in "An," the word that begins the phrase; that *A* is the first letter in the word "alien" within the sentence; and that *A* holds a medial position in the word, "space." Ages 5-up.

Pattern: Capitalized phrases and words carry underlined letters to emphasize selected guiding letters.

Views of Others

Anglund, Joan Walsh. *A Is for Always: An ABC Book.* Illustrated by the author. New York: Harcourt, Brace and World, Inc., 1968.

This title, and the others that follow, are associated with the topic of the points of view of others. In this alphabet Anglund directs the reader toward qualities to be achieved and maintained as the child grows. One oversize capital *A* is the center of a scene that shows one small child using a feather duster to dust around the toys found on shelves formed by the shape of the capital *E.* The next letter, *F*, is for fearless and shows one child who hangs by his knees from the arm of the letter. *G* is for generous and here another child shares a wedge of cheese with a nearby mouse. A boy or girl is reminded to show certain other behaviors and be obedient, kind, and mannerly. Pink uppercase letters are the focal points for all of the scenes of children. The word choices and pairs of uppper- and lowercase letters appear below the small scenes. Ages 4–6.

Pattern: Large capital letters are introduced by word choices that direct a child to complete reminders formed by the first two key words, "Always be———."

Belloc, Hilaire. *A Moral Alphabet: In Words of from One to Seven Syllables.* Illustrated by Basil T. Blackwood. Chelmsford, Eng.: Tindal Press, 1974.

First published in 1899 for older children who can appreciate the morals and humorous verse, here is included nonsense. These are verbal plays upon the morals popular during the time of Belloc's writings. Bits of daily life from the 1800s (*J* is for James, who thought it immaterial to pay his taxes, and met the tax collector with repartee) may have historical interest for adults but probably will have limited appeal for today's girls and boys. For *A*, Honest Archibald receives a book for a prize, and an accompanying moral about learning to brush your hair is offered from this irritating youth. *B* is for bear, the brave heroes who face the bear, and their decisive action to escape in their hour of need. Ages advanced 8-up.

Pattern: Small serif capitals in black introduce repetitive openings and rhymes with morals.

Berry, Cindi C. *Bible Alphabet Book.* Illustrated by Jack Gehring. Cincinnati: Standard Publishing Co., 1981.

Berry's alphabet book introduces some of the biblical personages. *N* is for Noah, *X* is for Xerxes, and *Y* is for the many years of Methuselah. In this paperback edition there is a letter-paragraph-picture arrangement for each selection. Ages 6-up.

Pattern: Each pair of upper- and lowercase cursive letters introduces a personage from the Bible in a descriptive paragraph.

Burgess, Gelett. *Goop Tales Alphabetically Told: A Study of the Behavior of Some Fifty-two Interesting Individuals, Each of Which While Mainly Virtuous, Yet Has Some One Human and Redeeming Fault.* Illustrated. New York: Dover Publications, Inc., 1973.

In this reprint of an ABC of verses, each child has one vice and many virtues. For example, Abednego (named because to bed he could not go) is neat, smiles, and does not cheat. Zelphinia (who thinks of herself only) always obeys any rule taught in her home or school. Each child is introduced alphabetically by name in serif capitals in bold type. Ages advanced 8-up.

Pattern: Guiding serif capitals in bold type are introduced by children's names and accompanying verses in sequence.

Ciardi, John. *An Alphabestiary.* Illustrated by Milton Hebald. New York: J. B. Lippincott Company, 1966.

In this ABC, Ciardi encourages a reader to watch an animal to see what the animal tells the reader about people. Selections include choices such as a nannygoat who loves a billygoat, a porcupine who yields his points when pressed (a typical play on words), and two rats who go aboard Noah's ark. For each animal in this bestiary, there is a moral to read in the rhyming verses. Ages advanced 8-up.

Pattern: Each guiding letter matches initial letter in the name of an animal described in rhyming verses with morals.

DeLage, Ida. *The ABC Christmas.* Illustrated by Roger Beerworth. Champaign, Ill.: Garrard Publishing Company, 1978.

The ABC Christmas has full-color holiday scenes by Roger Beerworth. *D* is for Daddy, who reads a holiday story; *S* is for Santa's sack; and *N* is for the written note that the children leave for Santa Claus. Key words are in capitals in boldface and found a second time in the text beneath each illustration. Ages 6-up.

Pattern: Illustrations of Christmas introduce guiding capitals and key words in capitals seen in boldface.

DeLage, Ida. *ABC Santa Claus.* Illustrated by Judith Gwyn Brown. Champaign, Ill.: Garrard Publishing Company, 1978.

Holiday scenes are in full color. The elves add oil to the toy trains for *O*. They paint toys for *P* and sing carols as Santa plays the music on a violin for *M*. Both capitals and word choices in capitals are seen in boldface. Key words are repeated again in the text beneath the illustrations. Ages 6-up.

Pattern: Actions of Santa's elves identify word choices and guiding letters found in capitals and in boldface type.

Downs, Kathy. *My ABC Zoo Book.* Photography by Robert Cushman Hayes. Cincinnati: Standard Publishing Company/ Standex International Corporation, 1983.

In alphabetical order twenty-six animals are reviewed by Lori's family through a trip to the zoo. The text points out that God made the animals, that God gave a baby elephant a mother that loves her, and that God gave the owl his big eyes to see in the dark. Additional information is given about each animal and is inserted over full-color illustrations. *A* is for the alpaca with a shaggy fur coat, *B* is for a bear swimming in the water, and *C* is for the camel with its strong legs and padded feet for desert living. Upper- and lowercase serif letters in either white or black are found in the corners of the illustrations. Ages 4-up.

Pattern: Narrative writing and full-color photographs of zoo animals introduce key words, accompanying capitals, and lowercase letters.

Duvoisin, Roger. *A for the Ark.* Illustrated by the author. New York: Lothrop, 1952.

Recommended. In Duvoisin's retelling about the ark that Noah built, the animals enter the ark in alphabetical order. The manuscript-style letters are in bold type through the sentences. In addition, large colorful serif capitals emphasize the sequence. The accumulated letters are shown periodically in sequence. A boy or girl sees that an alphabetical arrangement helps one tell a story. After the rains stop and the ark comes to rest on the ground, the animals whose names begin with *Z* are now the first to leave the ark. In this retracing, a child identifies the names of the animals from Z to A. Ages 6–8.

Pattern: With retracing, black capitals and word choices in black are found in ABC sequence within the sentences about Noah and the ark.

Gorey, Edward. *The Eclectic Abecedarium.* Illustrated by the author. New York: Adama Books, 1983.

Underneath each one of the small black-and-white drawings is a short couplet. Best suited for adults or an older sophisticated student, these words hold meanings beyond those first thought of by the reader. For instance, what does it take to move a fan? Elan. When should one find tasks to do? In a queue. While there are no letters to show the alphabetical sequence, the capitals in the words—e.g., "Alms," "Bird," "Crumbs," guide the arrangement. Ages 13-adult.

Pattern: Sophisticated rhyming couplets introduce selected words that are presented in the alphabetical sequence.

Kramer, Janice. *Christmas ABC Book.* Illustrated by Don Pallarito. St. Louis: Concordia Publishing House, 1965.

A is for angel, *B* is for Bethlehem, and *C* is for child on the opening pages of this alphabet book. Capitals in colors and rhyming couplets are inserted over the full-page illustrations in full color (a decorated tree, the wrapped presents) for a child interested in seeing and hearing about Christian values. Ages 5–6.

Pattern: Uppercase letters, some serif and some sans serif, are introduced by rhyming couplets and key words about Christmas shown in capitals in bold type.

Lalicki, Barbara, compiler. *If There Were Dreams to Sell.* Illustrated by Margot Tomes. New York: Lothrop, Lee and Shepard, 1984.

Recommended. A complete verse from Mother Goose, or a phrase from a poem such as Longfellow's *The Village Blacksmith*, and an illustration accompany each serif capital and lowercase letter in black located in the page corners. There are selections by others, too—Coleridge, Dickinson, Keats, and Donne. The choice for *B* is bee and Dickenson's words about a bee's experience. *E* stands for elves and Pope's words from *The Rape of the Lock*. A Teachers' Choice from the National Council of Teachers of English. Ages 6-up.

Pattern: Guiding uppercase and lowercase letters in black are emphasized by capitalized key words and selected lowercase words in lyrical selections.

Larson, Rayola Cramer. *Alphabet Talk*. Illustrated by Lucille R. Perry. Bountiful, Utah: Horizon Publishers, 1980.

From *A* is for angels and *B* is for baptism to *Y* is for young and *Z* is for Zion, a child finds a picture and a rhyme for each guiding capital. Each word choice is capitalized in bold type. At the foot of each page is an accompanying explanatory paragraph for every key word. Along with the letters *LDS* on the cover, the Latter Day Saints orientation is seen in such choices as *J* for "Joseph" (first prophet), *M* for "missionaries" (who preach the gospel and go two by two), and *T* is for "temples" (places to do eternal things). Ages 7-up.

Pattern: With stylized capitals in black and informative paragraphs, key words in capitals in bold type are found in rhymes.

Lisowski, Gabriel. *On the Little Heart: Word and Music for the Popular Yiddish Classic, Oif'N Pripitchik*. Illustrated by the author. New York: Holt, Rinehart and Winston, 1978.

Recommended. During the troubled times for the Jewish people of eastern Europe, this lullaby was sung. With the music by Mark Warshawski, the words tell of hope and coping and being strong. Ages 6 up.

Pattern: The lyrics and rhythm of a lullaby present sounds of the Yiddish language and symbols of Judaism.

Rosenberger, Francis Coleman. *An Alphabet*. Charlottesville: University Press of Virginia, 1978.

Guided by large, colorful serif capitals, Rosenberger's epigrammatic poetry is arranged from "Able was I" for *A* to "Zebu,

Zed, Zen" for Z. These poems are short, concise, pointed, and satirical. Each poem addresses a single thought or event and usually ends with a witticism. For instance, *T* is for Truman. Harry Truman, a former U. S. president, is seen as quite human and then compared to other statesmen. *H* is for Shirley Hazzard and her comment about novelty often being confused with quality. One final page contains the poet's notes about each one of the epigrams. For example, Hazzard's comment is credited to *The New York Times Book Review.* Ages 14-adult.

Pattern: Poems about single events, people, or their thoughts conclude with witticisms.

Stifle, J. M. *ABC Book About Christmas.* Illustrations from Arch Books Series, Concordia Publishing House. St. Louis: Concordia Publishing House, 1981.

The story of the Nativity is told page by page. Each page presents a letter, personage, or place. Serif capitals in color are centered on the pages and begin traditional phrases—e.g., *X* is for——, *Y* is for——, and *Z* is for——. Explanatory paragraphs follow the phrases. The choices of key words include "Chi-Rho," "Emmanuel," and "Messiah." Framed, full-color illustrations are seen. Ages 7-up.

Pattern: Similar introductory phrases for the letters include serif capitals and capitalized word choices.

Taylor, Kenneth N. *Big Thoughts for Little People: ABC's to Help You Grow.* Illustrated by Kathryn E. Shoemaker. Wheaton, Ill.: Tyndale House Publishers, Inc., 1983.

Values of Christian living such as courtesy and good manners are emphasized in this ABC. On each double-page spread, the colorful serif capital is illuminated with small objects whose names begin with the letter. Some key words mention such negative behaviors as lying, quarreling, and yelling. For each letter there are questions for a child to answer and a Bible verse to learn. In each illustration is a visual challenge. There are hiding ladybugs to seek and additional objects to locate whose names begin with the selected letter. Ages 7-up.

Pattern: Serif capitals precede explanatory sentences, questions, accompanying illustrations, and Bible verses to memorize.

Tobutt, Christine. *The Christmas Story Alphabet Frieze*. Illustrated by Margaret Chamberlain. Belleville, Mich.: Lion Publishing Company, 1984.

In this alphabet are four pull-out panels that show a full-color alphabet about the Christmas story. *C* is for camels that carried the wise men, *F* is for fields where the shepherds looked after their sheep, and *W* is for the wise men who watched for the star. Ages 5-up.

Pattern: With oversize guiding letters and initial letters of word choices in red, traditional beginnings of sentences, such as *A* is for——show capitalization and punctuation.

Van Stockum, Hilda. *The Angel's Alphabet*. Illustrated by the author. New York: Macmillan, 1948.

Beginning with *A* for angels and archangels, Van Stockum's verses face illustrated recto pages. Pen-and-ink sketches illustrate the friendly morals and are in black-and-white. Van Stockum's six children helped write this alphabet. Cherubim is for *C* and dominations (other angels with swords) stands for *D*. *O* is for obedience—e.g., looking before crossing the street, cleaning the ears, keeping shoes on, eating supper, and being careful of small things. One verse is a pledge that all chicks and puppies will be safe, that captive birds shall be set free, and that the reader will watch where he or she walks to avoid harming small insects. There is an emphasis on being kind, on recognizing the battle of good against evil, and on sharing with others. Ages 5-up.

Pattern: Rhyming verses offer titles as key words to identify illuminated capitals.

Watson, Jane Werner. *ABC Is for Christmas*. Illustrated by Sally Augustiny. Racine, Wisc.: Western Publishing Company, Inc., 1974.

Full-page and full-color illustrations in this holiday alphabet show such scenes as angels ringing a golden bell, an elf constructing a dollhouse, and Santa Claus driving his sleigh. Several scenes and key word choices refer to the Nativity and services at a church. Other pictures show home activities such as quiet times, opening presents, and trimming a tree. Still other settings are outside ones—

e.g., carolers singing, skiing in the snow, and visiting a snow-capped village by bus. With capitals and lowercase letters in colors inserted over the illustrations, does a child associate *K* for kings with *W* for wise men in these two illustrations? For every letter each rhyming couplet begins with an opening similar to *A* is for ————. Ages 4- up.

Pattern: With capitals and lowercase letters in colors inserted over the illustrations, lines with similar beginnings include key words and rhymes linked across two or more pages.

Wersba, Barbara. *Twenty-six Starlings Will Fly Through Your Mind*. Illustrated by David Palladini. New York: Harper and Row, 1980.

Emily is learning to read, and the alphabet, with *A* in the lead, shows Emily different images. *B* is searching for butterflies, *C* is for the moon's cousin, and *D* is for dancers and dreams. Each stylized capital is inserted into its appropriate illustration and is seen again in an accompanying verse. Wearing a clown's hat, one *M* rides a merry-go-round and waves to *N*. *O* reflects the shape of the moon. A single *T* stands on a beach and holds wires for telegram messages. There are characters to meet and events to see for every letter. Ages 10-up.

Pattern: Each stylized capital is accompanied by images created by poetic words.

Whitehead, Pat. *Christmas Alphabet Book*. Illustrated by Deborah Colvin Borgo. Mahwah, N.J.: Troll Associates, 1985.

In the *Christmas Alphabet Book*, Santa is late beginning his trip around the world. During his trip a child is introduced to the letters. *H* is for "hurry." *I* is for "instant" and *J* is for "jiffy." *M* is for "a million things" Santa must do. Pairs of capitals and lowercase letters and word choices are consistently found in the upper corners of the pages. A word-for-word cassette is available for a read-along time. Ages 3–7.

Pattern: Capitals, lowercase letters, and key words are introduced in progressive story format and follow the forward movement of the sequence.

Ways We See Things

Adler, David A. *Finger Spelling Fun*. Illustrated by Dennis Kendrick. New York: Franklin Watts, 1980.

In this section, several alphabet books, such as Adler's, show different ways for a child to see symbols of language. Here a black-and-white illustration shows the finger-spelling sign for each capital letter. To encourage a child to see the signs and their usefulness, Adler includes several activities. A young viewer is invited to send a message, to answer several riddles in signs, and to participate in a spelling bee with finger spelling. Ages 7-up.

Pattern: Each letter is introduced with an appropriate finger spelling sign.

Alda, Arlene. *Arlene Alda's ABC: A New Way of Seeing*. Illustrated by the author. Millbrae, Calif.: Celestial Arts/Dawne-Leigh Book, 1981.

Alda points out that certain objects in the world around us resemble letters. Recognizing such objects can be a visual game for a young boy or girl. Alda shows objects from the environment in striking, clear photographs, and each photograph shows a shape of a letter as it may be found in a child's surroundings. For instance, the shape of *M* is seen in the lines of a peaked roof. One round headlight reflects the shape of the letter *O*. The shape of *X* is shown by the entwining of two slender tree trunks. Accompanying capitals and lowercase serif letters stand beside full-color illustrations. Is the young viewer ready to see similarities in like shapes of letters? Can the child relate a lowercase letter to an uppercase one? Is the child able to see the differences in unlike letters? Ages 5-up.

Pattern: Selected objects in the environment resemble alphabet letters and introduce black or white upper- and lowercase serif letters.

Anno, Mitsumasa. *Anno's Alphabet: An Adventure in Imagination*. Illustrated by the author. New York: Thomas Y. Crowell Company, 1975.

Recommended. Anno shows a child the way letter shapes are seen when cut from wood. Wood blocks and cut shapes form the letters in this imaginative ABC. The margins present additional objects. A child discriminates visually to determine what is unusual about each of the letter shapes. A child may predict the names of the other objects on the pages. For verification there is a guide that gives the names of the objects that are found. A California state Department of Education-recommended recreational reading. Ages 5–8.

Pattern: Each central letter-shape is emphasized by objects whose names can be predicted and verified.

Asch, Frank. *Little Devil's ABC*. Illustrated by the author. New York: Charles Scribner's Sons, 1979.

Capitals are introduced in several ways. First, each capital consistently is seen, patterned, and decorated in the corner of the page. Second, each capital leads to additional words and illustrations. Each key word is labeled and illustrated, too, and each illustration carries the text of a short episode. A finger-spelling sign appears for each letter. Ages 6–9.

Pattern: To introduce patterned capitals there are illustrated key words, finger spellings, and short episodes.

Balian, Lorna. *Humbug Potion: An ABC Cipher*. Illustrated by the author. Nashville: Abingdon Press, 1984.

Balian uses numeral symbols along with letters to communicate meaning. Balian asks a child to decipher a magic beauty potion for a homely witch. The recipe is written in a secret code: *A* is 1, *B* is 2, and so on. At the foot of each page a child finds directions. A child looks at the numerals on the end pages to find a correlating letter and writes needed words. Replacing each numeral with a letter of the alphabet, a child breaks the code. In one example Balian directs a child to add an old house 11-5-25 to the potion. Each decoded word is the key word for the object (eggs, urn, key) and the selected letter on the page. The end pages show all of the letters and their matching numbers for the code. Several patterns challenge a child's observation skills. First there is the pattern of replacing each numeral with a letter to decipher the word. Next there is a pattern of accumulation in the detailed clutter that gathers and increases around the witch's cauldron. A pattern also exists in the small subplots that involve the same characters on each page—the hovering cat, the small mice, and the helping crow. The child notices their actions from page to page. Ages 7–9.

Pattern: Narrative writing in ABC progression, accumulation, subplots, and deciphering a number code emphasize the letters.

Barry, Katharina. *A Is for Anything: An ABC Book of Pictures and Rhymes*. Illustrated by the author. New York: Harcourt, Brace and World, 1961.

In Barry's illustrations a selected letter is used as a part of the sketching pattern to form an object whose label begins with the selected letter. For example, the letter *T* is repeated many times to form a railroad track for the engine of a train, and the letter *L* in a series makes the mane of a lion. Ages 7-up.

Pattern: With rhyme, shapes of letters are included in sketches of objects the names of which begin with the guiding letters.

Beisner, Monica. *A Folding Alphabet Book*. Illustrated by the author. New York: Farrar, Straus and Giroux, 1979.

Beisner's couplets in rhyme introduce the objects that shape themselves into letters. After a boy or girl reads about an elephant that is strong or about flags flying all day long, the child turns over this folding book to see the object take a letter's shape. One elephant sits up with its outstretched trunk; the trunk and the rest of the elephant's body-shape form the letter *E*. For the letter *F*, a child sees two bright purple flags flying outward from the poles to make the shape of *F*. In this arrangement, can a child recognize the letter shapes in a series of pictures from left to right? Ages 4–6.

Pattern: In descriptive couplets with rhyming words, key objects take the shapes of letters found in illustrations.

Bonini, Marinella. *I Can Be the Alphabet*. Illustrated by the author. New York: Viking Kestrel, 1987.

Bonini gives children easy directions about how to bend or turn their bodies to form the letters of the alphabet. For the letter *A*, a child bends over at the waist, folds his or her arms across the front of the knees, and moves the feet apart to show how the shape can be formed with body posture. With full-color illustrations, the small pages of this ABC unfold in an accordion format, making it easy for a child to display the sequence in a room at home or in a classroom environment. Ages 2–6.

Pattern: Body postures introduce letters.

Bourke, Linda. *Handmade ABC: A Manual Alphabet.* Illustrated by the author. Reading, Mass.: Addison-Wesley, 1981.

Each guiding letter of Bourke's alphabet appears in a textured, black-and-white illustration along with objects the names of which begin with the letter. Recto pages show the finger positions for the signs for letters. Verso pages present the guiding letters and show objects in borders. Scallops introduces the letter S, which has the most objects to identify: stitches, stars, stripes, and scar. Six letters (*D*, *J*, *Q*, *U*, *X*, and *Y*) are accompanied by single objects (diamonds, jewelery, quilt, unbuttoned, X ray, and yarn). On two final pages is a list of the capitals and the names that identify the objects. Ages 4-up.

'Pattern: With finger spelling, guiding letters appear as capitals on pages with illustrated objects the names of which begin with appropriate letters.

Bove, Linda. *Sign Language ABC.* Illustrated by Tom Cooke. Prepared in cooperation with the National Theater of the Deaf. New York: Random House/Children's Television Workshop, 1985.

With Jim Henson's Sesame Street Muppets, this ABC introduces a child to sign language, an expressive way to communicate. Word choices express actions, feelings, and concepts such as opposites. Each guiding letter appears as both a capital and a lowercase letter in black on a single page. There is a color photograph of Bove signing the letter, along with clearly labeled photographs of Bove signing additional words beginning with the guiding letter. For *A*, Bove signs the words for airplane, alligator, and apple. Arrows on the pictures show a child how to move hands or fingers. Muppet characters dramatize the words in an accompanying full-color drawing—e.g., Ernie is the pilot of a pink biwing plane, and an alligator, eating an apple, is the a copilot.

More of Linda Bove's finger-spelling signs are seen in *Sesame Street Sign Language Fun* (Random House/Children's Television Workshop, 1980). In this one, signs for the letters of the alphabet are found in full-color photographs on the endpapers, while signs for opposites, actions, and feelings are introduced in the body of the book. Ages 4–8.

Pattern: Each letter appears in both capital and lowercase forms in black on a single page along with signs for words, labeled photographs of the words, and a Muppet drawing.

Chaplin, Susan. *I Can Sign My ABC's*. Illustrated by Laura McCaul. Washington D. C., Gallaudet College Press, 1986.

This hardcover book holds full-color illustrations. Each verso page contains a sign for a letter in the alphabet and an ABC frieze with the guiding letter in blue. Each recto page shows a child with the key object and word. Ages 2–6.

Pattern: Letter-object-hand sign arrangement.

Charlip, Remy, and Mary Beth Miller. *Handtalk: An ABC of Finger Spelling and Sign Language*. Illustrated by George Ancona. New York: Four Winds Press/Scholastic, 1974.

Here is an introduction to two ways in which a child can see language. First, there is finger spelling, the way boys and girls can see words that are formed letter by letter with the fingers. Second, there is signing, the way children see the signs that are made with the hands to show whole words such as "Hello" or an idea such as "gigantic" or "enormous." Each letter appears on a double-page spread along with photographs of the finger positions for the letter, the spelling of a key word, and the sign or signs for another word choice. For instance, for *B*, a child sees how to make the letter in finger spelling, how to spell a key word, "butter," and how to sign the name for bug. A California State Department of Education-recommended core reading. Ages 7-up.

Pattern: Each serif capital in black or white appears consistently in the corners of the double-page spreads along with photographs of gestures that show finger spellings and signings of word choices.

Coletta, Irene, and Hallie Coletta. *From A to Z: The Collected Letters of Irene and Hallie Coletta.* Illustrated by Hallie Colletta. Englewood Cliffs, N.J.: Prentice-Hall, Inc., 1979.

Recommended. In the Coletta's alphabet a child sees rebus rhymes. A viewer is asked to identify the pictures to get clues for the rhymes. A rhyme about a horsehoe crab (xiphosuran) introduces the letter *X*. Rhyming Words about an acrobat introduces the letter *A*, about a baker introduces *B*, and about a camel introduces *C*. Ages 6-up.

Pattern: Each rebus rhyme about an alphabetical object introduces a letter.

Craig, Helen. *The Mouse House ABC.* Illustrated by the author. New York: Random House, 1979.

Craig's tiny alphabet book with its slipcase and small pages presents illustrations showing upper- and lowercase serif letters in the corners. Mice pose near, on, and around objects that take the shapes of letters. With blue yarn two mice knit the shape of the letter *J*, nibble on cheese formed in the shape of a *D*, and nail boards together to form the letter *N*. Ages 4-6.

Pattern: Shapes of letters are introduced by tiny mice and their interaction with objects in their surroundings.

Davar, Ashok. *Talking Words: A Unique Alphabet Book.* Illustrated by the author. New York: Bobbs-Merrill, 1969.

In this alphabet, Davar selects nouns for the alphabetic sequence and lets each noun provide a clue about what the word names by illustrating the clue. To show a child what the word "leopard" labels, there are spots on the letters in the word. Each letter in the word "king" wears a crown and the first *E* in the word "elephant" has an elephant's trunk. What additional words can a child select to illustrate with visual clues? Is the child ready to identify an attribute of an object and then draw that attribute in the object's name? Ages 7-8.

Pattern: For each letter, a word gives a clue about what the word means by the way the word looks on the page.

Dowdell, Dorothy. *Secrets of the ABC's*. Illustrated by Marilue Johnson. Fayetteville, Ga.: Oddo Publishing, 1965.

Large block capitals in black are introduced with short explanations about how our letters began to take shape. Each letter of the alphabet became a letter in a different way. *A* began as a drawing of the head of an ox, *B* began as a picture word and was a floor plan of a house, and *C* was first drawn to look like the head and the neck of a camel. With these examples, and others, a young viewer sees the ways that other people have looked at the alphabet symbols. Full-color illustrations and examples of past ways that each letter was written are included. Ages 7-up.

Pattern: Full-color illustrations and repetitive beginnings— e.g., I am *A*, I am *B*—begin explanatory sentences about each letter and show ways each evolved into its present form.

Edens, Cooper. *A Phenomenal Alphabet Book*. Illustrated by Joyce Eide. La Jolla, Calif.: Green Tiger Press, 1982.

With plays on words, Edens tells an imaginative story about magic weeks during a visit at the seashore. The words the reader finds in the text are literally and visually shown in a facing illustration. During these magical weeks a prizewinning eggplant is seen. The illustration shows gaily colored eggs at the top of a large green plant. A single ladder reaches up to the nearest eggs. One evening, a mystery (miss-tree) is encountered. The face of a golden-haired miss peeks from the foliage of a tall green tree. Traveling to the airport, a U-turn is made. In the picture a white woolly ewe pulls a cart along a U-shaped road. Ages 7-up.

Pattern: Narrative writing in ABC progression with selected words in color and visual identification of their interpretation in the illustrations.

Emberley, Ed. *Ed Emberley's ABC*. Boston: Little, Brown, 1978.

Recommended. In this interesting alphabet an activity of an animal begins in the first scene, continues in the second and third scenes to form part of a letter's shape, and ends in a fourth one as the total shape of a selected letter. For example, to show the formation of the capital *E* in manuscript, one large elephant selects three white eggs with his trunk and begins to arrange them on a carpet. The arrangement builds in the second and third scene. In the fourth a child sees a capital *E* formed from the arrangement of the eggs. Underneath the last scene is the key word, "ELE-PHANT," in capitals. The capital letter *E* is emphasized in blue. This alphabet is useful for a child's visual conceptualization of the formation of the capital letters in manuscript. Ages 6–7.

Pattern: Capitals and key words in capitals are introduced by animals and their actions, which form letter shapes.

Fisher, Leonard Everett. *Alphabet Art: Thirteen ABCs from Around the World.* Illustrated by the author. New York: Four Winds Press, 1978.

These thirteen alphabets show different symbols, the various ways that people write language. Among them is a flowing rhythm in the Arabic characters, a variety of symbols for the syllable sounds of the Cherokee language, and the many Chinese characters that can represent either complete ideas, total words, or sounds of syllables. In contrast to the visual flow of the Arabic characters, a group of angles, arcs, circles, and lines shows the Eskimo symbols that represent sounds and combinations in language. To show the useful flexibility of the Japanese symbols, Katakama (one of the two syllabaries used in Japan) also is presented. In addition, Devanagari, an alphabet for Sanskrit literature and the alphabetic ancestor to the altered Thai and Tibetan alphabets, is shown. Ages 7-up.

Pattern: For each of thirteen alphabets there is a brief introduction and a reproduction of the characters in use today. Characters are in color with English equivalents and pronunciation guides.

Freeman, Don. *Add-a-Line Alphabet.* Illustrated by the author. San Carlos, Calif.: Golden Gate Junior Books, 1968.

Each bright red capital in Freeman's alphabet receives added lines and takes the shape of an animal. The letter *A* is the basis for an anteater, a *B* becomes a bear, and a *C* is a sleeping cat. As capitals in red manuscript, the letters in the alphabet are reviewed again on a concluding page. Ages 7-up.

Pattern: With the addition of lines, each large capital turns into the shape of an animal.

Fuller, Catherine Leuthold. *Beasts: An Alphabet of Fine Prints.* Illustrated. Boston: Little, Brown, 1968.

Illustrated with Fuller's choices from the Cleveland Museum of Art and the Achenbach Foundation for Graphic Arts in San Francisco, this alphabet features a collection of old prints, ways illustrators have seen things in the past. For example, in Goya's *A Way of Flying,* there is a gliding man, capped with a helmet that is a replica of a bird's head and beak. This human glider floats on large feathered wings and clasps wires for guidance with both hands and feet. He is joined by three queer birds in this scene, entitled "*Q* is for Queer Bird." Fuller points out two other prints that have exceptional details in this volume: *I* for Imaginary Ox (Horned, wreathed, winged ox) and *N* for the Nonesuch Beast (seven-headed creature with sharp claws, scales, padded paws, and a spiraling tail). Ages 7-up.

Pattern: For each letter there is a old print selected for its clear details and impressions.

Gasiorwicz, Nina and Cathy. *The Mime Alphabet Book.* Illustrated by Nina Gasiorwicz. Minneapolis: Lerner Publishing Company, 1971.

In the large full-page black-and-white photographs by Nina Gasiorwicz, there are miming actions by Cathy Gasiorwicz. Each action introduces a word choice and an oversize, outlined letter in black. Ages 5-up.

Pattern: Miming actions are labeled with key words whose initial letters and sounds may be matched with guiding lowercase letters and their sounds.

Gathrid, Jonathan. *Alphabots.* Illustrated by the author. San Diego, Calif.: Slawson Communications, Inc., 1985.

Gathrid's metal robots form the shapes of the capital letters in this ABC. Shaped as an *R,* one robot carries his portable radio. The *M* robot admires himself in a mirror, while the *N* robot chases a butterfly with a net. A young listener begins to recognize that any sound that can be spoken can be represented by a letter. Is a boy or girl ready to look at some of the objects on the pages and name them? Is any child interested in hearing the sounds in the word that is the name of a selected object? Ages 4–5.

Pattern: Robots form shapes of capital letters and pose with object choices.

Hoban, Tana. *A, B, See!* Photographs by the author. New York: Greenwillow, 1982.

Recommended. From a collection of objects whose names begin with *A—apple, abacus, asparagus, acorn, arrow,* and *airplane—*to *zipper* as the single Z object, a young viewer sees familiar things in black-and-white photograms, photos taken with an prolonged light source. An alphabet frieze in gray at the foot of each page shows each selected letter in enlarged print in black. A California State Department of Education-recommended extended reading. Ages 5–6.

Pattern: Letter-photogram-frieze arrangement.

Johnson, Crockett. *Harold's ABC.* Illustrated by the author. New York: Harper and Row, 1963.

Recommended. Harold, with a purple crayon in his hand, takes a trip through the ABCs. An *H* becomes a fast horse, *J* is for jet, and *P* is for parachute, all ways that Harold travels on his trip. Explanatory sentences at the foot of each page guide the trip. This small book may be the basis for an adult's retelling in an enlarged format on the chalkboard. An adult may recount this story, or parts of it, from memory while sketching the transformed letters into objects on the chalkboard. For an easier story to sketch, one that focuses on only one letter, the letter *T*, select *T for Tommy* (Garrard, 1971) retold by Joan Lexau. Starting with a sketch of the *T*, a house with windows, chimneys, and grass is sketched. The route that Tommy follows during his walk is added to the sketch along with an S for his friend Sally. The path they walk along as they play catch with a ball is sketched. When the children have finished playing, the story, too, is finished. As this story ends, a child sees that the sketching made during the story has formed a great big cat. Ages 4–8.

Pattern: Black manuscript capitals appear as parts of objects in the story.

Krieger, David L. *Letters and Words*. Illustrated by the author. New York: Young Scott Books,1969.

With Kreiger's book a young child may become familiar with some of the different shapes of the letters seen in the surroundings. For each letter there are several type styles and both uppercase and lowercase letters. To show that letters can be placed together to form words, there are pictures of objects with the labels superimposed on them. For instance, the pictures of faucet, flower, and fish show their names in black boldface. A child is invited to find a selected letter in several words on each page. Some of the pictured objects show that some words may begin with a letter, end with a similar letter, or have the letter in the middle of the word. Considering Z, a child finds Z as the final letter in "fez," as a middle letter in "blazer," and as an initial letter in "zipper." Ages 5-up.

Pattern: Seen in variety of type styles, capitals and lowercase letters appear again in initial, medial, and final positions in selected labels for pictured objects.

Leander, Ed. *Q Is for Crazy*. Illustrated by Josef Sumichrast. New York: Harlin Quist, Inc., 1977.

In Leander's ABC verses a child is challenged to look and see what happens to the ABCs when one flitting fly lands in a spoonful of alphabet soup. Each letter found in the soup is featured by capitals in the four-line rhyme. In Sumichrast's illustrations, different people, animals, and objects form the shapes of the letters in the alphabet. Each verse contains unusual associations and unusual turns with the names of the letters for a child to hear. For example, a saw that cuts wood is the object for the letter *B*. The saw takes the shape of a capital *B* to remind a reader to be inside near a fire in a storm and to remember that the saw cuts the wood to keep a reader warm. Someone bites into a chocolate popsicle and leaves it in the shape of a *Y*. The verse asks, why did someone stop eating the popsicle? An E-15 aircraft takes the shape of *H* to complement the verse about an airplane hanging high in the sky. Ages 5-up.

Pattern: Each verse holds unusual word-choice associations with objects seen in the shapes of selected letters.

Lichtner, Schotmer. *Alphabet Drawings*. Illustrated by the author. Milwaukee: Morgan Press, 1973.

The shapes of the letters are found somewhere in each one of Lichtner's small black-and-white lines drawings. A penknife opens up to form the stems of the letter *K*, the wings of gulls form the *W*, and a cheerleader with raised arms leads a yell for the team for *Y*. For *N*, there is a ruffled neck of a dress on an aristocratic lady and a small black outlined form of a nude, a selection with which some viewers might be uncomfortable. Several complete sequences are shown. One *A* to *Z* arrangement contains adjacent letters backed with webbed lines, another holds letter shapes formed by the posture of a cow, while a third shows letters made of squibble lines. Still another arrangement shows *Z* as the dominant letter, while *A* is hidden partially in the design among the other letters. In another, serif capitals look as though they have been tossed onto a table and then outlined in sequence. In the final sequence, manuscript capitals form a left-hand margin from *A* to *Z*. Ages 13-Adult.

Pattern: Recognition of letter shapes within small black-and-white line drawings.

MacDonald, Suse. *Alphabatics*. Illustrated by the author. New York: Bradbury Press, 1986.

Recommended. Similar to *The Alphabeast Book: An Abecedarium* is this alphabet book. Each letter, like Schmiderer's letters, expands, shrinks, or is manipulated into a shape of an object the name of which begins with the letter itself. MacDonald looks at each letter and turns it into something that is new and different. The letter *K* forms the body of a kite that lifts and changes shape. The ark introduces the letter *A*, a clown stands for *C*, and a jack-in-the-box represents *J*. From letter to object there is a change that takes place in several stages in each illustration. For instance, in the first stage the letter *J* is seen. In the second stage the lowercase *J* is shown in a vertical flip. In the third stage the shape of the letter is repeated over and over. In the final step the repeated *J*s form the body of the jack-in-the box. MacDonald adds a face, ruff, hat, and streamers to complete the shape. A Junior Literary Guild Selection. Ages 3-up.

Pattern: In stages, each letter changes into an object the name of which begins with the letter.

McMillan, Bruce. *The Alphabet Symphony: An ABC Book.* Illustrated by the author. New York: Greenwillow, 1977.

Recommended. McMillan's book is useful for visual awareness. This ABC has black-and-white photographs of musical instruments. Accompanying each large black-and-white photograph is a second small insert that shows the part of the musical instrument that matches the shape of a particular letter in the alphabet. On several final pages is a review of the letters and another photographic review of the parts of the instruments. Can the child recognize the musical instruments and then identify the letter shapes in the parts of specific symphony instruments? There are smaller inserts on the final pages that help to review all of the letters. Ages 7-up.

Pattern: Musical instruments of a symphony have shapes that resemble forms of letters.

McNaughton, Colin. *Colin McNaughton's ABC and 123.* Illustrated by the author. Garden City, N. Y.: Doubleday and Company, Inc., 1976.

Small serif capitals in black stand alone and introduce repetitive beginning-sentence stems that explain the illustrations about nonsense situations. Two boys ride a bike toward a metal gate to show gate-crashing, and a chorus line of three potatoes dressed in top hats, long jackets, and spats on their black shoes, carry canes to illustrate potatoes in their jackets. In a barn, children climb a ladder to the top of hay bales stacked high and take turns jumpimg into a tall pile of hay to illustrate hay fever. Ages 7-up.

Pattern: Similar traditional stems such as *Q* is for———and *R* is for———begin lines in this nonsense alphabet.

Mendoza, George. *The Marcel Marceau Alphabet Book.* Photographs by Milton H. Greene. Garden City, N.Y.; Doubleday and Company, Inc., 1970.

A child may want to imitate some of Marcel Marceau's poses that mime words for the letters. Who will mime the word for *A, awake?* For *L, love?* for *T, tightrope?* Shown in the black-and-white photographs are several action words (*vanish, escape*), mood words (*happy, quiet*), and object words (*cape, kite*). Are there more words a child can identify as ones that name objects? Which additional words show actions? Moods? Ages 5-up.

Pattern: Miming poses lead to key words and their initial letters.

Miller, Barry. *Alphabet World.* Illustrated by the author. New York: Macmillan, 1971.

Capitals in colors guide a child in looking for similar shapes in these black-and-white photographs of objects in the environment. After determinimg a letter's stylized shape and name, the child's choice may be verified by placing an overlay sheet on top of the illustration. For a self-check, each sheet shows a brightly colored letter and where it can be found in the shape of an object in the photograph. With this one a child sees the forms of letters in the shapes of traffic lights and fire escapes, fences and gates, handles of hot and cold water faucets, stair railings, pencil sharpeners, and other objects found inside and outside of buildings. Ages 5-up.

Pattern: Shapes of letters are found in objects in the environment.

Neumeier, Marty, and Byron Glaser. *Action Alphabet.* Illustrated by the authors. New York: Greenwillow,1985.

Recommended. In this active ABC, the letters play the part of the word choices they represent, and where appropriate they show the action for their parts. For example, the serif capital *A* in black is the acrobat on the high wire to illustrate the word choice "acrobat." The capital *B* completely fills the page to illustrate the word "big." The capital *C* appears with a crack in its shape to illustrate the word "crack." Some unusual sights to see are the footprints that *W* makes after a walk, a twisted *T*, and an *L* being inserted into an envelope just like a sheet of paper. Ages 4-up.

Pattern: With capitals and lowercase letters on doublepage spreads, drawings of letters portray key words and show action.

Price, Marjorie. *Alphadabbles: A Playful Alphabet*. Illustrated by the author. New York: Pantheon, 1980.

In Price's book there are two alphabet presentations. In the first, artistic dabbles create designs or patterns for every letter. In the second, some space is left for a child to create original dabbles with letter shapes. For an activity that leads to expression, a child is invited to look at a selected letter and to create lines that follow its shape. The lines can magnify, minify, or stretch a letter. The impressions of the lines may be changed by placing corrugated cardboard or screening wire under drawing paper. In addition to reviewing Price's work, a child can visualize the letter from any direction. What would the letter look like from the top, the bottom, the back, or sides? The child can imagine what it would be like to walk inside the letter and look out at other letters in a word or in the alphabet sequence. Ages 6-up.

Pattern: Designs transform letters through enlargement, reduction, stretching, or squeezing.

Rebman, Sybil. *Animal Alphabet*. Illustrated by the author. San Diego, Calif.: Green Tiger Press, n.d.

From alligator and Baa-lamb to yak and zebra, all of the capital letters that make up a particular animal's name are used to draw the animal's shape. This visual playfulness helps a child recognize all of the letters that spell a certain animal's name. Black serif capitals begin each repetitive beginning stem (*O* for the ostrich) in each four-line verse. The letters in the name of the animal are found in the verse and matched to the letters that make the shape of the animal in the accompanying illustration. Each verse gives information about the animal—e.g., the alligator has a leathery hide, the lamb was born in spring, and the caterpillar spins a cocoon. Beside each verse, a pattern of red animal silhouettes is seen. The animals stand in, near, and around the single serif capitals in black that introduce the verses. Ages 6-up.

Pattern: Letters of animal names form animal shapes. Names of animals are repeated in rhyming verse.

Rey, Hans August. *Curious George Learns the Alphabet*. Illustrated by the author. Boston: Houghton Mifflin, 1963.

Recommended. The man in the yellow hat teaches George, the curious little monkey, that letters comes in two sizes, big and small. After introducing each upper- and lowercase letter in sequence, the author-artist transforms each letter into an object the name of which begins with that letter. As one example, when a tail, a bill, and some feet are added to a black manuscript capital *B*, the letter forms part of the final shape of a bird. Within the story line are reviews of the alphabetic sequence. Each manuscript upper-case and lowercase letter in black is introduced with a repetitive beginning stem—e.g., This is a big———and this is a small———. Each letter is part of a pattern that forms the shape of the object. Ages 7-up.

Pattern: Narrative writing in ABC progression as letters change into objects.

Schmiderer, Dorothy. *The Alphabeast Book: An Abecedarium.* Illustrated by the author. New York: Holt, Rinehart and Winston, Inc., 1971.

Recommended. Every letter of the alphabet turns into an alphabetical creature. In a four-panel sequence, a young viewer sees each letter transformed into an animal or insect. In the first panel the letter *W* is seen alone. In the next two panels the letter is changed and details are added. In the last panel the child sees the alphabeast. For instance, in the one final panel for *W*, the child finds an alphabetical worm. Ages 5-up.

Pattern: Letters are transformed into alphabet beasts.

Weil, Lisl. *Owl and Other Scrambles.* Illustrated by the author. New York: E. P. Dutton, 1980.

Every word makes its own picture with the scrambled capitals of the name of the object. What is the picture? A clue is on every page in the scrambled letters. A child self-checks by reviewing the answers on a final page. There is an alphabet frieze at the foot of each page with the initial letters identified for the words that are scrambled. If a child recognizes the left-to-right sequence of letters in words, it is possble to identify the sequence by pointing to the first letter in the object's scrambled name, the second letter, and so on. Ages 7-up.

Pattern: Letters in an object's name are arranged to make the shape of the object.

Wordless Stories for Creating Patterns

Arnosky, Jim. *Mouse Numbers and Letters*. Illustrated by the author. New York: Harcourt Brace Jovanovich, 1982.

Several wordless alphabet books in this part of the bibliography present opportunities for a child to create individual patterns in prose or poetry. One wordless ABC, *Mouse Numbers and Letters* by Arnosky can become the stimulus for oral or written composition of a poem or a story. In one section, "Mouse Letters," a small mouse tries to shape the capital letters from small sticks and twigs found on the ground. To shape an *A* is easy, but a capital *B* requires more of the mouse's strength as he bends a twig into the curved shapes of the *B*. In the cartoonlike illustration for the letter *F*, the mouse balances the letter on his nose until a snap of the upper twig causes the letter and the mouse to tumble. Pulling the upper curve of the letter *G* into its final shape, the mouse pulls too hard. The twig springs back and tosses the mouse forward as if he were pole-vaulting. Putting an icepack on his bumped head, the mouse returns to form a capital *H*. The crossbar of the *H* makes a resting place for the injured mouse. The bar slips and down goes the mouse, now angry enough to kick one twig into two pieces. The pieces, in turn, form the stems for the capital *K*. Placing one twig across a cavern, the mouse walks across the twig, slips, and grabs the twig with his hands to break his fall. As the mouse holds onto the twig, the twig responds to the weight of the mouse and first forms a U-shape and then a V-shape. At Z, the tired mouse sleeps near the shape of the letter. This book without words offers scenes for each letter, which encourages a child to tell the story. Ages 5-up.

Pattern: Visual patterns of letters are shaped from twigs and branches by a small mouse.

Arnosky, Jim. *Mouse Writing*. Illustrated by the author. New York: Harcourt Brace Jovanovich, 1983.

In Arnosky's second wordless alphabet book with its blue-bordered scenes, a child follows the ice-skating tracks left by two small mice as they cut the shapes of each upper- and lowercase letter in blue cursive script in the ice. The big mouse, Cap, and the small mouse, LC, follow the models and the handwriting patterns from those of Zaner-Bloser, Inc., 1980. One bird, a curious friend, follows along. If a child were to tell someone about these two mice, what words could be used? What writing patterns could be selected? What words could be chosen to describe the mice as they skate, fall, and leap into the air? The mice sail past trees and into snowbanks and up the inclined plane of a fallen tree trunk. Sometimes the mice twirl to gain speed to trace a shape. At Z, the tired mice rest on a bank, remove their skates, and LC is carried home by Cap. Ages 6-7.

Pattern: Shapes of cursive letters are shown by ice-skating patterns of mice.

Montrestor, Beni. *A for Angel: Beni Montresor's ABC Picture-Stories*. New York: Alfred A. Knopf, 1969.

Each one of Montresor's double-spread pictures forms a base for a child's story. For example, along with other objects in the picture-story for *B*, one boy rides a bike in a rowboat, and a bird is in a boot. What story might be started? What story sentence might be dictated to start a beginning? To support a child's search for a title, Monstresor includes a list of titles for the picture-stories on a final page. Ages 6-7.

Pattern: On each page black arrows point from the selected letter to the objects.

Rockwell, Anne. *Albert B. Cub and Zebra: An Alphabet Story-book*. Illustrated by the author. New York: Thomas Y. Crowell Company, 1977.

Recommended. This is a wordless mystery for young children. Zebra is abducted, and his friend, Albert Bernhardt Cub, searches on every page in alphabetical places all around the world. A young child looks at the pictures and dictates the happenings to read the story to an adult. An older child may look for actions and objects the labels of which begin with the selected letter for the page. Albert begins his search in a backyard, and continues on to visit a circus, the dock, a department store, and France. After Z, the author includes the story in small print and names some of the objects in the ABC illustrations. Some of the names in blue will stretch a child's vocabulary. Is a child able to find still more objects or actions? Ages 4–8.

Pattern: In wordless mystery, framed, full-color illustrations introduce objects and actions to emphasize the large upper- and lowercase serif letters in black.

References

Allen, Roach Van, and Claryce Allen. *Teacher's Resource Book: Language Experiences in Early Childhood.* Chicago: Encyclopaedia Britannica Educational Corporation, 1969.

American Library Association. *Realities: Educational Reform in A Learning Society.* Chicago: American Library Association, 1984.

Atwell, Margaret A. "Predictable Books for Adolescent Readers." *Journal of Reading* 29 (October 1985):18-22.

Barbe, Walter B., ed. *Basic Skills in Kindergarten: Foundations for Formal Learning.* Columbus, Ohio: Zaner-Bloser, 1980.

Barrett, T. C. "The Relationship Between Measures of Prereading Visual Discrimination and First-Grade Reading Achievement: A Review of the Literature." *Reading Research Quarterly* 2 (1965): 51-76.

Blatt, Gloria T. "Playing with Language." *The Reading Teacher* 31 (February 1978): 490.

Bond, G. L., and Dykstra, R. "The Cooperative Research Program in First-Grade Reading Instruction." *Reading Research Quarterly* 2 (1967): 5-142.

Bridge, Connie A., Peter N. Winograd, and Darlene Haley. "Using Predictable Materials vs. Preprimers to Teach Beginning Sight Words." *The Reading Teacher* 36 (May 1983): 884-91.

Bromley, Karen D'Angelo. "Teaching Idioms." *The Reading Teacher* 37 (December 1984): 272-76.

Bronson, David B. "Towards a Communication Theory of Teaching." *Teachers College Record* 78 (1977): 453.

Butler, Dorothy. *Babies Needs Books.* New York: Atheneum, 1980.

California State Department of Education. *Recommended Readings in Literature: Kindergarten Through Grade Eight*. Mirko Strazicich, ed. Sacramento: California State Department of Education, 1986.

Canella, Gaile S. "Providing Exploratory Activities in Beginning Reading Instruction." *The Reading Teacher* (December 1985): 284–88.

Carlson, Ann D. *Early Childhood Literature Sharing Programs in Libraries*. Hamden, Conn.: The Shoe String Press, Inc., 1985.

Cazden, Courtney B. *Child Language and Education*. New York: Holt, Rinehart and Winston,1972.

———. "Play with Language and Metalinguistic Awareness: One Dimension of Language Experience." *International Journal of Early Childhood* 6 (1976):13.

Chambers, Dewey Woods and Heath Ward Lowry. *The Language Arts: A Pragmatic Approach*. Dubuque, Iowa: Wm. C. Brown, 1975.

Chandler, Judy, and Marcia Baghban. "Predictable Books Guarantee Success." *Reading Horizons* 26 (April 1986): 167–77.

Chomsky, Carol. "Stages in Language Development and Reading Exposure." *Harvard Educational Review* 42 (1972): 1–33.

———. "After Decoding, What?" *Language Arts* 53 (March 1976): 288–96.

Chukovsky, Komei. *From Two to Five*. Translated by Miriam Merton. Berkeley: University of California Press, 1978.

Cianciolo, Patricia Jean. "Use Wordless Picture Books to Teach Reading, Visual Literacy, and to Study Literature." *Top of the News* 29 (April 1973): 226–34.

Clay, M.M. *Reading: The Patterning of Complex Behavior*. Aukland, N.Z.: Heinemann Educational Books, 1972.

Cohen, Dorothy H. "The Effects of Literature on Vocabulary and Reading Achievement." *Elementary English* 45 (February 1968): 209–13.

Combs, Martha. "Developing Concepts about Print with Patterned Sentence Stories." *The Reading Teacher* 38 (January 1985): 415–17.

Crowell, Doris C., Alice J. Kawakami, and Jeanette L. Wong. "Emerging Literacy: Reading-Writing Experiences in a Kindergarten." *The Reading Teacher* 40 (November 1986): 144–51.

Cunningham, Patricia. "The Clip Sheet." *The Reading Teacher* 33 (Janaury 1980): 474–76.

Davidson, Janet E., and Robert J. Sternburg. "What Is Insight?" *Educational Horizons* 64 (Summer 1986): 177–79.

deHirsch, K., Jansky, J., and Langford, W. S. *Predicting Reading Failure: A Preliminary Study.* New York: Harper and Row, 1966.

Dickerson, Dolores Pawley. "A Study of the Use of Games to Reinforce Sight Vocabulary." *The Reading Teacher* 36 (October 1982): 46–51.

Dinan, Linda L., and Anne Haas Dyson. "Viewpoints: Writing." *Language Arts* 19 (Summer, 1980): 157–62.

Downing, John. "How Children Think about Reading." *The Reading Teacher* 23 (1969): 217–30.

———. "The Child's Conception of 'A Word.'" *Reading Research Quarterly* 9 (1973–74): 568–82.

Durrell, D., and Murphy, H. "Reading in Grade One." *Journal of Education* 146 (1962): 14–18.

Dykstra, R. "Auditory Discrimination Abilities and Beginning Reading Achievement." *Reading Research Quarterly* 1 (1966): 5–34.

Edds, Maryann. "Bookwords: Using a. Beginning Word List of High Frequency Words from Children's Literature K-3." *The Reading Teacher* 38 (January 1985): 418–23.

Ellis, D.W., and Preston, F.W. "Enhancing Beginning Reading Using Wordless Picture Books in a Cross-Age Tutoring Program." *The Reading Teacher* 37 (1984): 692–98.

Emans, Robert. "Children's Rhymes and Learning to Read." *Language Arts* 55 (Nov.-Dec. 1978): 937–40.

Forester, A. D. "What Teachers Can Learn from Natural Readers." *The Reading Teacher* 31 (November 1977): 160–66.

Geller, Linda Gibson. *Wordplay and Language Learning for Children.* Urbana, Ill.: National Council of Teachers of English, 1985.

Gipe, Joan P. "Use of a Relevant Context Helps Kids Learn New Word Meanings." *The Reading Teacher* 33 (January 1980): 398– 402.

Glass, G. G., and Burton, E. H. "How do They Decode? Verbalizations and Observed Behaviors of Successful Decoders." *Education* 94 (1973):58–64.

Goodall, M. "Can Four Year Olds 'Read' Words in the Environment?" *The Reading Teacher* 37 (1984): 478–82.

Hajek, Ellen. "Whole Language: Sensible Answers to the Old Problems." *Momentum* 15 (May 1984): 39–40.

Harms, Jeanne McLain, and Lucille J. Lettow. "Fostering Ownership of the Reading Experience." *The Reading Teacher* 40 (December 1986): 324–30.

Hart, Leslie A. "Programs, Patterns, and Downshifting in Learning to Read." *The Reading Teacher* 37 (October 1983): 5–13.

Healey, Jack. *Teaching Writing K Through 8.* Berkeley: Instructional Laboratory, University of California, 1978.

Hoersten, K. "Games Children Play." *The Columbus Dispatch Magazine* (13 April 1969): 52–54, 61.

Hollingsworth, Paul M. "An Experiment with the Impress Method of Teaching Reading." *The Reading Teacher* 24 (November, 1970): 112–14.

Holt, John. *How Children Learn.* New York: Pitman Publishing Corporation, 1968.

Hoskisson, Kenneth. "Learning to Read Naturally." *Language Arts* 56 (May 1979): 491.

Hoskisson, Kenneth, and B. Krohm. "Reading by Immersion: Assisted Reading." *Elementary English* 51 (September 1974): 832–36.

Huey, E. B. *The Psychology and Pedagogy of Reading.* Originally published in 1908. Cambridge: M.I.T. Press, 1968.

Johns, Jerry L. "Predictable Pattern Books." *Handbook for Remediation of Reading Difficulties.* Englewood Cliffs, N.J.: Prentice-Hall, Inc., 1986.

Kellough, Richard D., and Patricia L. Roberts. *A Resource Guide for Elementary School Teaching: Planning for Competence.* New York: Macmillan Publishing Company, Inc.,, 1985.

Krashen, S. *Inquiries and Insights: Essays on Language Teaching, Bilingual Education, and Literacy.* Hayward, Calif.: Alemany Press, 1985.

Lamme, Linda. "Library Programs for Infants and Toddlers: An Educator's View." From speech at Florida Library Association Annual Meeting, Orlando, Florida. Tallahassee: Florida State Library, May 1979, 2–4, 7–8.

LeFevre, C. A. *Linguistics and the Teaching of Reading.* New York: McGraw-Hill, 1964.

Lehr, Fran. "ERIC/RCS Report: Instructional Scaffolding." *Language Arts* 62 (October 1985): 667-71.

Loban, Walter. *The Language of Elementary School Children.* Urbana: National Council of Teachers of English, 1963.

Lutz, Elaine. "ERIC/RCS Report: Invented Spelling and Spelling Develoment." *Language Arts* 34 (November 1986): 742-44.

McClure, Amy A. "Predictable Books: Another Way to Teach Reading to Learning Disabled Children." *Teaching Exceptional Children* 17 (Summer 1985): 67-73.

Martinez, Miriam, and Nancy Roser. "Read It Again, the Value of Repeated Readings During Storytime." *The Reading Teacher* 38 (April 1985): 782.

Marzano, Robert J. "A Cluster Approach to Vocabulary Instruction: A New Direction from the Research Literature." *The Reading Teacher* 38 (November 1984) 168-73.

Mason, George C. *A Primer on Teaching Reading: Basic Concepts and Skills of the Early Elementary Years.* Itasca, Minn.: Peacock Publishers, 1981.

Mavrogenes, Nancy A. "What Every Reading Teacher Should Know About Emergent Literacy." *The Reading Teacher* 40 (November 1986): 174-78.

May, Frank. *To Help Children Communicate.* Columbus, Ohio: Charles E. Merrill, 1980.

Milner, E. "A Study of the Relationship Between Reading Readiness in Grade One School Children and Patterns of Parent-Child Interaction." *Child Development* 22 (1951): 95-112.

Noyce, Ruth M., and James F. Christie. "Using Literature to Develop Children's Grasp of Syntax." *The Reading Teacher* 34 (December 1980): 298-304.

Odegaard, Jim, and Frank May. "Creative Grammar and the Writing of Third Graders." *Elementary School Journal* 73 (September 1972): 156-61.

Pickert, Sarah M. "Repetitive Sentence Patterns in Children's Books." *Language Arts* 55 (January 1978): 16-18.

Rhodes, Lynn K. "I can Read: Predictable Books as Resources for Reading and Writing Instruction." *The Reading Teacher* 34 (February 1981): 511-18.

Rosso, B. R., and Emans, R. "Children's Use of Phonic Generalizations." *The Reading Teacher* 34 (November, 1981): 653-58.

Ruddell, R. B. "The Effect of Oral and Written Patterns of Language Structure on Reading Comprehension." *The Reading Teacher* 18 (1965): 270–75.

Sampson, Delores. "Children and Books." *Insights into Open Education.* 16 (December 1983): 2–9.

Schonell, F. J. *The Psychology and Teaching of Reading, 4th Ed.* New York: Philosophical Library, 1961.

Sharp, Peggy A. "Reading the Write Way." *Early Years* (Nov.-Dec. 1985): 40–41.

Smith, F. "Learning to Read by Reading." *Language Arts* 53 (March 1976): 297–99, 322.

———. "The Role of Prediction in Reading." *Elementary English* 52 (1975): 305–11.

———. *Reading Without Nonsense, Second Edition.* New York: Teachers College Press, 1985.

Taylor, Gail Heald. "Scribble in First Grade Writing." *The Reading Teacher* 38 (October 1984): 4–8.

Tompkins, Gail E., and Mary Beth Webeler. "What Will Happen Next? Using Predictable Books with Young Children." *The Reading Teacher* 36 (February 1983): 498–502.

Tovey, D.R. "The Psycholinguistic Guessing Game." *Language Arts* 53 (March 1976): 319–22.

———. "Children's Grasp of Phonics Terms vs. Sound-Symbol Relationships." *The Reading Teacher* 33 (1980): 431–37.

Tyson, Eleanore S., and Lee Mountain. "A Riddle or Pun Makes Learning Words Fun." *The Reading Teacher* 35 (November 1982): 170–73.

United States Department of Education. *What Works: Research about Teaching and Learning.* Washington, D.C.: Department of Education, 1986.

Veatch, Jeannette. *How to Teach Reading with Children's Books, Second Edition.* New York: Richard C. Owen Publishers, 1968.

Wagner, Cynthia. "Factors Influencing Young Children's Response to Literature." *The California Reader* 19 (Spring 1986): 8–11.

Wepner, Shelley B. "Linking Logos with Print for Beginning Reading Success." *The Reading Teacher* 38 (March 1985): 633–39.

White, Mary Lou. "Fiddling with Fancy Words for Vocabulary Building." *Ohio Reading Teacher* 14 (January,1980): 19-21.

Whitehead, Robert J. *A Guide to Selecting Books for Children.* Menuchen, N.J.: The Scarecrow Press, 1984.

Williams, M. S., and J. D. Knafle. "Comparative Difficulty of Vowel Sounds and Consonant Sounds for Beginning Readers." *Reading Improvement* 14 (Spring 1970): 2-10.

Wingert, R. C. "Evaluation of a Readiness Training Program." *The Reading Teacher* 22 (1969): 325-28.

Woodburn, Mary Stuart. "A Strategy for Using Predictable Books." *Early Years* 15 (April 1986): 45-46.

Zaner-Bloser, Inc. *Creative Growth with Handwriting: Elements of Legible Cursive Handwriting.* Columbus: Ohio: Zaner-Bloser, Inc., 1974.

Index

Hyman, Jane, 195
Hyman, Trina Schart, 59

I Can Be the Alphabet (Bonini), 220
I Can Sign My ABC's (Chaplin), 222
I Found Them in the Yellow Pages (Farber), 185
I Live in the City ABC (Moore), 169
I Love My Anteater with an A (Ipcar), 51, 107
I Packed My Trunk (Waller), 42–43
I Unpacked My Grandmother's Trunk: A Picture Book Game (Hoguet), 8, 41
I Used to Be an Artichoke (McGinn), 6, 156
Ick's ABC (Gwynne), 175
Idalia's Project ABC/Proyecto ABC: An Urban Alphabet Book in English and Spanish (Rosario), 169, 199
If I Say ABC (Porter Productions), 73
If There Were Dreams to Sell (Lalicki), 10, 213
Illsley, Velma, 165
In a Pumpkin Shell: A Mother Goose ABC (Anglund), 24, 148–49
Incredible Animals from A to Z (Robinson), 29, 182
Indian Two Feet and the ABC Moose Hunt (Friskey), 31, 122
Inquiries and Insights: Essays on Language Teaching, Bilingual Education, and Literacy (Krashen), 240
Ipcar, Dahlov, 51, 95, 107
Isadora, Rachel, 166
It's the ABC Book (Harada), 73
Ivens, Dorothy, 113
Izawa, Tadasu, 135, 153

Jambo Means Hello: Swahili Alphabet Book (Feelings), 192
Jansky, J. 3, 239

Jefferds, Vincent, 196
Jewell, Nancy, 138
John Burningham's ABC (Burningham, 1964), 70
John Burningham's ABC (Burningham, 1967), 70
John Burningham's ABC (Burningham, 1985), 70
Johns, Jerry L., 240
Johnson, Crockett, 19, 227
Johnson, Jean, 29, 186
Johnson, Laura Rinkle, 143
Johnson, Marilu, 224
Johnstone, Anne Grahame, 111, 148
Johnstone, Janet, 148
Join in with Us! Letters: An Action Alphabet (O'Callaghan), 13, 112
Jolly Days (Booth), 177
Jones, Kathryn Amanda, 104

Kahn, Peggy, 196
Kahn, Ruth E., 187
Karas, G. Brian, 130–31
Katamura, Satoshi, 16, 104
Kawakami, Alice J., 4, 238
Keani, 96
Keats, John, 10, 11, 13, 214
Kellogg, Steven, 13, 90–91
Kellough, Richard D., 23, 240
Kelly, Donna, 105
Kendrick, Dennis, 218
Kennedy, X. J. (Charles Joseph), 153
Kent, Jack, 26, 97
Kepes, Juliet, 157
Keys, Robert, 171
King, Colin, 44
King, Tony, 105
Kingdon, Jill, 30, 181
King's Cat Is Coming, The (Mack), 21, 126
Kinkaid, Eric, 180
Kinkaid, Lucy, 180
Kitchens, Bert, 11, 59
Kittens' ABC, The (Newberry), 34, 139